THE AIR PILOT'S MANUAL

Volume 1

Flying Training

Trevor Thom

Airlife

England

Nothing in this manual supersedes any legislation, rules, regulations or procedures contained in any operational document issued by Her Majesty's Stationery Office, the Civil Aviation Authority, the manufacturers of aircraft, engines and systems, or by the operators of aircraft throughout the world.

Text, Copyright © 1987 Trevor Thom.
Original Illustrations & Diagrams, Copyright © 1987
Trevor Thom & Robert Johnson.

ISBN 1 85310 014 5

First edition published 1987
by Airlife Publishing Ltd.

This second revised edition published 1987.
Reprinted 1988

Printed in England by Livesey Ltd., Shrewsbury.

Airlife Publishing Ltd.

7 St. John's Hill, Shrewsbury, England.

THE AIR PILOT'S MANUAL Vol. 1

Flying Training

EXERCISES

to Bill Vowell

EDITORIAL TEAM

Trevor Thom.
A current Boeing 727 Captain with Ansett Airlines of Australia, Trevor is active in the *International Federation of Airline Pilots' Associations (IFALPA)*, based in London, and is a member of the *IFALPA Aeroplane Design and Operations Group*. He was recently appointed IFALPA representative to the *Society of Automotive Engineers` (SAE) – Aerospace*, a body which makes recommendations to the aviation industry, especially the manufacturers. Prior to his airline position Trevor worked as a lecturer in Mathematics and Physics, and also as an Aviation Ground Instructor and a Flying Instructor. He is a double degree graduate from the University of Melbourne and also holds a Diploma of Education.

John Fenton.
A Flying Instructor since 1970, John is joint proprietor and assistant CFI of Yorkshire Flying Services at Leeds/Bradford. He is a PPL Examiner and was recently awarded the Bronze Medal by the Royal Aero Club for his achievements and contributions to air rallying. John has also made considerable contributions to the field of flying instruction in this country and pioneered the use of audio tapes for training.

Peter Godwin.
Currently Chief Flying Instructor at the London School of Flying, Elstree, Peter has amassed over 7000 instructional flying hours, embracing periods as Chief Pilot for an Air Charter and Freight organisation, and head of the Advanced Flying Training Unit and also CFI at Gulfstream School of Flying, Denham. He is both a PPL and CPL Instrument Rating Examiner.

Edward Pape.
Director of the Manchester School of Flying and a former Chief Flying Instructor of the Lancashire Aero Club, Edward has over 3000 instructional flying hours and is dedicated to Private Pilot training.

Ronald Smith.
A senior Aviation Ground Instructor, Ron's twenty years in aviation include considerable time as a flying instructor, specialised flying in remote areas, fish-spotting, and a period operating his own Air Taxi Service. He is an active member of *California Wheelchair Aviators* and holds a Commercial Pilot's Licence.

Robert Johnson.
An experienced aviator, Bob drew most of the diagrams, designed the cover, and prepared the final edit and layout of the manuals for printing. His aviation experience includes flying a *Cessna Citation* executive jet, a *DC-3* and light aircraft as Chief Pilot for an international University based in Switzerland, and seven years as a First Officer on *Fokker Friendship*, *Lockheed Electra* and *McDonnell Douglas DC-9* airliners. Prior to this he was an Air Taxi Pilot and also gained technical experience as a Draughtsman on Airborne Mineral Survey work in Australia.

ACKNOWLEDGEMENTS

We greatly appreciate the input that has been made by the following:

The Civil Aviation Authority, numerous Flying Schools throughout the UK, Jim Hitchcock and Bill Ryall; Bill Constable, Don Hutchison, Lindsay Ingram and Rick James. Also, Brian Hill, Robyn Hind and Marc Vogel for photographs; ARV, Cessna, Gulfstream American, King Radio, Piper and Slingsby for technical material, and of course Airtour International Ltd., and Robert Pooley Ltd.

'Good, clear Knowledge
minimises
Flight Training Hours'

INTRODUCTION

BECOMING A PILOT.

Every Pilot begins as a Student Pilot whether his or her aim is to fly for a hobby or to fly for a career.

Fig.1. Becoming A Pilot.

Learning to fly does not take long – within the first 20 hours of flying training you will have learned the basic skills. Since the training period is so short, good habits must be developed right from the start. Patterns formed in the first few hours will stay with you throughout your flying life and so, to gain the maximum benefit from each hour in the air and to develop good habits, you should be well prepared. This manual will help you to do this.

An advanced formal education is not a requirement to become a Pilot although the English Language is required for radio calls and a knowledge of basic mathematics is useful. Beyond that, no special academic skills are required.

The basic training **aeroplane** is simple in design and straightforward to operate. It has a control column (or control wheel) to raise or lower the nose and to bank the aeroplane, a rudder to keep it in balance, and a throttle to supply engine power. The largest and fastest airliners have basically the same controls.

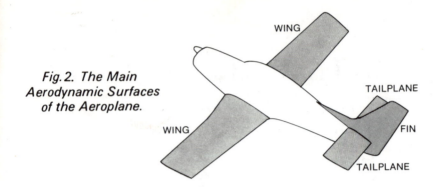

Fig. 2. The Main Aerodynamic Surfaces of the Aeroplane.

HOW AN AEROPLANE FLIES.

When not in flight, an aeroplane is supported by the ground, but when airborne it must generate its own support. This it does by modifying the flow of the air over the wings, generating a force known as Lift.

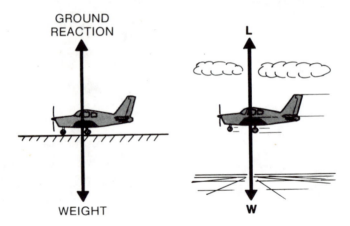

Fig. 3. In Flight, the Aeroplane is Supported by Lift.

The air is made up of many molecules, all of which are moving at high speed and in random directions, even though the parcel of air itself might be stationary. The molecules act like small tennis balls, bouncing off any surface that they come in contact with and exerting a force on it.

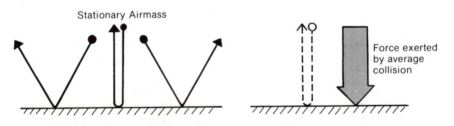

Fig. 4. Static Pressure Exerted by a Stationary Parcel of Air.

The size of the force is greatest when the collision is 'head-on' and becomes less with glancing blows. All of these small forces, when added up over an area, exert a pressure on the surface. This is known as **static pressure.**

If the parcel of air is moving relative to the surface, the collisions are more likely to be glancing blows rather than 'head-on', and so the pressure exerted on the surface will be less. **The faster the air flows** past the surface, **the lower the static pressure** that it exerts.

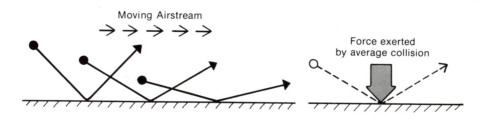

Fig. 5. Static Pressure Decreases with the Speed of Airflow.

A wing is shaped so that the airflow speeds up over its upper surface. This results in a lower static pressure above the wing than below it and so a lifting force is created.

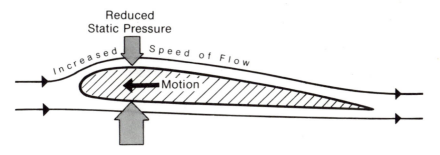

Fig. 6. The Airflow is Faster Over a Wing than Under It, Causing a Lower Static Pressure to be Generated.

NOTE: The decrease in static pressure with an increased speed of airflow is known in Physics as **Bernoulli's Principle.** It is usually stated as:

Static Pressure + Dynamic Pressure = a Constant Total Pressure
(related to speed)

The effect is the same when air flows past the wing as when the wing moves through the air – it is the **relative motion** of one to the other that is important.

The actual Lift generated by a wing depends upon its shape and also upon the angle at which the wing is presented to the airflow. This angle is known as the **angle of attack.** The greater it is in the flight range, the faster the air will travel over the upper surface of the wing and the lower the static pressure will be – thus, the greater the angle of attack, the greater the lifting ability of the wing. The practical result is that sufficient Lift to support the weight of the aeroplane can be generated at a lower airspeed.

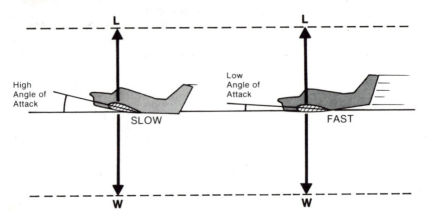

Fig. 7. In Level Flight the Aeroplane Can Fly Slower at High Angles of Attack.

A limit occurs when the aeroplane slows to an airspeed at which the angle of attack reaches a critical value. Beyond this angle of attack the **smooth airflow** over the wing breaks down and becomes **turbulent,** causing a marked decrease in Lift. The wing is then said to be **'stalled'**. Chapter 10a of this manual discusses the recovery from a stall in detail.

The force that opposes the motion of the aeroplane through the air is called *Drag.* In 'straight and level flight', **Drag** is balanced by **Thrust** from the propeller.

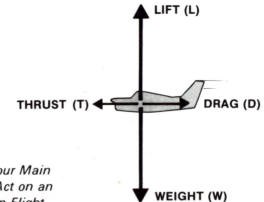

Fig. 8. The Four Main Forces That Act on an Aeroplane In Flight.

To control the aeroplane, **Control Surfaces,** operated from the cockpit by the Pilot, are used to alter the airflow around the wings and the tail-section. This causes different aerodynamic forces to be generated, and thus allows the Pilot to manoeuvre the aeroplane as desired.

The fore-going pages are a brief summary of the basic Principles of Flight. Volume 4 of this series covers this topic in greater depth and prepares you for the technical examination on the aeroplane – Aircraft (General).

BE PREPARED FOR YOUR FLYING LESSONS.

The cockpit is a difficult place in which to learn, so adequate pre-flight preparation is essential. For each training flight you should have a clear aim and be thoroughly prepared in order to achieve it. Ideally, the actual training flight should be an illustration of principles which you already understand, rather than a series of totally unexpected events.

For each stage of your training, this manual sets out:
* a clear aim;
* the principles and considerations involved;
* how to fly the manoeuvre; and
* the actual 'airwork'.

It will prepare you well and help to minimise your training hours (and your expense). As your training progresses, it can be used for revision. Earlier manoeuvres can be revised simply by scanning the sub-headings within the relevant chapter and referring to the Airwork pages, which act as a summary.

FLIGHT TESTS FOR THE PPL(A).

The culmination of your training is to demonstrate that you have achieved (or even surpassed) the required standard for the PPL(Aeroplanes). There are two tests involved:- the first checks your ability as a Pilot/Navigator, (which is done prior to carrying out your *solo* qualifying cross-country flight), and the second is the General Flight Test, right at the end of your training.

Details of the Navigation Flight Test have been included as an Appendix in Vol. 3 of this series (Air Navigation), and the General Flight Test is outlined at the end of this Volume.

THE AIR PILOT'S MANUAL.

This is a series of five volumes designed to prepare you for the Private Pilot's Licence according to the syllabus in the United Kingdom (and many other countries).

Volume 1: Flying Training.

Volume 2: Aviation Law (including Flight Rules and Procedures); Aeromedicine and Safety; Aviation Meteorology.

Volume 3: Air Navigation and Flight Planning.

Volume 4: The Aeroplane – technical, covering Aircraft (General) and Aircraft (Type) – (Principles of Flight; Airframe, Engines and Systems; Airworthiness and Performance).

Volume 5: Radio Navigation, Instrument Flying, IMC Rating and Night Rating.

SUBDIVISION OF EXERCISES

The order and subdivision of Flying Training Exercises follows our preferred sequence of instruction, and has been agreed with the CAA. Students may find these differ slightly from those used in some other syllabuses.

AIRWORK SUMMARIES

1

THE
AEROPLANE

1

THE AEROPLANE

The **Basic Training Aeroplane** consists of a **fuselage** to which the **wings,** the **tail,** the **wheels** and an **engine** are attached. A **propeller,** driven by the engine, generates **Thrust** to pull the aeroplane through the air. This enables the airflow over the wings to generate an aerodynamic force known as 'Lift' that is capable of supporting the aeroplane in flight. The aeroplane can fly without thrust if it is placed in a gliding descent.

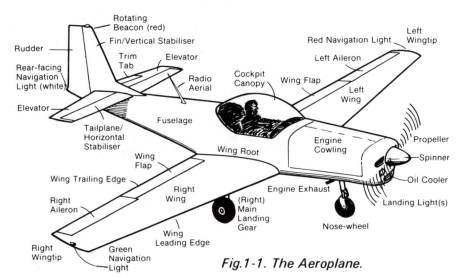

Fig.1-1. The Aeroplane.

The **tail section** of the aeroplane is situated some distance to the rear of the main load-carrying sections of the fuselage and provides a balancing or stabilising force much like the tail feathers on an arrow or a dart. The tail section consists of a **vertical stabiliser** (or fin) and a **horizontal stabiliser,** both of which are shaped to produce suitable aerodynamic forces

The Pilot and other occupants of the aeroplane are accommodated in the **cockpit,** usually in two-abreast seating – the Pilot-in-Command sitting on the left hand side. Various controls and instruments are available in the cockpit to enable safe and efficient operation of the aeroplane and its systems.

The **main controls** used to fly the aeroplane are the **flight controls** and the **throttle.** The throttle, which is operated by the Pilot's right hand, controls the power supplied by the engine/propeller combination. 'Opening' the throttle by pushing it forward increases the fuel/air supply to the engine, resulting in increased revolutions and greater power being developed. Pulling the throttle back, or 'closing' it, reduces the power.

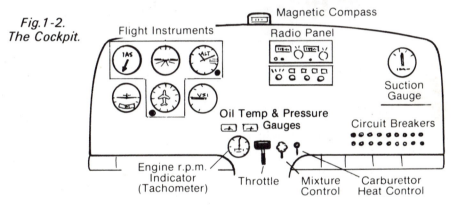

Fig.1-2.
The Cockpit.

Magnetic Compass

Flight Instruments

Radio Panel

Suction Gauge

Oil Temp & Pressure Gauges

Circuit Breakers

Engine r.p.m. Indicator (Tachometer)

Throttle

Mixture Control

Carburettor Heat Control

The **attitude** (or position in flight) of the aeroplane is controlled using the main **flight controls.** These are surfaces which, when deflected, alter the pattern of the airflow around the wings and tail causing changes in the aerodynamic forces that they generate.

- **The Elevator** (hinged to the trailing edge of the horizontal stabiliser) controls pitching of the nose up or down and is operated from the cockpit with fore and aft movements of the control column;

- **The Ailerons** (hinged to the outer trailing edge of each wing) control rolling of the aeroplane and are operated by sideways movement of the control column;

- **The Rudder** (hinged to the trailing edge of the vertical stabiliser) controls the yawing of the nose left or right and is operated by the rudder pedals.

Other flight controls include:
- the **Wing Flaps** (situated on the inner trailing edge of each wing); and
- the elevator **Trim Tab** (situated on the trailing edge of the elevator).

There will be other controls in the cockpit to operate the **cabin heating and ventilation systems.**

VARIATIONS IN DESIGN.

There are variations in design between different types, but **the same basic principles apply to all aeroplanes.**

Instead of a **control column** in the form of a 'stick', many aeroplanes are fitted with a **control wheel,** which serves exactly the same function. Moving the control wheel in or out operates the elevator, rotating it operates the ailerons. In this manual the term 'control column' refers to both types.

Fig.1-3. The Control Column and the Control Wheel.

Even though the aerodynamic sections of various aeroplane types serve the same basic functions, their actual location on the structure and their design can vary. For example, the wings may be attached to the fuselage in a high, low or mid-wing position; the horizontal stabiliser is sometimes positioned high on the fin (known as a T-tail), and the combined horizontal stabiliser and elevator is sometimes replaced by an 'all-flying tailplane' (or 'stabilator').

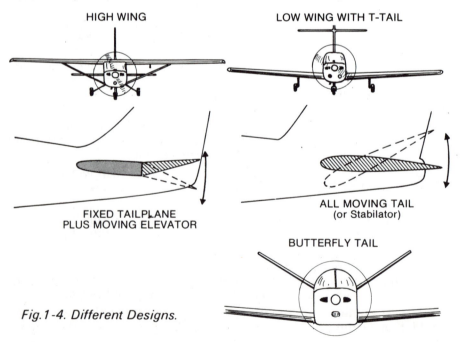

HIGH WING

LOW WING WITH T-TAIL

FIXED TAILPLANE
PLUS MOVING ELEVATOR

ALL MOVING TAIL
(or Stabilator)

BUTTERFLY TAIL

Fig.1-4. Different Designs.

Most modern training aeroplanes have a tricycle **undercarriage** consisting of two main wheels and a nose-wheel to provide support on the ground. Other aircraft have a tail-wheel instead of a nose-wheel. The nose-wheel on most types is connected to the **rudder pedals** so that movement of the pedals will turn it, assisting in directional control on the ground.

Most aircraft have **brakes** on the main wheels which are operated by pressing the top of the rudder pedals or by using a brake handle.

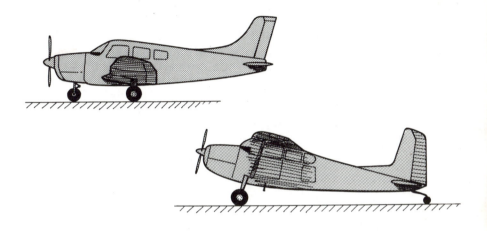

Fig.1-5. The Tricycle Undercarriage and the Tail-Wheel Type.

THE ENGINE AND PROPELLER.

The typical training aeroplane has a **piston engine** that uses **AVGAS** (aviation gasoline). The engine revolutions per minute (rpm) are controlled by the **throttle**. Attached to the engine is a fixed-pitch **propeller** (i.e. one whose blade angle cannot be altered) that converts the power from the engine into thrust. A measure of the power being developed is the engine **rpm** which is indicated in the cockpit on the **Tachometer** (or 'rev counter').

The **fuel** is usually stored in **wing tanks;** low-wing aeroplanes requiring a fuel pump to deliver it to the engine, high-wing aeroplanes usually relying on gravity. There are **fuel gauges** in the cockpit to indicate quantity, but it is good airmanship (common sense) to check the contents of the tanks visually prior to flight.

It is also wise to confirm that the fuel is both of the correct grade (which is identified by its colour) and that it is not contaminated – the most likely contaminant being water which is denser than AVGAS and gathers at the low points in the fuel system. The check is performed by inspecting a small sample taken from 'fuel drains' fitted at low points in the fuel system; for example from beneath each fuel tank.

The **Fuel Tank Selector** in the cockpit allows fuel to be supplied from each tank as desired or possibly from all tanks. It is vital that a tank containing fuel be selected. **Fuel management is a high priority item for the Pilot.**

Oil for **lubricating** and **cooling** the engine is stored in a sump in the engine compartment. Its quantity should be checked with a dip-stick prior to flight. There are two cockpit gauges in the oil system to register **Oil Pressure** and **Oil Temperature** when the engine is running. These gauges are often colour-coded, the normal operating range being shown as a green arc.

The fuel is mixed with air in a **carburettor** attached to the engine and passes through the induction system into the cylinders, where combustion occurs. The **Mixture Control,** situated near the throttle, is used to ensure that a suitable fuel/air mixture is provided to the engine by the carburettor. The **Carburettor Heat Control,** also located near the throttle, is used to supply hot air to protect the carburettor from ice.

The engine has **dual ignition systems** which provide sparks to initiate the combustion process in the cylinders. The electrical current for the sparks is generated by **two magnetos** geared to the engine. The dual ignition systems provide more efficient combustion and greater safety in the event of one system failing. An ignition switch in the cockpit is normally used to select *'BOTH',* although it can select the *'LEFT'* or *'RIGHT'* systems individually, as well as having an *'OFF'* position.

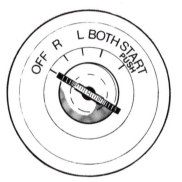

Fig.1-6. The Ignition Switch.

Most ignition switches have a further position, *'START',* which connects the battery to an **electric starter** to turn the engine over. Once the engine starts, the ignition switch is returned to *'BOTH'* and the red starter warning light (if fitted) should go out to verify that the starter motor has indeed disengaged.

THE ELECTRICAL SYSTEM.

The **battery** is a source of electrical power to start the engine and provides an emergency electrical back-up supply if the engine-driven alternator (or generator) fails.

The electrical system will have an **alternator** or a **generator** to supply various aircraft services such as some flight instruments, the radios, cabin lights, landing lights, navigation lights, the wing-flap motor, pitot heater and stall warning system. It is important that aeroplanes fitted with an alternator have a serviceable battery so that the alternator can come on-line.

The electrical system has an **ammeter** and/or **warning light** incorporated to verify that electrical current is flowing.

Note that the two magneto systems providing the ignition sparks to the engine are totally separate from the electrical system (alternator/generator, battery, circuit breakers and fuses). Each electrical circuit is protected from excessive current by a **fuse** or a **circuit breaker.**

One very useful electrical service is the **radio,** which is used for air/ground communications. It has an *ON/OFF* and **volume** control (usually combined in the one knob), a Squelch control to eliminate unwanted background noise, a **microphone** for transmitting and **speakers** or **headphones** for receiving messages.

Fig.1-7. Control Panel of a Typical Communications Radio.

THE INSTRUMENTS.

The panel in front of the Pilot contains various instruments which can provide important information – the main groups being the **Flight Instruments** (which are directly in front of the Pilot) and the **Engine Instruments** (which are generally situated near the throttle).

The **Flight Instruments** include an **Air Speed Indicator,** an **Attitude Indicator** to depict the aeroplane's attitude relative to the horizon, an **Altimeter** to indicate height, a **Vertical Speed Indicator** to show climb or descent, a **Direction Indicator** and a **Turn Co-ordinator** with an associated **Balance Ball.**

The instruments related to airspeed and height are operated by air pressure obtained from the **pitot-static pressure system,** whilst those related to attitude, direction and turning are operated by internal spinning **gyroscopes,** (with the exception of the **Magnetic Compass).** The gyroscope rotors may be spun electrically or by a stream of air induced by 'suction' from the vacuum system. The Magnetic Compass is usually located well away from the magnetic influences of the instrument panel and radio.

The engine instruments include the **Tachometer** (to read engine rpm), and the **Oil Pressure** and **Temperature** gauges. Some aircraft also have a **Cylinder Head Temperature** gauge.

Other instruments may include an **Ammeter** to monitor the electrical system and a **Suction** gauge for the vacuum system.

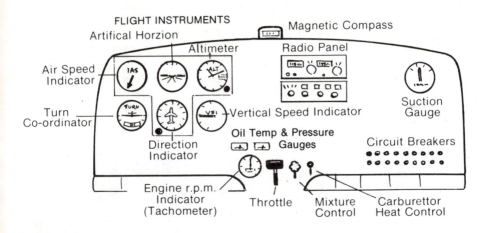

Fig.1-8. A Typical Instrument Panel.

OTHER ITEMS.

There may be a **fire extinguisher** provided in the cockpit, which should be checked for serviceability and security in its fitting. Light aircraft fire extinguishers are normally of the dry-chemical (powder) type which are non-toxic and the Pilot should make himself familiar with its operation.

Control locks may be carried to fit both internally to lock the control column and/or externally on the actual flight controls. Their purpose is to prevent control-surface movement and damage from the wind when the aeroplane is parked. It is vital of course that they be removed prior to flight.

A **pitot cover** may be carried to protect the pitot head from blockage by insects and water whilst the aeroplane is parked. It must be removed prior to flight if the Air Speed Indicator is to read correctly.

Wheel chocks may be carried, to place ahead of and behind the wheels when the aeroplane is parked as a precaution against movement. There may also be a **tie-down kit** of ropes, pegs and mallet to secure the aeroplane to the ground and prevent strong winds lifting the wings or tail. A **First Aid Kit** may be carried.

Written checklists are used in some aeroplanes to confirm that appropriate drills have been carried out, for example, the 'pre-take-off drill' or the 'engine fire drill'. The method of using checklists may be one of:
- carrying-out the items as the check list is read;
- carrying-out the items in-toto followed by confirmation using the checklist; or
- carrying-out the items without reference at all to a written checklist.

Vital drills are best committed to memory so that they may be actioned quickly and efficiently, followed by confirmation using a checklist if required. The procedures for your Training Organisation will be made quite clear by your Flying Instructor. If checklists are used, they must be carried in the cockpit.

EMERGENCIES

The Pilot's Operating Handbook for the particular aeroplane will specify the drills to be followed in coping with certain emergencies, for example:
- engine fire on start-up or taxying;
- engine fire in flight;
- engine-failure in flight followed by a forced landing;
- electrical fire;
- cabin fire; and
- brake failure.

If any problem occurs in flight, the most essential task for the Pilot is to **maintain flying speed and control the flight path of the aeroplane.** The emergency must be handled in conjunction with this primary task.

The more serious emergencies are considered in detail in the appropriate chapter of this manual, however, since you are about to commence flying training, and become part of the 'flight crew', you should have a basic awareness of emergency procedures even at this early stage.

FIRE

Fire is a hazard to aviation and is to be avoided at all costs. For a fire to occur, three things are required:
- fuel (AVGAS, oil, papers, fabric, cabin seating, etc.);
- oxygen (present in the air); and
- a source of ignition (cigarettes, matches, electrical sparks, etc.).

The usual method of extinguishing a fire is to eliminate one or more of these items, e.g. blanketting a fire with 'dry chemical' from a fire extinguisher to starve the fire of oxygen.

It is, of course, preferable that fire is prevented by keeping 'fuel' and possible sources of 'ignition' separate. For example, **when refuelling** an aeroplane, ensure that there is no smoking in the vicinity, that the aeroplane and refuelling equipment are adequately grounded to avoid the possibility of static electricity causing a spark, and that no fuel is spilled. As a precaution, however, a fire extinguisher should be readily available.

ENGINE FIRE DURING START-UP.

The best procedure in this situation is to keep the engine turning with the starter, but move the Mixture Control to *IDLE CUT-OFF* (or the Fuel Selector to *OFF)* to allow the engine to purge itself and the induction system of fuel. The fire will probably go out. If not, then further action should be taken:
Fuel – *OFF;*
Switches – *OFF;*
Brakes – *ON;*
Evacuate, taking the extinguisher.

ENGINE FIRE IN FLIGHT.

If there is an engine fire in flight, shut down the engine and do not restart it. Maintain flying speed.

A fire in flight will probably be caused by a leakage of fuel or oil under pressure, so a typical procedure to stop the leakage is:
- throttle – *CLOSED;*
- mixture – *IDLE CUT-OFF,* or Fuel Selector – *OFF* (so that fuel will be eliminated from the induction system and engine);
- ignition switches – *OFF;*
- cabin heat – *OFF* (to avoid fumes from the engine entering the cockpit).

ELECTRICAL FIRE.

A peculiar smell is often the clue that the fire is electrical. Switch off any associated electrical circuits. If required, a fire extinguisher can be used, but ensure that cabin ventilation is sufficient and the windows are open to remove smoke and toxic fumes from the cabin once the fire is out. An immediate landing is advisable. Whether or not to shut the engine down in flight is a command decision and will, of course, mean a forced landing without power.

A typical drill for an electrical fire is:
- master switch – *OFF* (to remove power from the electrical services);
- all other switches (except ignition) – *OFF;*
- cabin heat – *OFF;*
- fire extinguisher – use as required (and open fresh air vents);
- **on the ground,** shut down the engine and evacuate; **in flight,** decide whether to keep the engine running and make an early landing or shut down the engine and make an immediate forced landing.

CABIN FIRE.

A cabin fire may be caused by such things as a cigarette igniting a seat or other matter. The source of the fire should be identified and the fire eliminated using the fire extinguisher. **In flight,** maintain flying speed and a suitable flight path whilst the emergency is resolved; **on the ground,** consider an immediate evacuation after securing the aeroplane (shut down the engine, switches and fuel – *OFF,* brakes – *ON).*

BRAKE FAILURE.

If the brakes fail while taxying, then:
- throttle – *CLOSED*
- steer away from other aircraft and obstacles;
and, if a collision is imminent:
- STOP the engine (Mixture Control to *IDLE CUT-OFF):*
- fuel – *OFF;*
- ignition – *OFF;*
- master switch – *OFF.*

BEFORE
AND
AFTER FLIGHT

2a

PREPARATION FOR FLIGHT

To prepare for flight.

CONSIDERATIONS

The success of a flight depends very much upon thorough preparation. In the course of your training a pattern of regular pre-flight actions should be developed to ensure that this is the case. They must be based on the checks in the Pilot's Operating Handbook for your aeroplane.

Preparation for a flight commences well before you actually enter the aeroplane and consists of:

- Personal Preparation;
- satisfying the pre-flight Documentation requirements;
- 'Booking Out' the flight with the Air Traffic Service (ATS) Unit;
- the Pre-Flight Inspection of the Aeroplane;
- the Checks associated with Start-up and Taxying;
- the Pre Take-Off Check.

PERSONAL PREPARATION FOR FLIGHT.

The Pilot is the key person on any flight and must be properly prepared. If you are planning on a flight some days hence, then calm, unhurried and thorough long-term preparation a day or two ahead of time might be useful, be it preparing the maps for a cross-country flight or reading up on 'Turning' for an imminent lesson on that exercise.

Short term preparation involves such things as being properly equipped, arriving early enough at the aerodrome for any briefing or flight preparation to proceed in an unhurried manner, and carrying out the required pre-flight checks of the aeroplane calmly and thoroughly.

A typical list of items to check before even leaving home should include:
- am I fit to fly?
  - have I consumed alcohol in the last eight hours?
  - am I using pills, tablets, drugs, etc., that could impair my abilities?
  - do I have a cold, blocked nose, blocked ears or any other upper respiratory complaint?
- do I have the required equipment for this particular flight?
- am I suitably clothed? (natural fibres and materials are generally best, such as a cotton shirt, woollen slacks and leather shoes; these allow the body to 'breathe' as well as being somewhat fire-resistant).

PRE-FLIGHT DOCUMENTATION.

A high level of flight safety is maintained partly because of the thorough documentation required. Items that are recorded include the history of the aeroplane in terms of hours flown and maintenance carried out, and the details of each particular flight and the experience of the Pilot.

The Flight Authorisation Sheet:
Each flight must be authorised by your Flying Training Organisation and will be recorded on a Flight Authorisation Sheet with appropriate details. There may also be a book containing local rules and regulations appropriate to your flying training and which you should check prior to flight.

The Flight Plan and the Weather:
It is not usual to compile a Flight Plan prior to a local training flight, but it is a consideration during your more advanced training when cross-country flights will be undertaken. Weather is a consideration for every flight and, if a 'Weather Man' is available, you should consult with him, and also read through the appropriate weather forecasts or discuss the weather with your Flying Instructor.

Weight and Balance:
It is vital to the safety of every flight that no weight limit is exceeded and that the load is arranged to keep the Centre of Gravity within approved limits. The ability of the aeroplane to fly and be controllable depends upon this.

Most training aeroplanes, however, will be satisfactorily loaded with one or two persons on board and so there may be no need to actually compile a Load Sheet or check the Weight and Balance prior to every training flight. All the same, you should develop the habit of considering 'Weight and Balance' before each and every flight.

Airworthiness Documents:
It is a Pilot's responsibility to check certain documents prior to flight to **ensure that the aeroplane is airworthy.** These documents include:

- The Certificate of Airworthiness;
- The Maintenance Documents;
- The Aircraft Weight and Balance Schedule;
- The Aircraft Technical Log.

Do not accept responsibility for the aeroplane if it has defects which may make it unacceptable for flight. If in any doubt, discuss the matter with your Flying Instructor or with a Licensed Engineer.

BOOKING OUT.

'Booking Out' with the Air Traffic Service (ATS) makes them aware of your flight and allows them to document its progress and safe completion. You can book out with the ATS Unit in person before going to the aeroplane or by radio prior to taxying.

PREPARING THE AEROPLANE FOR FLIGHT.

The Pilot's Operating Handbook for your aeroplane will contain a list of items that must be checked during:
- the External Inspection of the aeroplane;
- the Internal Inspection;
- the Pre-start, Starting and After-starting checks;
- the Engine Power Check; and
- the Pre Take-Off Check.

At first, these checks may seem long and complicated but, as you repeat them thoroughly prior to each flight, a pattern will soon form. It is vital that these checks are carried out thoroughly, strictly in accordance with your Pilot's Operating Handbook. The comments that follow are only general comments that will apply to most aeroplanes, however they may or may not apply to yours.

THE EXTERNAL INSPECTION.

This can commence as you walk to the aeroplane and should include:
- the position of the aeroplane as being suitable for start-up and taxi (also, note the wind direction and the likely path to the take-off point);
- the availability of fire extinguishers and emergency equipment in case of fire on start-up (a very rare event, but it does happen).

A list of typical 'walk-around' items is shown below. Each item must be inspected individually, but do not neglect a general overview of the aeroplane. Be vigilant for things such as buckling of the fuselage skin or 'popped' rivets as these could indicate internal structural damage from a previous flight. Leaking oil, fuel forming puddles on the ground, or hydraulic fluid leaks from around the brake lines also deserve further investigation. With experience, you will develop a 'feel' for what looks right and what doesn't.

The **walk-around inspection** starts at the cockpit door:
- check or action that:
    - the Magneto Switches are *OFF;*
    - the fuel contents are indicated on the gauges;
    - the control locks are removed;
    - the flaps are lowered (in anticipation of an external inspection);
    - the brakes are set to *PARK.*
- Check the door to ensure that it is securely attached and can be latched correctly;
- Check the fuel contents by visually inspecting the tanks, replacing the fuel caps securely;
- Carry-out a fuel drain (following refuelling or on the first flight of the day) from the drain valves into a glass bottle, visually checking for water (which will sink to the bottom), for any sediment, and for correct colouration of the fuel;

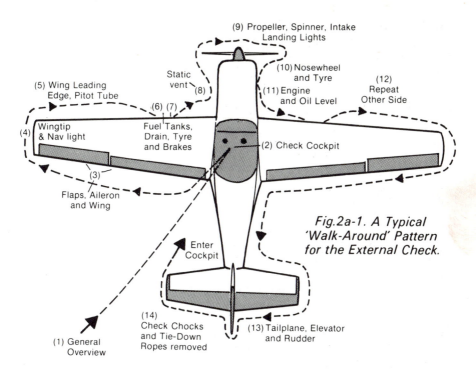

(9) Propeller, Spinner, Intake
Landing Lights

(10) Nosewheel
and Tyre

(12)
Repeat
Other Side

Static
vent

(8)

(5) Wing Leading
Edge, Pitot Tube

(11) Engine
and Oil Level

(6) (7)

Wingtip
(4) & Nav light

Fuel Tanks,
Drain, Tyre
and Brakes

(2) Check Cockpit

(3)

Flaps, Aileron
and Wing

Enter
Cockpit

*Fig.2a-1. A Typical
'Walk-Around' Pattern
for the External Check.*

(14)
Check Chocks
and Tie-Down
Ropes removed

(13) Tailplane, Elevator
and Rudder

(1) General
Overview

- Check the hydraulic lines to the wheel brakes for cracks and leaks and check that the brake disc is secure;
- Check the undercarriage leg and its attachment to the fuselage; popped rivets, buckling of the skin or other damage should be brought to the attention of an Engineer;
- Check the tyre for correct inflation, cuts and creep, and check that the wheel is secure;
- Check the undersurface of the fuselage for any buckling of the skin or other damage;
- Check the flap surfaces and flap actuating mechanism; check the trailing edge of the wing and aileron for free and correct movement (one up — one down);
- Check the wingtip and navigation light for damage and security;
- Check the leading edge of the wing for smoothness — contamination from ice, frost or insects can greatly diminish the lifting ability of the wing;
- Check that the cover is removed from the pitot tube (otherwise the Air Speed Indicator will not operate correctly in flight);
- Check that the fuel vent is clear (to allow pressures inside and outside the tanks to equalise as fuel is used and/or altitude is changed);
- Ensure that all inspection panels on the wing are secure;
- Check that the wing strut (if one exists) is secure at both ends;
- Check that the Static Vent is open and clean (for correct operation of the Air Speed Indicator, Altimeter and Vertical Speed Indicator);
- Check the nose section of the fuselage – loose screws, popped rivets and any buckling of the skin could indicate structural damage from a previous flight;

- Check the propeller for damage (especially nicks along its leading edge), cracks and security;
- Check the propeller spinner for damage, cracks and security;
- Check that the engine air intake and filter is clean, secure and not blocked by things such as a bird's nest, rags, etc.;
- Check the nose wheel and tyre;
- Check the nose oleo strut for correct extension (usually 2–3 inches) and the shimmy damper and other mechanisms for security;
- Open the engine inspection panel and check the oil contents (replacing the oil cap securely), inspect for any obvious loose cables or wires, cracked manifolds, etc., and then lock the inspection panel;
- Ensure that the windscreen is clean;
- Continue the check around onto the other side of the aeroplane;
- Check luggage lockers securely closed;
- Check radio aerials for security and no loose wires;
- Check all visible cables, lights, etc.;
- Check the tailplane, rudder, elevator (for free movement) and trim tab;
- Remove and stow tie-down ropes and chocks (provided the parking brake is on);
- Stand back and check the general appearance of the aeroplane.

It cannot be emphasised too greatly just how important this pre-flight inspection by the Pilot is. Even if you have no experience in mechanical things, you must train yourself to **look** at the aeroplane and notice things that do not seem right. Bring any items that you are unsure of to the attention of your Flying Instructor or an Engineer.

At this stage, you are now ready to seat yourself in the aeroplane and commence the Internal Inspection.

THE INTERNAL INSPECTION.

This should include:
- Confirm the brakes are – *ON* (parked);
- Fuel – *ON;*
- Seat position and harness;
- Ignition Switch (magnetos) – *OFF* (i.e the engine is not 'live');
- Master Switch – *ON* (for electrical services such as fuel gauges);
- Flight controls for full and free movement (elevator, ailerons, rudder and trim wheel or handle – set the trim to the take-off position);
- Engine controls for full and free movement (throttle, mixture control and carburettor heat control);
- Scan the instruments systematically from one side of the panel to the other for serviceability and correct readings;
- No circuit breakers should be popped nor fuses blown (for electrical services to operate);
- The microphone should be plugged in if you are to transmit on the radio;
- Safety equipment (fire extinguisher, first aid kit) on board;
- Loose articles stowed;
- Check lists available (if required).

Once the pre-flight inspection is completed and you are comfortable in your seat, the engine starting procedure can begin. This is covered in the next chapter.

2b

STARTING
AND STOPPING
THE ENGINE

AIM

To start and stop the engine.

CONSIDERATIONS

Prior to starting the engine, check that the surrounding area is suitable for start-up. The aeroplane should be on a surface suitable for taxying and well away from any buildings, fuel storage areas and public areas. The aeroplane should be parked facing in a direction that will not cause loose stones or gravel to be blasted back over other aircraft or into open hangars when the engine is running. Also, there should be no fuel spills in the vicinity as this creates a fire risk.

The engine then needs to be properly prepared for the start-up. The correct procedure for this is found in your Pilot's Operating Handbook.

THE PRE-START AND STARTING CHECK will include such items as:
- Brakes – *ON;*
- Unnecessary Electrical Equipment – *OFF;*
- Fuel – *ON;*
- Carburettor Heat Control – *COLD;*
- Mixture – *RICH;*
- Throttle – *CLOSED* (or cracked ¼ inch open);
- Fuel Primer – *LOCKED* (following 1—3 priming strokes, if applicable);
- Rotating Beacon – *ON* (as a warning to other people);
- 'All Clear' – the area around the aeroplane, especially near the propeller, should be *ALL CLEAR*. The Pilot is responsible for people around the aeroplane. Loudly call "CLEAR PROPELLER" to warn anyone that may be approaching the aeroplane;
- Starter – *ENGAGE* to crank the engine; then, once the engine has started, release the starter and check that it has disengaged (which, in most aeroplanes, is indicated by a red light going-out).

AFTER STARTING, various items to be checked may include:
- Starter Warning Light – *OUT;*
- Oil Pressure – sufficient pressure within 30 seconds of start-up (slightly longer in very cold weather);
- Set Idling rpm with the Throttle (usually 1,000 – 1,200 rpm) to ensure adequate cooling;
- Ammeter – indicating re-charging of the battery following the drain on it during start-up;
- Vacuum Gauge (if fitted) – check for sufficient suction to operate the gyro instruments;
- Magneto Check of the LEFT and RIGHT Magnetos individually, as well as with the Ignition Switch in the usual *BOTH* position (the rpm should decrease slightly on each individual magneto and return to the previous value when the switch is returned to *BOTH)* but, if the engine stops, then a problem exists;
- Radio – *ON*, correct frequency selected, volume set, and squelch set.

THE PRE TAKE-OFF CHECK OF THE ENGINE.

After the aeroplane has been taxied to the holding point or run-up bay prior to entering the runway, it is brought to a halt and the brakes parked whilst the **Pre Take-Off Vital Actions** are performed. One of these actions is a check of the engine. This is detailed in Section 12 of this manual.

SHUTTING-DOWN THE ENGINE.

There will be a shut-down procedure specified in the Pilot's Operating Handbook for your aircraft which will include such items as:
- Brakes – *PARKED,* with the aeroplane (ideally) pointing into any strong wind;
- ensure the engine is cool (having taxied or set 1,000 – 1,200 rpm for a minute or two should be sufficient);
- Magnetos – *CHECK:* both magnetos should be checked individually. There should be a slight rpm drop as you go from *BOTH* to an individual magneto, and a return to the set rpm when the switch is returned to *BOTH*

NOTE: Sometimes a 'DEAD-CUT' check is made by moving the Ignition Switch very quickly from *BOTH* to *OFF* and back to *BOTH,* to check that the engine will actually cut. It checks that *'OFF'* does indeed break the circuit to each magneto by earthing them. If this were not the case, then the engine and propeller would be 'LIVE' even with the magneto switch to *OFF.* An innocent movement of the propeller could start the engine unexpectedly — a dangerous situation! Certain engine manufacturers advise against this check as it may cause damage to the engine, especially if the switch is held too long in the *OFF* position. Seek your Flying Instructor's advice.

- Electrics – *OFF* (radio, lights, etc.);
- Mixture Control – *IDLE CUT-OFF,* (fully-out), to starve the engine of fuel and stop it running;
- After the engine stops, switch the Ignition *OFF* and remove the key;
- Consideration should be given to switching the Fuel Cock *OFF.*

PROBLEMS DURING START-UP

Most engine starts are uneventful if correct procedures are followed but, occasionally, a problem may occur.

A FLOODED ENGINE.

It is possible to flood an engine with too much fuel, making a start difficult and placing a strain on the Battery which supplies electrical power to the Starter Motor. If 'flooding' is suspected, adopt the following procedure:
• Ignition Switches – *OFF;*
• Throttle – *FULLY OPEN;*
• Fuel – *ON;*
• Mixture Control – *IDLE CUT-OFF* (i.e. no fuel supplied to the engine);
• **Crank** the engine through several revolutions with the Starter (which should clear the intake passages of excess fuel); then
• **Repeat the Starting Procedure** without priming the engine.

ENGINE FIRE ON START-UP.

Engine fires are a very rare event these days but they can still occur, possibly as a result of over-priming the engine with fuel. In such a case:

Starter – if still engaged, *CONTINUE CRANKING;*
Mixture Control – *IDLE CUT-OFF;*
Fuel Selector – *OFF;*
Throttle – *OPEN* (to allow maximum airflow through to purge the induction system and engine of fuel).

Once the fuel has been eliminated, the fire should stop. Release the Starter.

If the fire continues:
• Ignition Switch – *OFF;*
• Master Switch – *OFF;*
• Brakes – *ON;*
• Evacuate, taking any suitable fire extinguisher with you. Do not attempt to re-start the engine.

2c

POST-FLIGHT ACTIONS

The post-flight duties required of each Pilot are to:
- secure the aeroplane; and
- complete the post-flight documentation.

A flight is not really completed until the engine is shut-down and the aeroplane parked and secure. The post-flight documentation must be finalised, since it is **a requirement that certain records be kept** and that any faults in the aeroplane be made known so that **maintenance** action will be taken.

An aeroplane has a life of its own in the sense that it passes continually from the command of one Pilot to the command of another – the post-flight check of one being followed by the pre-flight check of the next. To a certain extent, each Pilot relies upon the fact that earlier Pilots have performed their duties, even though we must all **accept individual responsibility.**

SECURING THE AEROPLANE.

The aeroplane should not be left unattended unless it is adequately secured against movement and possible damage.

- Ensure that the parking brake is *ON* (if required) and that the wheel chocks are in place, in front of and behind the wheels;
- Carry-out a brief external inspection;
- Fit the pitot covers, control locks and tie down ropes if required;
- Secure the seat belts;
- If yours is the last flight of the day, consider refuelling to minimise overnight condensation of water in the fuel tanks;
- Lock the door and return the key.

POST-FLIGHT DOCUMENTATION.

- 'Book In' the flight if necessary with the Air Traffic Service Unit;
- Complete the **Flight Authorisation** sheet, recording the time and nature of the flight;
- Report any aeroplane defects to your Flying Instructor or to an Engineer and, when appropriate, note them on the maintenance document to ensure that necessary maintenance will be attended to and that the following Pilot will have a serviceable aeroplane;
- Complete your personal **Log Book.**

During your training, a de-briefing by your Flying Instructor will probably occur following the completion of your post-flight duties.

3

YOUR FIRST FLIGHT

3

YOUR
FIRST FLIGHT

This flight is not part of your formal instruction but rather an opportunity to get the 'feel' of being airborne. Your Flying Instructor, an experienced and professional Pilot, will use this first flight to let you experience some of the more common sensations of flying an aeroplane.

Sit comfortably in your seat and relax. Since you will be trained to become the Captain of your aeroplane, you may as well start by sitting in the left-hand seat – the Captain's seat by tradition and design. It needs to be positioned so that you can reach the appropriate controls comfortably with your hands and feet. The seat belt or harness should be firm.

Even though this may be your very first flight, it is important that your seat is positioned correctly, since the position of the natural horizon in the windscreen is a vital element in assisting the visual Pilot to fly accurately.

Fresh air is available through vents, and directing these towards your face and body improves the cockpit environment considerably for you.

Whilst **taxying out,** you can assist in maintaining a good **Look Out** for other aircraft and for obstructions.

During the **take-off** roll you should look well ahead. Maintaining a straight path down the runway, and also judging height above it, is best achieved by looking into the 'middle distance'. Develop good habits right from the start! Even though the take-off appears full of action, in reality it is a straightforward manoeuvre and you will soon master it.

As the aeroplane climbs, ground features take on a different perspective, being viewed more in plan than in profile – towns, roads, rivers, mountains and coastlines appearing as they would on a map. The sensation of speed also diminishes and the aeroplane feels like it is flying in slow motion.

You will have the opportunity to 'follow' your Instructor on the Flight Controls by placing:

- your left hand lightly on the control wheel (or control column);
- your right hand on the throttle or on your lap; and
- both feet lightly on the rudder pedals (with your heels on the floor to ensure that the toe brakes are not applied).

Fig.3-1. A Light Touch on the Controls.

During the course of your training, control will be passed from your Instructor to you and then back again quite frequently. Your Flying Instructor will say, "you have control" (or words to that effect), when he wishes you to take control. Upon hearing this instruction, you should place your hands and feet on the controls lightly, but firmly, and, once you feel comfortable to take control, respond by saying, "I have control". **Each change of control** should be preceded by an initial statement followed by a response from the other Pilot.

Fig.3-2. Be Clear At All Times as to Who Has Control.

Visual flying requires that the Pilot maintains a **high visual awareness of the environment outside the cockpit,** both to relate the attitude (or nose position) of the aeroplane to the natural horizon, as well as to **Look Out** for other aircraft, to check passage over the ground, and to remain clear of cloud.

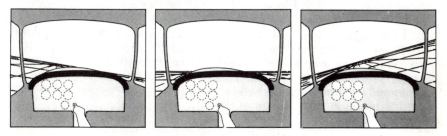

Fig.3-3. The View from the Cockpit.

The **position of other aeroplanes** in relation to your own is best described by using the **'Clock Code'**, based on a horizontal clock face aligned with the aeroplane's heading.

An aeroplane ahead of you, but higher, would be described as '12-o'clock high', whilst one slightly behind and below you on the left-hand side would be at '8-o'clock low'.

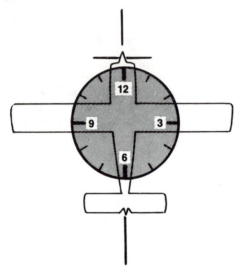

Fig.3-4. The Clock Code.

Note any landmarks that can assist in your return to the aerodrome and **remain well clear of cloud** at all times.

The aeroplane has instruments which can provide useful information regarding altitude, direction, airspeed and engine operation. The basic division is into **Flight Instruments and Engine Instruments.** An occasional glance at a particular instrument for one or two seconds is all that a visual Pilot requires – his visual awareness of the world outside the cockpit must not suffer.

As the **descent, approach and landing** proceed, the Pilot's workload increases. During the landing, you should again look into the 'middle distance', to allow better judgement in the **flare and touchdown** when you are making the landing. The approach and landing seems full of action, but it will not be long before you have mastered this manoeuvre!

A flight is not complete until the aeroplane is parked and secured, and the **post-flight duties** of the Pilot completed. Your first flight is now over, but a marvellous hobby or career awaits you. Preparing for the next flying lesson carefully on the ground by reading the appropriate chapter of this manual (as outlined by your Instructor) will ensure that you **derive the maximum benefit from your next lesson in the air.**

4

THE
CONTROLS

4a

THE PRIMARY EFFECT OF EACH MAIN FLIGHT CONTROL

AIM

To observe the primary effect of moving each main flight control.

CONSIDERATIONS

AN AEROPLANE MOVES IN THREE DIMENSIONS.

To describe an aeroplane's attitude or position in flight, three mutually-perpendicular reference-axes passing through the Centre of Gravity are used. Any change in aeroplane attitude can be expressed in terms of motion about these three axes.

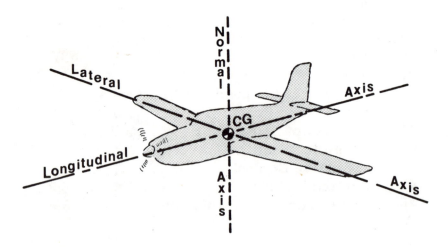

Fig.4a-1. Angular Motion is Described Using Three Reference Axes.

- **Motion about the lateral axis** is known as **pitching** (or motion in the pitching plane);
- **Motion about the longitudinal axis** is known as **rolling** (or motion in the rolling plane); and
- **Motion about the normal axis** is **yawing** (or motion in the yawing plane).

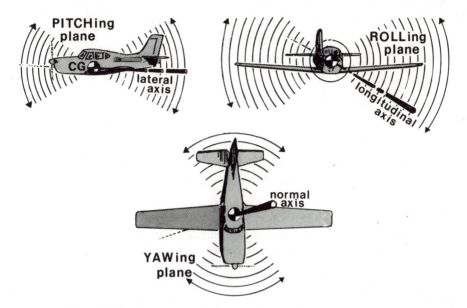

Fig.4a-2. Angular Motion Can Occur in Three Planes.

THE STABILITY OF AN AEROPLANE.

Stability is the natural ability of the aeroplane to remain in its original attitude or to return to it following some disturbance (such as a wind gust) without any action being taken by the Pilot.

Most training aeroplanes are reasonably stable in the **pitching plane.** If correctly trimmed, they will maintain steady flight with the Pilot flying 'hands-off'. In other words, the nose position relative to the horizon will remain reasonably steady without too much attention from the Pilot.

The stability of most aeroplanes in the **rolling** and **yawing** planes, however, is usually not as great as in the pitching plane. If the wings are moved from their level position (say by a gust), the aeroplane will eventually enter a descending spiral turn unless the Pilot actively does something about it – in this case by levelling the wings.

THE MAIN FLIGHT CONTROLS.

The Pilot controls motion about the three axes (or in the three planes) with the main flight controls:

- the Elevator controls Pitch;
- the Ailerons control Roll; and
- the Rudder controls Yaw.

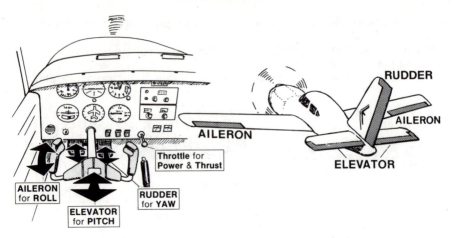

Fig.4a-3. The Three Main Flight Controls:
Elevator, Ailerons and Rudder.

THE ELEVATOR CONTROLS PITCHING.

The elevator is operated by fore and aft movements of the control column and controls pitching. The **conventional elevator** is a control surface hinged to the rear of the tailplane (also known as the horizontal stabilizer). Some aircraft have an **'all-flying tail'** (or 'stabilator') which is a single moving surface acting as both the tailplane and the elevator. Either type has the same effect on the aeroplane when the control column is moved.

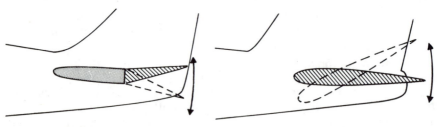

FIXED TAILPLANE
PLUS MOVING ELEVATOR

ALL MOVING TAIL
(or Stabilator)

Fig.4a-4. The 'Separate' Tailplane and Elevator, and the 'All-Flying' Tail.

Deflecting the elevator with the control column alters the airflow around the tailplane and changes the aerodynamic force generated by it. Moving the control column back deflects the elevator up, causing an increased speed of flow beneath the tailplane and reducing the static pressure in that area. This results in a downwards aerodynamic force on the tailplane, causing the aeroplane to rotate about its Centre of Gravity. The tail moves down and the nose moves up.

Fig.4a-5. The Elevator Controls Pitching.

The rate of pitching of the aeroplane increases with larger elevator deflections. At normal flight speeds, the movement of the control column can be quite small and may feel more like pressure changes than actual movements. Fore and aft movement of the control column is used to place the nose in the desired position relative to the horizon (i.e. to set the pitch attitude).

THE AILERONS CONTROL ROLLING.

The ailerons are hinged control surfaces attached to the outboard trailing edge of each wing. The ailerons in some aeroplanes are controlled by rotation of the control wheel and in other aeroplanes by left/right movements of the control column. The control column or control wheel therefore serves two functions:
1. Fore and aft movement operates the elevator.
2. Rotation or left/right movement operates the ailerons.

Fig.4a-6. A Control Column or a Control Wheel Perform the Same Function.

As one aileron goes down and increases the lift generated by that wing, the other aileron goes up and reduces the lift on its wing, causing the aeroplane to roll. For example, moving the control column to the left causes a roll to the left by raising the left aileron and lowering the right aileron.

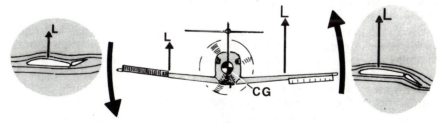

Fig.4a-7. A Roll to the Left.

The aeroplane will continue to roll whilst the ailerons are deflected, the roll rate being determined by the amount of aileron deflection. Holding the control column central places the ailerons in the neutral position and stops the roll.

THE RUDDER CONTROLS YAWING.

The third (and final) main flight control is the Rudder which is a hinged control surface at the rear of the fin (vertical stabilizer). The rudder is controlled with both feet on the rudder pedals. These pedals are inter-connected so that as one moves forward the other moves back.

Moving the left rudder pedal forward deflects the rudder to the left. This increases the speed of airflow on the right hand side of the fin, reducing the static pressure there and creating an aerodynamic force to the right. The aeroplane rotates about its Centre of Gravity and so, with left rudder, the nose yaws left. Conversely, moving the right rudder pedal forward yaws the nose of the aeroplane to the right.

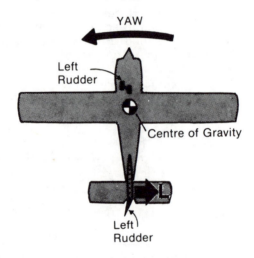

Fig.4a-8. The Left Rudder Pressure Yaws the Nose Left.

Yawing the aeroplane can be uncomfortable and is aerodynamically inefficient because it causes drag to increase. It is neither a comfortable nor efficient means of turning an aeroplane in flight; a yawing turn falls into the same category as trying to turn a bicycle without leaning it into the turn.

Although it can yaw the aeroplane, one of the main functions of the rudder is to **prevent unwanted yaw,** a function known as 'maintaining balanced flight'. This is indicated to the Pilot by the small balance ball on the instrument panel and also by the 'seat of his pants'. If the aeroplane is out of balance, the ball moves out to one side (and the Pilot, reacting in the same way as the ball, will feel pressed to the same side).

Balance can be restored by applying **same-side rudder pressure,** i.e. if the ball is out to the right, apply right rudder pressure (and vice versa).

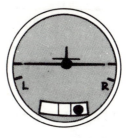

*Fig.4a-9. Apply
'Same-Side' Rudder Pressure
to Centre the Balance Ball.*

THE CONTROLS OPERATE RELATIVE TO THE AEROPLANE'S THREE AXES.

Each of the three primary aerodynamic controls operates in the same sense **relative to the aeroplane,** irrespective of its attitude in pitch or bank. For example, moving the control column forward will move the nose in a direction away from the Pilot even if (taking an extreme case) the aeroplane is inverted.

*Fig.4a-10. Motion is
Referred to the
Aeroplane Axes.*

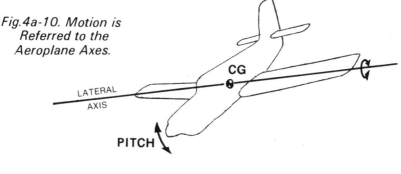

FLYING THE MANOEUVRE

Good flying requires the co-ordination of all three flight controls, however in this exercise we will use them individually. It is a necessary step because the individual effects need to be appreciated before smooth co-ordination of the flight controls in normal flight is possible.

From straight and level flight move each of the controls **individually** and relate the effects to the three axes. Repeat with the aeroplane banked.

AIRMANSHIP

You are training to be a visual Pilot so develop good habits early. **Look Out** of the cockpit most of the time, both to check the attitude of the aeroplane relative to the horizon and to look for other aircraft. Identify their position using the clock code. Follow the correct "You have control" – "I have control" procedures so that it is quite clear at all times who has control.

Hold the controls lightly and move them smoothly and fluently. Occasionally, large control movements are required to achieve the desired effect but, at normal flying speeds, firm pressures rather than large movements will achieve the desired effect.

AIRWORK 4a —

AIM: *To observe the primary effect of moving each main flight control during flight.*

(1) The Primary Effect of the Elevator is to Pitch the Aeroplane.

(a) Establish the aeroplane in steady, straight-and-level flight. Maintain a good *LOOK OUT*

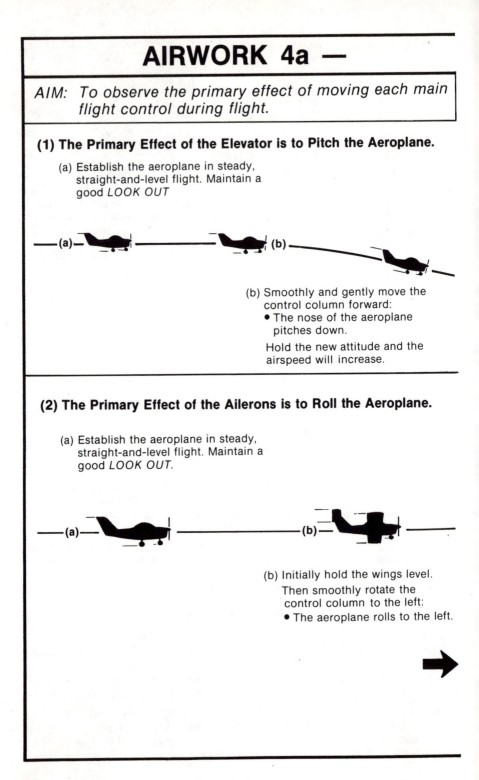

(b) Smoothly and gently move the control column forward:
   • The nose of the aeroplane pitches down.

   Hold the new attitude and the airspeed will increase.

(2) The Primary Effect of the Ailerons is to Roll the Aeroplane.

(a) Establish the aeroplane in steady, straight-and-level flight. Maintain a good *LOOK OUT.*

(b) Initially hold the wings level.
   Then smoothly rotate the control column to the left:
   • The aeroplane rolls to the left.

THE PRIMARY EFFECT OF EACH MAIN FLIGHT CONTROL

(c) Smoothly and gently move the control column rearward.
- The nose of the aeroplane pitches up.

Hold the new attitude and the airspeed will decrease.

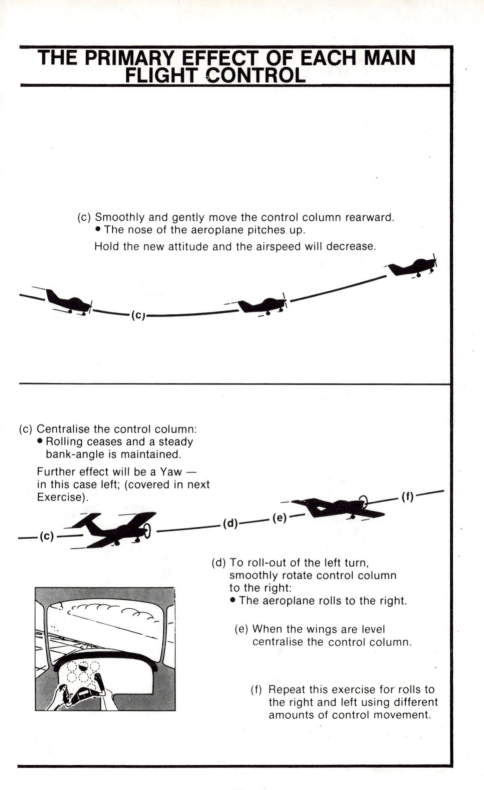

(c) Centralise the control column:
- Rolling ceases and a steady bank-angle is maintained.

Further effect will be a Yaw — in this case left; (covered in next Exercise).

(d) To roll-out of the left turn, smoothly rotate control column to the right:
- The aeroplane rolls to the right.

(e) When the wings are level centralise the control column.

(f) Repeat this exercise for rolls to the right and left using different amounts of control movement.

AIRWORK 4a (cont'd) —

(3) The Primary Effect of the Rudder is to Yaw the Aeroplane.

(a) Establish the aeroplane in steady, straight-and-level flight. Maintain a good *LOOK OUT*.

(b) Select a reference point on the horizon.

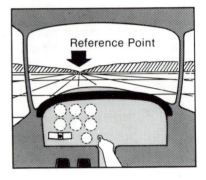

(c) Smoothly apply left rudder pressure:
  • The nose of the aeroplane yaws left (and the balance ball is thrown out to the right).

Left rudder – nose yaws left and balance ball thrown right.

(d) Centralise the rudder pedals (by removing left rudder pressure).

(e) Repeat using right rudder pressure and observe the reverse results.

THE PRIMARY EFFECT OF EACH MAIN FLIGHT CONTROL

(4) The Controls Work the Same when the Aeroplane is Not Flying Straight and Level.

(a) Establish the aeroplane in steady straight-and-level flight. *LOOK OUT.*

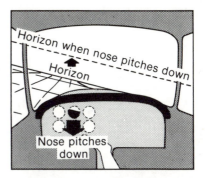

Aeroplane banked to the left – forward control column pressure still pitches the nose down.

(b) Bank the aeroplane with the aileron control:
- Forward pressure on the control column pitches the nose down and away from the Pilot;
- Aft pressure on the control column pitches the nose up and towards the Pilot.

(c) Set the aeroplane with a high nose attitude:
- Rotating the control column left causes the aeroplane to roll left;
- Rotating the control column right causes the aeroplane to roll right.

With a high nose attitude the aeroplane still responds to the aileron control – rolls right (and left).

(d) Bank the aeroplane with the ailerons:
- Pushing the left rudder pedal causes the nose to yaw left relative to the Pilot;
- Pushing the right rudder pedal causes the nose to yaw right relative to the Pilot.

Intentionally Blank

4b

THE FURTHER EFFECT OF EACH MAIN FLIGHT CONTROL

AIM

To observe the further effect of moving each main flight control.

CONSIDERATIONS

OPERATING A SINGLE FLIGHT CONTROL CAN HAVE MORE THAN ONE EFFECT.

When either the ailerons or rudder are used individually there is both a primary and a secondary (or further) effect.

ROLL CAUSES YAW — THE FURTHER EFFECT OF AILERONS.

Banking the aeroplane tilts the Lift force generated by the wings. A sideways component of the Lift force now exists, causing the aeroplane to 'slip' towards the lower wing. In this **sideslip,** the large keel surfaces behind the Centre of Gravity (such as the fin and the fuselage) are struck by the airflow which causes the aeroplane's nose to yaw in the direction of the sideslip. The nose will drop and a spiral descent commence (unless prevented by the Pilot levelling the wings).

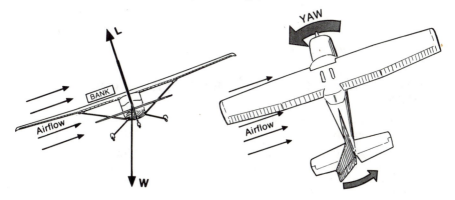

Fig.4b-1. Bank Causes Sideslip Followed by Yaw.

Moving the ailerons with left/right movements of the control column has two effects – a **roll** followed by **a yaw**. Therefore:
• **the primary effect of the ailerons is to roll the aeroplane; and**
• **the further effect is to yaw the aeroplane.**

YAW CAUSES ROLL — THE FURTHER EFFECT OF RUDDER.

Applying rudder will yaw the nose of the aeroplane – a yaw to the left if left rudder pressure is applied, a yaw to the right if right rudder is applied.

As a result of the yaw, the outer wing will tend to rise because:
• it is moving faster than the inner wing and so generates more lift; and
• the aeroplane will continue to move in its original direction due to inertia, causing the outer wing, if it has dihedral, to be presented to the airflow at a greater angle of attack, generating increased lift. ('Dihedral' describes a wing that is angled up towards the wingtip.)

Operating the rudder, therefore, causes **yaw followed by roll** and unless the Pilot takes corrective action (by preventing unwanted yaw with opposite rudder or by levelling the wings) a spiral descent will result.

When rudder is applied:
• **the primary effect is to yaw the aeroplane; and**
• **the further effect is to roll the aeroplane.**

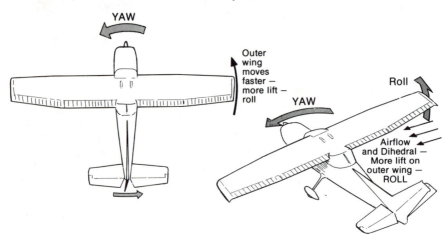

Fig.4b-2. Rudder Causes Yaw Followed by Roll.

THE FURTHER EFFECT OF THE ELEVATOR IS AN AIRSPEED CHANGE.

The primary effect of elevator is to change the pitch attitude. For example, by moving the control column back the nose is raised.

Following a pitch change, the inertia of the aeroplane (i.e. its resistance to any change) will cause it to follow the original flight path for a brief period. The airflow will then strike the wings at a greater angle of attack and, as a consequence, they will generate a different aerodynamic force. Drag will increase, causing the aeroplane to slow down. Thus, raising the nose with the elevator will lead to an airspeed decrease.

Conversely, by moving the control column forward, the nose is lowered and the airflow will strike the wings at a lesser angle of attack, less Drag will be created and so the airspeed will increase. Thus, lowering the nose with the elevator will lead to an airspeed increase.

When deflected by moving the control column, **the elevator has:**
- **the primary effect of pitching the aeroplane; and**
- **the further effect of changing the airspeed.**

SLOW   FAST

Fig.4b-3. The Further Effect of Elevator is to Change the Airspeed.

NOTE: When the elevator changes the pitch attitude of the aeroplane, it will gradually settle at a new airspeed. Whether the aeroplane climbs, descends or stays at the same level depends upon the power that is set. The effect of power is discussed shortly.

FLYING THE MANOEUVRE

Established in straight and level flight, observe the effects of moving each main flight control individually. Allow time after the initial effect for the further effect to become apparent. The effects should be related to the three aeroplane axes.

Observing the effects of each of the main flight controls is a prelude to learning how to co-ordinate their use to achieve smooth, comfortable and efficient flight.

AIRMANSHIP

Maintain a good **Look Out,** both with respect to the horizon and landmarks as well as looking for other aircraft. Be very clear at all times about who has control of the aeroplane. When you have control, exert gentle, but firm and positive pressures on the controls as required.

AIRWORK 4b —

AIM: *To observe the further effect of moving each main flight control.*

(1) Roll Causes Yaw — The Further Effect of the Ailerons.

(a) Establish straight and level flight,
maintaining a good *LOOK OUT*

(b) Remove your feet from the rudder pedals.

(c) Apply aileron by moving
the control column:
- The aeroplane banks and then, because of the resulting sideslip,
yaws towards the lower wing, i.e. the nose drops into the turn.

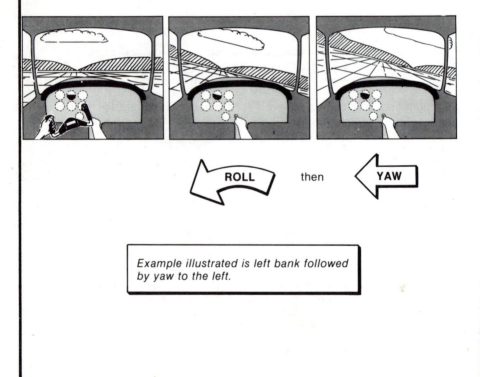

ROLL   then   YAW

> *Example illustrated is left bank followed
> by yaw to the left.*

THE FURTHER EFFECT OF EACH MAIN FLIGHT CONTROL

(2) Yaw Causes Roll — the Further Effect of the Rudder.

(a) Establish straight-and-level flight, maintaining a good *LOOK OUT*.

(b) Take your hands off the control column.

(c) Apply rudder pressure.

(d) The aeroplane yaws and then, because of the yaw, rolls in the same direction.

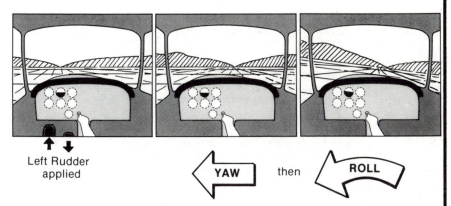

Left Rudder applied

YAW   then   ROLL

Left yaw produces a roll to the left.

NOTE: THE EFFECTS SEEN IN Nos. 1 and 2 WILL ALSO BE THE SAME WHEN THE AEROPLANE IS BANKED, IS CLIMBING, OR IS DESCENDING.

(3) Changing the Pitch Attitude Alters the Airspeed — the Further Effect of the Elevator.

(a) Establish straight-and-level flight, and *LOOK OUT*.

(b) Ease the control column forward:
  • The nose pitches down and the airspeed increases.

(c) Ease the control column back:
  • The nose rises and the airspeed decreases.

4c

THE ART
OF TRIMMING

AIM

To use the trim to relieve prolonged control pressures.

CONSIDERATIONS

TRIMMING IS VITAL TO ACCURATE FLIGHT.

All training aeroplanes have an elevator trim that can relieve the Pilot of steady fore and aft pressures on the control column. Some aeroplanes also have a rudder trim to relieve steady pressures on the rudder pedals.

The trim is used to relieve prolonged control pressures in steady conditions of flight, such as straight and level, climbing and descending. The trim should not be altered in transient manoeuvres, such as turning.

Using the trimming devices can ease the work load on the Pilot tremendously, so the effect of trim and how to use it correctly should be clearly understood at an early stage.

TRIM CONTROL WHEEL
(sometimes in ceiling)

ELEVATOR TRIM TAB

Fig.4c-1. The Elevator Trim Tab and Trim-Wheel.

42

WHY IS TRIM NEEDED?

The elevator is controlled by fore and aft movement of the control wheel and is used by the Pilot to hold the desired pitch attitude. If this requires a steady pressure, then flight becomes quite tiring, making precision flight almost impossible. Trim can be used to relieve this steady pressure on the control column and, used precisely, can reduce it to zero.

Trim is **not** used to alter the attitude of the aeroplane; it is only used to relieve pressure.

ELEVATOR TRIM CAN HOLD THE ELEVATOR DEFLECTED.

Elevator trim in most aeroplanes is achieved using a small 'trim tab' located on the trailing edge of the elevator. The trim tab is operated by a trim-wheel (or handle) in the cockpit. **The purpose of the trim tab** is to hold the elevator displaced with an aerodynamic force, rather than a force that the Pilot exerts via the control column.

If the trim tab is deflected downwards, the airflow over the upper surface of the elevator speeds up, reducing the static pressure. An aerodynamic force now exists to deflect the elevator upwards.

RELIEVING CONTROL PRESSURES WITH THE TRIM.

A steady back pressure exerted by the Pilot on the control column to hold the elevator up can be relieved by winding the trim-wheel back. This deflects the trim tab down, reducing the static pressure above it. If the static pressure is sufficiently low for the elevator to remain deflected upwards to the same degree, then the Pilot need not continue to hold steady back pressure on the control column. Flying now becomes less tiring.

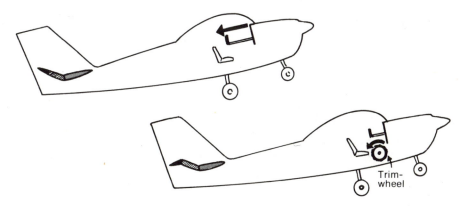

Fig.4c-2. Using Elevator Trim
to Relieve Steady Pressures on the Control Column.

NOTE: The description above applies to the 'aerodynamic' trim tab that is found on most aeroplanes. On others, however, trimming is achieved by applying a spring loading to the control column to relieve the Pilot.

RE-TRIMMING.

The demands placed upon the elevator change from time to time and so re-trimming will be necessary:
- after a **new pitch attitude** is selected;
- after a **power change;**
- after a **configuration change** (e.g. alteration of flap position);
- after a **change** in the position of the **Centre of Gravity** (say as fuel burns off, passengers move, baggage is shifted or parachutists depart).

Whenever a steady pressure is required on the control column in steady flight, then trim it out.

FLYING THE MANOEUVRE

Correct trimming is achieved by moving the trim-wheel in a natural sense. If you are holding back pressure on the control column, then wind the trim wheel back, gradually releasing the pressure so that the pitch attitude does not change.

Conversely, if forward pressure is needed to maintain pitch attitude, then wind the trim-wheel forward until there is no steady pressure required on the control column.

Whilst you are trimming the aircraft, the pitch attitude should not change.

NOTE: In aircraft fitted with a rudder trim the same procedure is used. With the aeroplane in balance, trim-off any steady rudder pressure without allowing the nose to yaw.

AIRMANSHIP

Maintain a good **Look Out.**

Do not be reluctant to use the trim. If you feel a steady pressure then trim it off, but do not use the trim in transient manoeuvres such as turns.

Trimming is an art. As you develop the skill of trimming an aeroplane, smooth and precise flying becomes much easier.

AIRWORK 4c —

AIM: *To use the trim to relieve steady pressures on the control column.*

(1) Trimming the Aeroplane Correctly.

> *This involves use of the pitch trim-wheel or control.*

To trim the aeroplane correctly in pitch:

- Hold the desired pitch attitude with pressure on the control column; then

- Without looking, place your hand on the trim-wheel and trim (in a natural sense) to relieve pressures so that the desired attitude is held without exerting any pressure on the control column. If the load is high, trim quickly. As the load reduces, trim more finely. Gradually, the pressure on the control column can be relaxed.

Pitch-trim
Control wheel

CONTINUED OVERLEAF

THE ART OF TRIMMING

(2) Getting the Feel of Incorrect Trim.

(a) To get the feel of incorrect trim, fly straight and level, holding the desired pitch attitude with elevator.

(b) Then, without letting the pitch attitude change, gradually wind the trim-wheel fully forward:
  - You will need considerable back pressure on the control column to hold the nose up in the level flight attitude.

(c) Gradually wind the trim-wheel back until the control column back pressure is again reduced to zero.

(d) Repeat the procedure, winding the trim fully aft this time, noting the considerable forward pressure required on the control column to maintain the level flight attitude.

NOTE: This is not a normal procedure. It is done only for you to experience the effect of incorrect trim, which makes flying almost impossible.

(3) Common Situations Requiring Re-Trimming.

Practise trim changes by holding a particular pitch attitude and then:
  (i)   adopt a new pitch attitude;
  (ii) change the power setting, or
  (iii) change the aircraft configuration (e.g. lower flaps).

After each change, hold the pitch attitude constant for a short period (10 or 20 seconds) and allow the aeroplane to settle into the new flight path and/or airspeed before re-trimming.

  - If a strong pressure is required on the control column then it is advisable to relieve most of it fairly quickly and then, after the aeroplane has settled down, trim more finely.

NOTE: Trim is used to relieve steady control pressure. It is not used to trim-off pressures that are only transient, such as those in a turn. For aeroplanes fitted with a rudder trim these exercises can be repeated. The same technique applies – use rudder trim to relieve steady pressures on the rudder pedals which are necessary to balance the aeroplane.

*The use of the word '**Trim**' throughout the Manual implies use of the elevator trim, and also use of the rudder trim, where fitted.*

46

4d

THE EFFECT OF AIRSPEED AND SLIPSTREAM

AIM

To observe the effect of an increased speed of airflow over the control surfaces.

CONSIDERATIONS

INCREASED AIRFLOW INCREASES CONTROL EFFECTIVENESS.

The effectiveness of the three main flight controls and the rate at which the aeroplane moves in all three planes (pitch, roll and yaw) depends upon:
- the amount of control deflection;
- the airflow over the control surface, which can be increased by:
  – a higher airspeed; and/or
  – slipstream from the propeller.

THE FLIGHT CONTROLS ARE MORE EFFECTIVE AT HIGHER AIRSPEEDS.

The elevator, ailerons and rudder will all experience an increased airflow when the aeroplane is flying at a higher airspeed. Each control will feel firmer and only small movements will be required to produce an effective response.

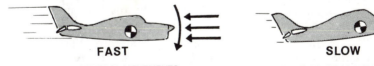

FAST
SMALL CONTROL MOVEMENTS
VERY EFFECTIVE

SLOW
SAME CONTROL MOVEMENT
NOT VERY EFFECTIVE

Fig.4d-1. All of the Flight Controls are More Effective at High Airspeeds.

Conversely, at low airspeeds the airflow over each of the flight controls is less and their effectiveness is reduced. The elevator, ailerons and rudder will all feel 'sloppy' and large movements may be required to produce the desired effect.

THE SLIPSTREAM INCREASES RUDDER AND ELEVATOR EFFECTIVENESS.

The slipstream from the propeller flows rearwards around the aeroplane in a corkscrew fashion, which increases the airflow over the tail section, making the rudder and elevator more effective.

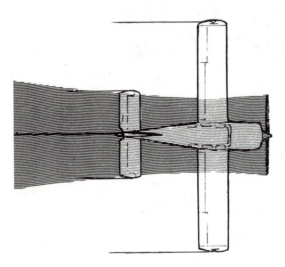

Fig.4d-2. The Slipstream Increases Elevator and Rudder Effectiveness.

The ailerons, being outside the slipstream airflow, are not affected by it and will remain 'sloppy' at low airspeeds irrespective of the power set. The elevator on T-tail aircraft may also be somewhat out of the slipstream and therefore not affected by it to the same extent as the rudder.

THE SLIPSTREAM CAUSES A TENDENCY TO YAW.

The slipstream from the propeller flows back in a corkscrew fashion over the tailplane, meeting the fin at an angle of attack. This generates a sideways aerodynamic force, which tends to yaw the nose of the aeroplane. The Pilot can balance this yawing effect with rudder pressure.

Slipstream effect is most pronounced under conditions of high power and low airspeed (e.g. during a climb) when the 'corkscrew' is tighter and its angle of attack at the fin is greater.

The direction of the yaw resulting from the slipstream effect depends upon the direction of propeller rotation. If the **propeller rotates clockwise** when viewed from the cockpit (as is the case for many modern training aircraft) the slipstream passes under the fuselage and strikes the fin on its left-hand side. This causes a **tendency for the nose to yaw left,** which can be balanced with right rudder.

If the **propeller rotates anti-clockwise** as seen from the cockpit (e.g. the Tiger Moth, Chipmunk, and the ARV Super 2 recently certified in the UK), the slipstream passes under the fuselage and strikes the fin on the right-hand side. The **nose will tend to yaw right** and will require left rudder to balance.

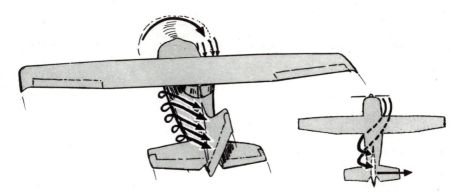

Fig.4d-3. Slipstream Tends to Yaw the Aeroplane.

FLYING THE MANOEUVRE

To observe the effect of airspeed on the flight controls, first establish a glide (to eliminate the effect of slipstream) at a high airspeed and operate each of the three main flight controls. Each one will feel firm and be effective.

Then raise the nose to glide at a lower airspeed and operate each of the three main flight controls. Each will feel 'sloppy' and less effective than before.

Next apply climb power, maintaining the same low airspeed by raising the nose. This will introduce a strong slipstream effect, but keep the airspeed effect constant. The elevator and the rudder, being in the slipstream, will feel firm and effective. The ailerons, which are outside the slipstream, will still feel 'sloppy' and less effective.

AIRMANSHIP

Maintain a high visual awareness. Keep an eye out for other traffic and remain aware of the position of the aeroplane and the direction to be flown back to the aerodrome. Exert firm, positive, but smooth control over the aeroplane.

AIRWORK 4d —
EFFECT OF AIRSPEED AND SLIPSTREAM

AIM: *To observe the effect of increased airflow over each of*
the main flight control surfaces as a result of:
- *Airspeed*
- *Slipstream.*

(1) The Effect of Airspeed:

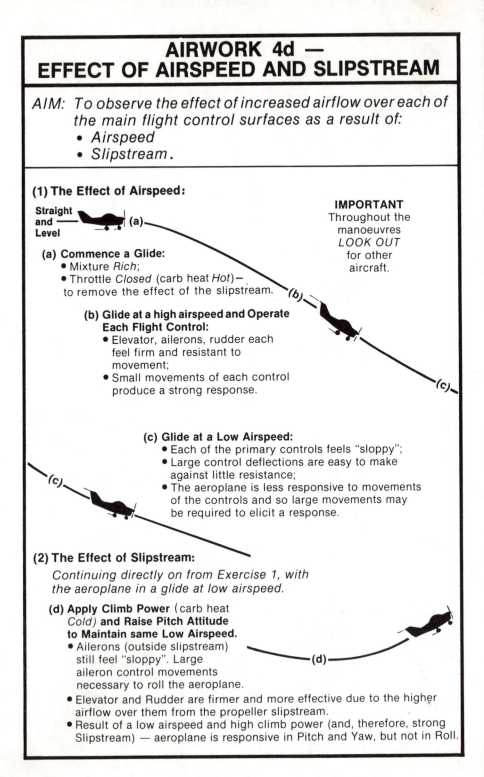

Straight and Level — **(a)**

IMPORTANT
Throughout the
manoeuvres
LOOK OUT
for other
aircraft.

(a) Commence a Glide:
- Mixture *Rich*;
- Throttle *Closed* (carb heat *Hot*) —
to remove the effect of the slipstream.

(b)

(b) Glide at a high airspeed and Operate Each Flight Control:
- Elevator, ailerons, rudder each feel firm and resistant to movement;
- Small movements of each control produce a strong response.

(c)

(c) Glide at a Low Airspeed:
- Each of the primary controls feels "sloppy";
- Large control deflections are easy to make against little resistance;
- The aeroplane is less responsive to movements of the controls and so large movements may be required to elicit a response.

(c)

(2) The Effect of Slipstream:

Continuing directly on from Exercise 1, with the aeroplane in a glide at low airspeed.

(d) Apply Climb Power (carb heat *Cold)* **and Raise Pitch Attitude to Maintain same Low Airspeed.**
- Ailerons (outside slipstream) still feel "sloppy". Large aileron control movements necessary to roll the aeroplane.

(d)

- Elevator and Rudder are firmer and more effective due to the higher airflow over them from the propeller slipstream.
- Result of a low airspeed and high climb power (and, therefore, strong Slipstream) — aeroplane is responsive in Pitch and Yaw, but not in Roll.

4e

THE EFFECTS OF POWER CHANGES

AIM

To observe the effects of applying and removing power, then to counteract any undesirable tendencies resulting from power changes.

CONSIDERATIONS

Pushing the throttle in (or 'opening' it) increases power, which is indicated by increased rpm on the tachometer. This causes the propeller to rotate faster and generate **increased thrust. Pulling the throttle out** (or 'closing it') **reduces power.**

REDUCING POWER CAUSES A PITCH-DOWN TENDENCY.

Most aeroplanes are designed so that, if power from the engine is lost, the aeroplane will 'automatically' assume the glide attitude without action being taken by the Pilot. This is a safety feature designed into the aeroplane to ensure that flying speed is maintained in case of engine failure.

In normal flight, when power is reduced with the throttle, the tendency for the nose to pitch down still occurs but can be counteracted with back pressure on the control column.

INCREASING POWER CAUSES A PITCH-UP TENDENCY.

When adding power, the reverse effect occurs; the nose will tend to pitch up. This can be counteracted with forward pressure on the control column.

CHANGING POWER ALSO CAUSES A YAWING TENDENCY.

Adding power increases the slipstream effect on the tail of the aeroplane, causing the nose to yaw to the left (for propellers rotating clockwise when viewed from the cockpit). This yawing tendency can be counteracted with right rudder pressure to keep the aeroplane balanced (i.e. balance ball centred).

Conversely, **reducing power** reduces the slipstream effect on the tail, causing a yawing tendency in the other direction, which can also be counteracted with opposite rudder.

Some aircraft are fitted with rudder trim which is used to trim-off any steady pressure on the rudder pedals, e.g. on the climb.

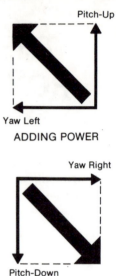

Fig.4e-1. The Effects of Power Changes (for a clockwise-rotating propeller).

THE MIXTURE SHOULD BE RICH FOR SIGNIFICANT POWER CHANGES.

Under certain conditions the fuel/air mixture can be 'leaned' using the Mixture Control in the cockpit (a procedure considered later in this section). Opening the throttle to a high power setting with the mixture lean can cause damage to the engine, so it is usual to have the mixture fully **RICH** prior to making any significant power changes.

WHEN CLOSING THE THROTTLE, PROTECT YOURSELF AGAINST CARBURETTOR ICE.

The air mixing with fuel in the carburettor is cooled and, if moisture is present, there is always the possibility of ice forming, even at temperatures of +25°C and higher. This can block the flow of induction air/fuel to the cylinders, and so, if you intend to close the throttle for a prolonged period, apply full hot carburettor heat.

FLYING THE MANOEUVRE

OPERATE THE THROTTLE SMOOTHLY.

The engine has moving parts which should not be subjected to shock treatment, so operate the throttle smoothly. As a guide to how rapidly the throttle should be opened, from idle power to full power should take approximately the same time as to count '1-2-3'. This also applies when closing the throttle.

INCREASING POWER.

Increasing power (clockwise-rotating propeller) will cause the nose of the aeroplane to:
● rise; and
● yaw left.

These unwanted tendencies can be counteracted with:
● forward pressure on the control column to hold the desired attitude; and
● right rudder pressure to prevent the unwanted yaw and keep the ball centred.

Residual pressures can then be trimmed-off.

DECREASING POWER.

Decreasing power will cause the nose of the aeroplane to:
● drop; and
● yaw right.

These unwanted tendencies can be counteracted with:
● back pressure on the control column to maintain the desired attitude; and
● left rudder pressure to balance the unwanted yaw.

Residual pressures can then be trimmed-off.

AIRMANSHIP

Maintain a high visual awareness. **Look Out** for other aircraft and note landmarks so that you do not get lost. Make full use of the natural horizon when holding the pitch and bank attitude.

Have the Mixture Control in full RICH prior to any significant power changes.

When about to reduce power, consider whether you need protection from carburettor ice. If so, (and this is usually the case when reducing the power to idle), apply full hot carburettor heat before closing the throttle.

When changing power, consider the engine. It has lots of reciprocating and rotating parts moving at high speeds and any sudden shock to the system is not good for it. Move the throttle smoothly and handle the engine with care. Monitor the engine gauges, especially during the climb when high power is set and there is reduced cooling because of the lower airspeed.

Handle the aeroplane smoothly, but firmly. Anticipate the effect of power changes — be prepared to hold the desired pitch attitude and prevent unwanted yaw.

AIRWORK 4e —
EFFECT OF MAKING POWER CHANGES

AIMS: 1. To observe the effect of changing power.
2. To counteract undesirable tendencies resulting
from power changes.

(1) The Effect of Changing Power:

(a) Trim the Aeroplane to
Cruise Straight and Level:
- Remove your hands
  from the control column
  and your feet from the
  rudder pedals.

(b) Smoothly Open
the Throttle to
Full Power:
- Nose pitches
  up and
- yaws*.

(c) Smoothly close
the Throttle:
- Nose pitches
  down and
- yaws**.

* left in most
training aeroplanes

** right in most
training aeroplanes

(2) The Correct Pilot Response When Changing Power:

(a) When Increasing Power:
- Hold desired nose attitude
  with elevator (forward
  pressure);
- Balance with rudder
  pressure;
- Trim.

(b) When Reducing Power:
- Hold desired nose attitude
  with elevator (back
  pressure);
- Balance with rudder
  pressure;
- Trim.

NOTE:
A good means of practising this is to maintain the straight and level
pitch attitude with the nose on a reference point on the horizon.

Smoothly move the throttle from idle to full power and back again,
anticipating the changes and holding pitch attitude constant and
balancing the unwanted yaw.

INCREASING AIRSPEED (BY LOWERING THE NOSE) WILL CAUSE AN
INCREASE IN ENGINE R.P.M. WITHOUT ANY THROTTLE MOVEMENT.

4f

THE EFFECT OF USING FLAPS

To observe the effect of altering the flap position and to control the aeroplane smoothly during flap alteration.

CONSIDERATIONS

The flaps are attached to the inboard trailing edge of each wing. They are operated from the cockpit — in some aeroplanes electrically by a switch and, in others, mechanically by a lever. They operate symmetrically on each wing.

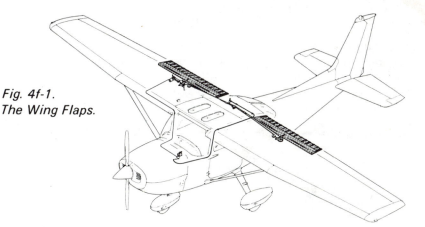

Fig. 4f-1.
The Wing Flaps.

Flaps alter the shape of the wings and the airflow around them. This changes the **lifting ability** of the wings, altering both the Lift and Drag generated. In a sense, flaps create new wings. They are used to:
- **generate the required Lift at a lower speed** (allowing safe flight at low airspeeds as well as reducing take-off and landing distances);
- **increase Drag** and steepen the descent path on approach to land;
- **improve forward vision** as a result of the lower nose attitude.

The flaps may be used to serve various purposes simultaneously; for example, to steepen the descent path while at the same time allowing better forward vision and safe flight at a lower airspeed.

As the flaps are lowered the changes in lift and drag will cause a pitching tendency. This will result in the aeroplane 'ballooning' unless counteracted with pressure on the control column. Conversely, when flap is raised, there will be a pitching tendency in the opposite direction and a tendency to sink.

Once attitude and power changes are complete, and the airspeed has stabilised at the desired value, these pressures can be trimmed-off. In general, a **lower pitch attitude** is required to achieve the same airspeed when flaps are lowered compared to when the wings are 'clean'.

T.E. Flaps extended along with change
of pitch attitude

Fig.4f-2. Flaps Require a Lower Pitch Attitude.

The initial stages of flap are sometimes called **'lift flaps',** because the lifting ability of the wing is increased considerably even though there is the cost of a small amount of extra drag. **Flaps allow the required lift to be generated at a lower speed.**

The larger flap settings are sometimes called **'drag flaps',** because they cause a marked increase in Drag for little improvement in lifting ability. If airspeed is to be maintained, the increased drag must be balanced by either:
- additional thrust; or
- a greater component of the weight force acting along the flight path (achieved by steepening the descent).

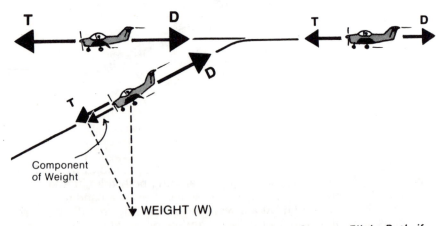

Component
of Weight

WEIGHT (W)

Fig.4f-3. Flaps require Increased Power or a Steeper Flight Path if Airspeed is to be Maintained.

THE FLAP OPERATING RANGE.

To avoid overstressing the structure, ensure that the airspeed is less than the maximum speed allowed for flap extension (VFE). This figure is stated in the Pilot's Operating Handbook and is shown on the airspeed indicator as the high speed end of the white arc.

Two straight and level stalling speeds (at maximum aircraft weight) are available on the Air Speed Indicator:
1. With full flap — the low speed end of the white band;
2. With a 'clean' wing — the low speed end of the green band.

They mark the approximate minimum flying speeds straight and level that the aeroplane is capable of in these configurations.

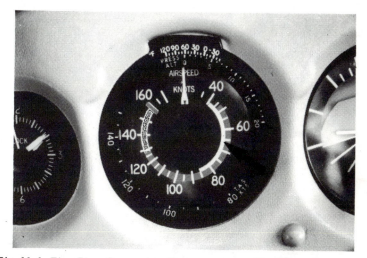

Fig.4f-4. The Flap Operating Range on the Air Speed Indicator.

FLYING THE MANOEUVRE

Raising or lowering large amounts of flap may cause large changes in pitch attitude and in the trim required. For this reason it is usual to operate the flaps in stages, re-trimming after each selection.

To operate the flaps:
- lower (or raise) one stage at a time;
- hold the desired pitch attitude with elevator and make any necessary power changes;
- trim off the steady pressure on the control column.

AIRMANSHIP

Do not exceed the maximum flap operating speed (VFE) and do not raise them below the 'clean' stalling speed.

AIRWORK 4f −

AIMS: (a) To observe the effect of altering flap position.
(b) To control the aeroplane smoothly during flap alteration.

(1) Changing Flap Position Causes a Pitching Tendency.

(a) With the wing 'clean" (i.e. flaps up), establish straight and level flight.

(b) Reduce the airspeed to within flap operating range (white arc on ASI) and re-trim. (Higher nose attitude required to maintain height as airspeed is reduced.)

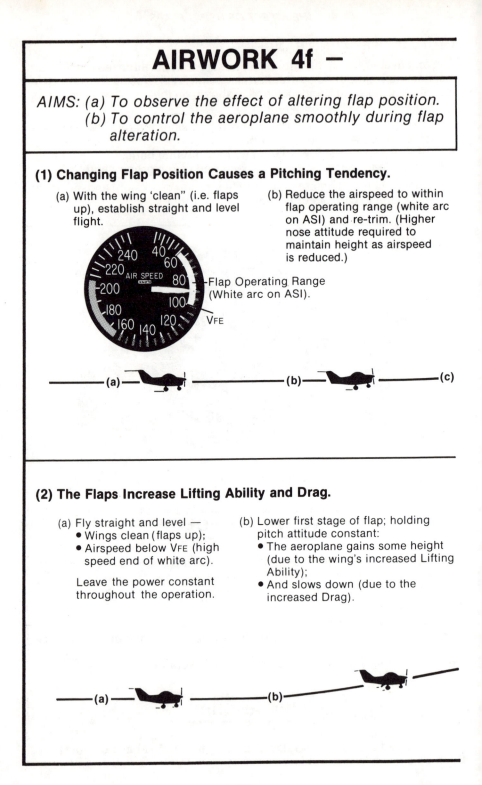

Flap Operating Range (White arc on ASI).

V_{FE}

(2) The Flaps Increase Lifting Ability and Drag.

(a) Fly straight and level —
  • Wings clean (flaps up);
  • Airspeed below V_{FE} (high speed end of white arc).

Leave the power constant throughout the operation.

(b) Lower first stage of flap; holding pitch attitude constant:
  • The aeroplane gains some height (due to the wing's increased Lifting Ability);
  • And slows down (due to the increased Drag).

THE EFFECT OF USING FLAP

(c) To illustrate the pitching tendency when lowering the flaps, remove your hands from the control column — (although normally you never do this).
Lower flap in stages (using a firm, steady movement if the flaps are manually operated).
● Note the pitching tendency.

Trim for the desired attitude.

(d) To illustrate the pitching tendency when raising the flaps, once again temporarily remove your hands from the control column.

Raise the flaps fully in one selection (an incorrect procedure not used in normal operations):
● Note the effect.

(There will most likely be a strong pitching tendency, accompanied by a height loss.)

Re-establish straight and level flight and re-trim.

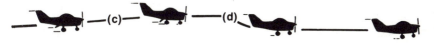

NOTE: In normal flap operations you will control any unwanted pitching tendency when flap is changed with pressure on the control column.

(c) Lower the nose to **maintain height** and re-trim:
● Notice the lower nose position — improved vision — and lower airspeed.

(d) Lower the rest of the flaps in stages and maintain height by lowering the nose; re-trim after each flap selection:
● Notice the lower airspeed as the extra Drag slows the aeroplane.

(e) Raise the flaps in stages and maintain height by raising the nose; re-trim after each selection:
● Note the higher airspeed resulting from the reduced Drag.

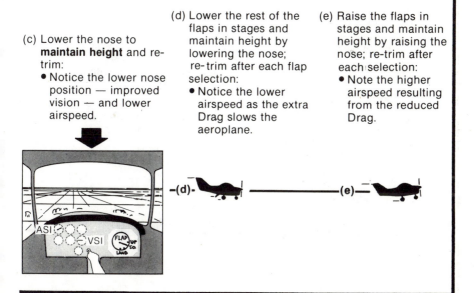

AIRWORK 4f (cont'd) —

(3) Using Flaps to Steepen the Descent Path.

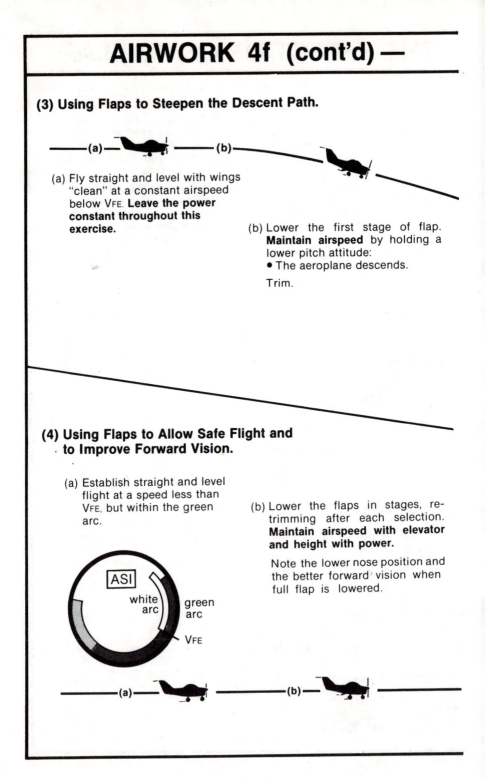

(a) Fly straight and level with wings "clean" at a constant airspeed below V_{FE}. **Leave the power constant throughout this exercise.**

(b) Lower the first stage of flap. **Maintain airspeed** by holding a lower pitch attitude:
- The aeroplane descends.

Trim.

(4) Using Flaps to Allow Safe Flight and to Improve Forward Vision.

(a) Establish straight and level flight at a speed less than V_{FE}, but within the green arc.

(b) Lower the flaps in stages, re-trimming after each selection. **Maintain airspeed with elevator and height with power.**

Note the lower nose position and the better forward vision when full flap is lowered.

THE EFFECT OF USING FLAP

(c) Repeat for each stage of flap until full flap is extended. Note:
- A lower nose attitude is required to maintain a constant airspeed;
- Improved forward visibility;
- Increased rate of descent

This is similar to an approach to land.

(d) Raise the flaps in stages, re-trimming after each selection.
Resume straight and level flight.

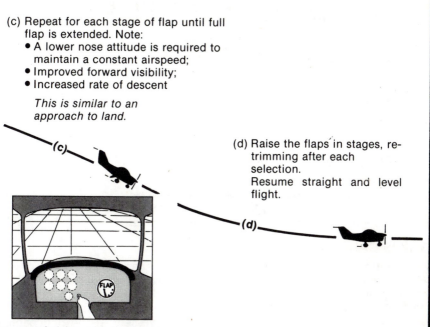

Improved vision with flap down.

(c) Reduce airspeed to a figure just less than the clean stalling speed (i.e. to below the green arc on the ASI).

Maintain height with power.

- The aeroplane can fly quite comfortably at lower airspeeds with flaps extended compared to when the wing is "clean".

(d) Increase speed (by applying power) and raise the flaps in stages, re-trimming after each selection.

Do not raise the final stage of flap until you are above the "clean" stalling speed (low speed end of green arc).

4g

CARBURETTOR HEAT

AIM

To operate the Carburettor Heat Control correctly.

CONSIDERATIONS

WHY IS CARBURETTOR HEAT NECESSARY?

Vaporisation of the fuel causes cooling in the carburettor, which may reduce the temperature to below freezing. If the air is sufficiently moist, ice may form in the induction system, partially blocking the flow of fuel/air to the cylinders. **Carburettor Ice** can occur at Outside Air Temperatures of +25°C or more and affects engine power adversely — the noticeable effects including:

- **a drop in rpm;**
- **rough running;** and
- **possible engine stoppage.**

The Carburettor Heat Control, which is usually a knob situated near the throttle, can be used to direct hot air into the carburettor to prevent ice forming or to melt any ice which has already formed. Being less dense than cold air, **hot air** lowers the mass of each fuel/air charge burned in the cylinders, reducing the maximum power available from the engine. Consequently, as carburettor heat is applied, the engine rpm will drop. **If ice is present,** the rpm will rise following the initial drop as the ice is melted by the warm air.

As a precaution when operating at low rpm it is usual to apply *FULL HOT* carburettor heat, such as in a prolonged descent. The control is returned to *FULL COLD* when higher power is required (and if protection from carburettor ice is not required).

In many aeroplanes, the hot air for carburettor heat is supplied from around the engine exhaust and is unfiltered (unlike the cold air which is filtered in the normal engine air intake). For this reason, it is usual to taxi with the carburettor heat control in the full *COLD* position to avoid introducing dust and grit into the engine as this would seriously affect engine life.

AIRWORK 4g —
USE OF CARBURETTOR HEAT

AIM: To learn the correct use of Carburettor Heat.

(1) If Carburettor Icing is Suspected (rough running &/or r.p.m. decay):
- Apply *FULL* carburettor heat (by pulling the carb heat control knob fully *OUT*);
- Note drop in r.p.m. (due to the less dense air now entering the engine cylinders);
- If carburettor icing was present and has been melted, a slight rise in r.p.m. will occur following the initial drop;
- Push Carb Heat knob to *FULL COLD*. Note r.p.m. rise (denser air is now entering the cylinders).

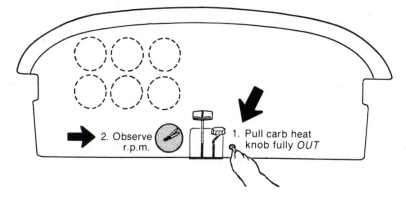

2. Observe r.p.m.

1. Pull carb heat knob fully *OUT*

(2) Using Carburettor Heat as a Precaution.
(Normal Procedure on descent and approach-to-land.)

(a) When reducing power to IDLE:
- Select carb heat to *FULL HOT*
- Throttle *CLOSED*

(b) When about to increase power:
- Carb heat to *FULL COLD* (if hot air to carburettor no longer required);
- Apply power with the throttle, as required.

NOTE:
Your flying training organisation's procedure for using Carb Heat as a Precaution may differ from that given above, in which case you should follow it. (There may be variation in the order of operating the throttle and carb heat when both reducing and increasing power, perhaps due to manufacturer's recommendations).

If in doubt as to the correct procedure to follow, consult your flying instructor.

4h

THE MIXTURE CONTROL

AIM

To operate the Mixture Control correctly.

CONSIDERATIONS AND OPERATION

The Mixture Control is usually a red knob situated near the throttle. Its two functions are:
1. to 'lean' the mixture and achieve optimum fuel usage; and
2. to cut-off fuel to the carburettor and stop the engine.

Air density decreases with increasing height. This results in a lower weight of air being mixed with the same weight of fuel in the carburettor as an aeroplane climbs. Thus, **the 'fuel/air' mixture becomes richer as height is gained** and an increasing amount of fuel will remain unburned because of the reduced air available for the combustion process. This fuel is wasted in the exhaust.

Corrective action to avoid the fuel wastage is usually taken on a high level cruise (usually above 5000 ft and when the power is less than 75% Maximum Continuous Power). This action is called **'leaning'** the mixture and is accomplished by moving the Mixture Control partially out, which reduces the weight of fuel mixing with the air being taken into the carburettor.

As the 'fuel/air' mixture is leaned and returns to its optimum value, the engine rpm will show a slight increase. Leaning the mixture past the optimum ratio will cause the rpm to fall, at which point the Mixture Control should be moved back-in slightly to the rich side of optimum. It is preferable to **operate an engine slightly on the rich side** than too lean (when detonation may occur and damage the engine). Note that **range figures** published by the manufacturer assume cruising with the mixture correctly leaned.

Moving the Mixture Control fully out to the **Idle Cut-Off** position cuts-off fuel to the carburettor completely. This is a safe way of shutting an engine down, since there will be no fuel left in the cylinders or induction system.

AIRWORK 4h —
USE OF THE MIXTURE CONTROL

AIM: To operate the Mixture Control (red knob) correctly.

(1) To Lean the Mixture at Altitude:
(for improved range and fuel economy)

- Set desired engine r.p.m. (with the throttle);
- Slowly move red Mixture Control knob *OUT* towards lean position;
- Observe the r.p.m. rise. If r.p.m. doesn't rise, return mixture to *RICH*;
- Continue moving Mixture Control *OUT* until a **slight drop** in r.p.m. occurs;
- Move the knob *IN* slightly to restore maximum r.p.m. It might be advisable to move the Mixture Control slightly further in so that the mixture is slightly on the rich side, (too-rich is preferable to too-lean), where r.p.m. will be slightly lower than peak value.

NOTE:
Whenever the power setting or cruise level are changed, repeat the above procedure.

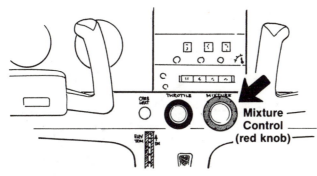

Mixture Control (red knob)

(2) On Descent:
Prior to commencing descent and reducing power:
- Select Mixture to *FULL RICH*.

(3) After Landing:
To stop the engine:
- Close the throttle (pull it fully out) to reduce engine r.p.m.;
- Move the Mixture Control to *IDLE CUT-OFF* by pulling it fully out — (this starves the engine of fuel);
- Complete other actions as per the procedure in your Pilot's Operating Handbook.

4i

USING THE RADIO

Most aeroplanes are equipped with at least one high quality communications set. It will operate in the Very High Frequency (VHF) radio band. Such a set, which is known as a **VHF-COM,** is both a transmitter and a receiver and is quite simple to operate. VHF provides high quality 'line-of-sight' communications and is the usual form of communication used in aviation.

Many VHF-COM sets are combined in the same unit as a radio NAVigation receiver — the whole unit being called a COM/NAV or **NAV/COM.** It is usual for the COM set to be on the left hand side.

Connected to the radio are:
- a microphone for transmitting;
- speakers and/or headphones for reception;
- the electrical Master Switch (and possibly an Avionics Power Switch) to connect the power supply to the radio;
- an Audio Control Panel (in some aircraft) to connect the radio set to the microphone and the speaker or headphones.

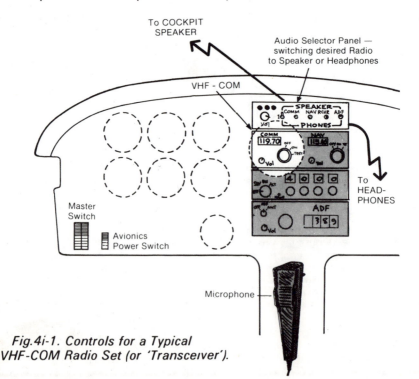

Fig.4i-1. Controls for a Typical
VHF-COM Radio Set (or 'Transceiver').

SWITCHING ON THE VHF-COM.

1. Check the **Master Switch ON**
   (& **Avionics Power Switch** if applicable).
2. Switch the **Radio ON.**
3. Select the **Desired Frequency.**
4. Select **Audio** to speaker of appropriate radio.
5. Adjust the **Volume** to desired level and adjust 'squelch' control (if fitted) to cut out undesired background noise.
6. Check that the **Microphone** is plugged in correctly.
7. Select the **Transmitter** to the desired radio, e.g. VHF No. 1.

Squelch.

The function of 'Squelch' is to eliminate unwanted weak signals that cause background noise ('static' or 'hash'). 'Noise' makes it difficult to hear the desired stronger signals. Some squelch controls are automatic and others manual. Your Flying Instructor will advise you on your particular set.

To adjust the squelch manually:
• turn the Squelch control up high (i.e. clockwise) until background noise or hash is heard; then:
• rotate the squelch knob anti-clockwise until the noise just disappears (or is at least at an acceptably low level). This causes the unwanted noise from weak signals to be suppressed allowing only the strong signals to be heard.

NOTE: Turning the squelch **right down** may also cut out the signal that you want to hear as well as the unwanted noise if you are not careful.

What If The Radio Doesn't Work ?

Occasionally you may find that the set is not functioning correctly. If so then follow a simple fault-finding procedure:
1. Check switching as above in 'Switching the VHF-COM Radio ON';
2. Check the Circuit Breakers or Fuses.

TRANSMITTING.

Before Transmitting:
• Listen out on the frequency to be used and avoid interference with other transmissions;
• Before you commence transmitting determine what you want to say. The CAA publication CAP 413 contains the correct terminology and there are also other excellent publications and learning aids available.

The Microphone.

There are various types of microphone, each having its own operating characteristics. They are the **hand-held microphone** which has a transmit switch incorporated on it, and the **boom microphone** attached to a headset worn by the pilot, and which has its transmit switch situated usually in a convenient position on the control column.

Training aeroplanes are usually equipped with a hand-held microphone.

Fig.4i-2. The Hand-Held and the Boom Microphone.

When using a microphone the following rules are generally satisfactory:
- actuate the transmit switch before commencing to talk and do not release it until after your message is completed;
- speak with the microphone one or two centimetres from your lips;
- do not significantly vary the distance between your lips and the microphone;
- speak directly into the microphone and do not speak to one side of it.

The microphone is used like a telephone, except that:
- the transmit button must be depressed for you to transmit;
- whilst transmitting, most radio sets are unable to receive simultaneously;
- only one transmission from one station within range can occur on the frequency in use without interference. **Whilst you are transmitting, no-one else can.**

NOTE: Your COM set will continue to transmit as long as the transmit switch is depressed, even if you are not speaking. This will block out other stations that may be trying to call on that particular frequency. **So at the end of your transmission ensure that the transmit switch (or 'mike button') is released.**

THE TRANSPONDER.

A Transponder unit is fitted in most light aircraft and when 'squawking' enables an Air Traffic Radar Controller to identify a particular aircraft more easily on his screen. There is no voice communication through the transponder. Transponder code selection is accomplished by dialling in the required code with the knobs. When selecting a new code avoid passing through the emergency codes (7700 EMERGENCY, 7600 RADIO FAILURE and 7500 UNLAWFUL INTERFERENCE) when the transponder is switched ON, unless you really want to activate one of them.

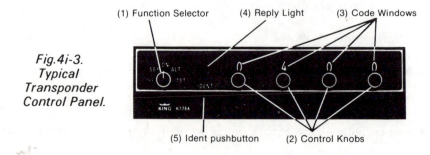

(1) Function Selector   (4) Reply Light   (3) Code Windows

Fig.4i-3. Typical Transponder Control Panel.

(5) Ident pushbutton   (2) Control Knobs

4j

CABIN HEATING AND VENTILATION

Your comfort and well-being is most important to flight safety, so maximise it with correct use of the cabin ventilation and heating systems as explained in The Pilot's Operating Handbook. Ventilation generally improves the cockpit environment quite significantly.

The hot air for cabin heating is usually taken from around the engine exhaust system. To protect the occupants of the aeroplane from any fumes escaping from a leaking exhaust system, it is good practice to use the fresh air vents in conjunction with cabin heating. Carbon monoxide, which is colourless, odourless and dangerous, is present in the exhaust gases and ventilation provides good protection against it!

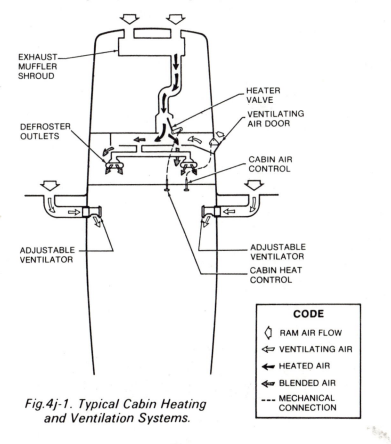

Fig.4j-1. Typical Cabin Heating and Ventilation Systems.

Intentionally Blank

5

TAXYING
AN
AEROPLANE

5

TAXYING
AN
AEROPLANE

AIM

To manoeuvre the aeroplane safely on the ground.

CONSIDERATIONS

USE POWER AND BRAKES TO CONTROL TAXYING SPEED.

Power is used to commence taxying an aeroplane. The effects of wheel friction and the brakes are used to stop it.

Like all objects, an aeroplane has inertia and is resistant to change, so it requires more power to start moving than to keep moving. Once the aeroplane is rolling at taxying speed, the power can be reduced simply to balance the frictional forces and any air resistance so that a steady speed is maintained. On a straight and smooth taxiway with no obstructions, a **fast walking pace** is a safe taxying speed and this can be judged by looking ahead and to the left of the aeroplane. In a confined area, the ideal speed is somewhat less.

The **amount of power** required to maintain taxying speed depends upon the ground surface and its slope – a rough, upward-sloping grassy surface requiring much more power than a flat, sealed taxiway. **High power** may also be required to **turn the aeroplane,** especially at low speeds.

To slow the aeroplane down, the power should be reduced. Friction may cause the aeroplane to decelerate sufficiently, otherwise the brakes can be used gently, but firmly.

Generally speaking, **power should not be used against brakes.** It is a waste of energy and can lead to overheated brakes and increased brake wear. There are some aircraft, however, which have engines requiring a high idling rpm, and occasional braking may be required to avoid the taxying speed becoming excessive.

Toe Brakes are situated on top of each rudder pedal. They are individually applied using the ball of each foot. Normally the Pilot taxies with his heels on the floor and the ball of his feet on the rudder pedals, thereby avoiding inadvertent application of the toe brakes. **When braking is needed,** he slides his feet up and, with the ball of each foot, applies the toe brakes as required. To brake the aeroplane whilst taxying in a straight line, the toe brakes should be applied evenly.

Rudder Pedals

Using Rudder   Using Toe Brakes

Fig.5-1. Using Rudder and Using Toe Brakes.

Brakes should be used gently so that the aeroplane responds smoothly – harsh braking being avoided except in an emergency. For a normal stop, a good technique is to relax the braking pressure (or perhaps even release it) just as the aeroplane comes to a halt. The resulting stop will be smooth.

Differential braking is available by pressing each toe brake individually. This is useful both for turning sharply and for maintaining directional control when taxying in a strong crosswind.

Test the Brakes early. Once taxying has commenced from the parked position, the power should be reduced and the brakes tested, but in a manner that causes the aeroplane to respond smoothly.

During extended taxying, the brakes should be tested occasionally, and they should certainly be tested just prior to entering a congested tarmac area. Pay due caution to the ground surface, especially in wet weather when taxiways and tarmacs can become slippery. Always have an escape route in mind to avoid collisions in case the brakes fail to stop the aeroplane.

Ensure that the Taxi Path is Clear. Allow for the fact that the wings of an aeroplane are wide and the tail-section is well behind the main wheels. Maintain a good **Look Out** ahead and to the sides. If the taxi path is obscured by the nose, then turns slightly left and right will permit a better view.

Should you unfortunately run into something whilst taxying, **stop** the aeroplane, **shut-down** the engine, set the brakes to **PARK** and investigate. **Do not fly!**

BE AWARE OF THE GROUND SURFACE.

Ensure that propeller clearance will be adequate when taxying in long grass or over rough ground, especially if there are small ditches or holes since striking grass or the ground can seriously damage the propeller. Loose stones or gravel picked up and blown back in the slipstream can also damage both the propeller and the airframe. Damage may even be caused to other aeroplanes or persons quite some distance behind. So **when taxying on loose surfaces, avoid the use of high power as much as possible.**

Small ridges or ditches should be crossed at an angle so that the wheels pass across the obstruction one at a time. This will minimise stress on the undercarriage and avoid the nose pitching up and down excessively, which not only stresses the nose-wheel but also puts the propeller at risk. **Large ditches or ridges should be avoided.** If necessary, park the aeroplane and investigate.

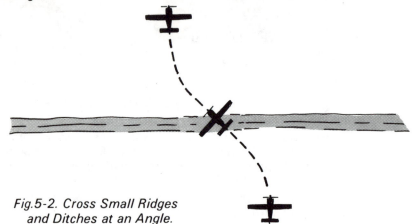

Fig.5-2. Cross Small Ridges and Ditches at an Angle.

ALLOW FOR WIND EFFECT WHEN TAXYING.

The flight controls should be held in a position to avoid either the tail or a wing being lifted by a strong wind.

When taxying into a strong headwind, hold the control column either neutral or back. This holds the elevator neutral or up, and the tail down, and takes the load off the nose-wheel.

When taxying with a strong tailwind, hold the control column forward to move the elevator down. This stops the wind lifting the tailplane from behind.

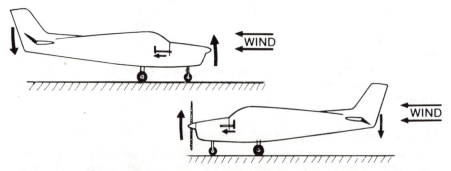

Fig.5-3. Taxi Into-Wind with the Control Column Neutral or Back, and Taxi Downwind with the Control Column Forward.

A **crosswind** will try to weathercock the aeroplane into-wind because of the large keel surfaces behind the main wheels. Using the rudder pedals, especially if nose-wheel steering is fitted, should provide adequate directional control, but, if not, then use differential braking.

To avoid a crosswind from ahead lifting the into-wind wing, raise its aileron by moving the control column into-wind.

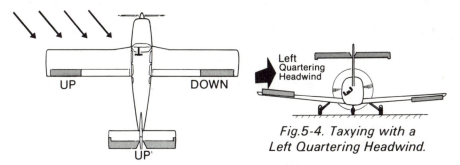

UP   DOWN

UP

Left Quartering Headwind

Fig.5-4. Taxying with a Left Quartering Headwind.

To avoid a crosswind from behind lifting the into-wind wing, lower its aileron so that the wind cannot get under it, by moving the control column out-of-wind.

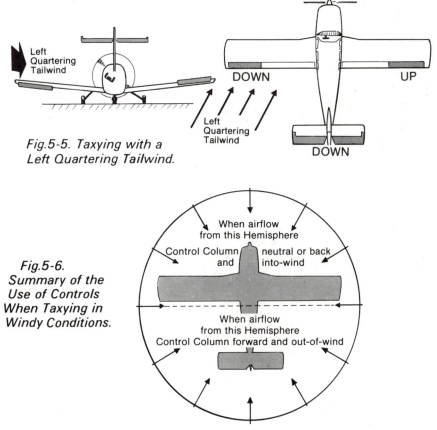

Left Quartering Tailwind

DOWN   UP

Left Quartering Tailwind

DOWN

Fig.5-5. Taxying with a Left Quartering Tailwind.

Fig.5-6. Summary of the Use of Controls When Taxying in Windy Conditions.

When airflow from this Hemisphere Control Column neutral or back and into-wind

When airflow from this Hemisphere Control Column forward and out-of-wind

TAXYING RULES.

Taxying frequently occurs on crowded tarmacs and taxiways. Five simple rules understood and followed by all Pilots makes life easier for everybody.

1. Regardless of any ATC (Air Traffic Control) clearance, it is the duty of the Pilot to do all possible to avoid collision with other aircraft or vehicles.
2. Aircraft on the ground must give way to aeroplanes landing or taking-off, and to any vehicle towing an aircraft.
3. When two aircraft are taxying and approaching head on or nearly so, each should turn right.
4. When two aircraft are taxying on converging courses, then the one that has the other on its right must give-way, and should avoid crossing ahead of the other aircraft unless passing well clear.
5. An aircraft which is being overtaken by another has right-of-way. The overtaking aircraft must keep out of the way by turning left until past and well clear.

If in any doubt — STOP.

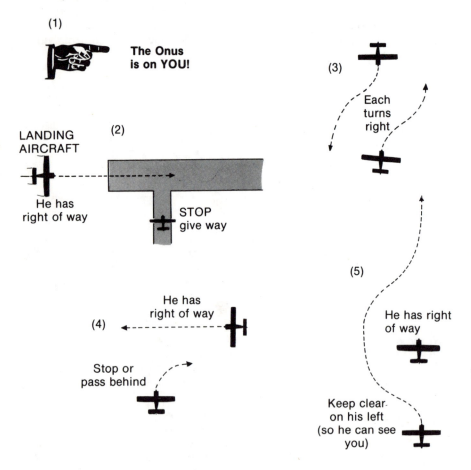

Fig.5-7. *Five Rules for Taxying.*

MARSHALLING.

Although **the Pilot is ultimately responsible** for the safety of the aeroplane on the ground, no matter who gives him guidance, taxying guidance on a tarmac area may be given by a marshaller. Some of the basic signals are illustrated below, but a Pilot should only follow them if he considers it safe to do so.

On a crowded tarmac or in very strong winds, it may be preferable to have wingtip assistance from experienced personnel, or to shut-down the engine and move the aeroplane by hand or with a tow-bar.

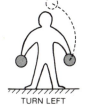

| MOVE AHEAD | TURN LEFT | TURN RIGHT | SLOW DOWN | STOP |

Fig.5-8. Some Useful Marshalling Signals.

STOP ENGINE

BRAKE FAILURE.

If the brakes fail:
- close the throttle;
- steer away from other aircraft and obstacles and towards a high friction surface if possible (e.g. grass).

If a collision is imminent:
- Mixture Control— *IDLE CUT OFF* (to stop the engine by purging it of fuel);
- Fuel — *OFF*;
- Ignition — *OFF*;
- Master Switch — *OFF*.

When stopped, chock the aeroplane.

CHECKS WHILST TAXYING.

Several items are checked once clear of the tarmac area and moving along on a straight taxiway. The **rudder** should be checked for full and free movement and 'directional' **flight instruments** for correct operation:

Turning left:
- the Compass and Direction Indicator should decrease in heading;
- the Turn Co-ordinator should indicate a left turn; and
- the Balance Ball should show a skid to the right, i.e. 'Turning left, skidding right'. (The Attitude Indicator should stay level.)

Turning right:
- the Compass and Direction Indicator should increase in heading;
- the Turn Co-ordinator or Turn Indicator should indicate a right turn;
- the Balance Ball should show a skid to the left, i.e. 'Turning right, skidding left'. (The Attitude Indicator should stay level.)

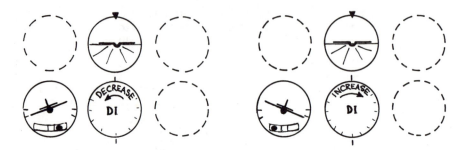

Fig.5-9. 'Turning Left, Skidding Right' and 'Turning Right, Skidding Left'.

THE MANOEUVRE

Before commencing to taxi, have a reasonable idea of the path that you will follow to the take-off position, taking note of the surface and the position of other aircraft. If required, obtain a taxi clearance from ATC by radio. Ensure that tie-down ropes and chocks have been removed before releasing the park brake.

Test the brakes shortly after the aircraft starts to roll. Maintain a suitable taxying speed for the conditions and avoid using power against brake, (unless a high idling speed is required for better engine cooling). Cross ridges and small ditches at an angle, avoiding long grass and rough ground, and have an escape route in mind in case of brake failure. On the taxying run, check the rudder and flight instruments for correct operation.

Once the aeroplane is stopped, the park brake should be applied and the engine set to idling speed.

AIRMANSHIP

Maintain a good **Look Out** ahead and to either side. Follow the accepted taxying rules and do not blast debris back over your aeroplane, other aeroplanes or into hangars.

Operate the throttle and brakes smoothly so that there are no sudden stops, starts or turns. Do not use power against brakes and maintain a listening watch on the radio if appropriate.

AIRWORK (Groundwork) 5 — TAXYING AN AEROPLANE

AIM: To manoeuvre the aeroplane safely on the ground.

(1) To Commence Taxying;
LOOK OUT;
- Survey the area around the aeroplane for obstructions and other aeroplanes. Consider the taxying surface.
- If "permission to taxi" is required at your airfield, obtain this by radio prior to taxying;
- Loosen the throttle friction nut and reduce the power to idle.
- Release the parking brake.

Moving-off:
- Release the Parking Brake;
- Apply sufficient power with the throttle to get the aeroplane moving forward; then
- reduce the power to idle and gently test the brakes.
- Apply sufficient power to recommence taxying;
Then:
- reduce power as necessary to maintain a safe taxying speed (a fast walking pace).

(2) Taxying the Aeroplane:
Steering is not possible until the aeroplane is rolling forward.
- Control direction with the rudder pedals and, if necessary, differential braking. An increased slipstream over the rudder may assist also;
- Gently test the brakes from time to time without bringing the aeroplane to a stop;
- Remember to allow plenty of clearance for the wing tips and tail;
- Hold the control column suitably to counteract any wind effect from the side or behind;
- Cross rough surfaces slowly and at an angle.
- Monitor engine pressure and temperature gauges for correct engine operation and adequate cooling.

(3) Stopping the Aeroplane
(a) To stop the Aeroplane:
- Anticipate by a few seconds;
- Close the throttle;
- Allow the aeroplane to roll to a stop; and
- if necessary, gently apply the brakes, releasing them just as the aeroplane stops so that coming to a halt is smooth.

(b) When completely stopped, set the brakes to *PARK* and set the correct engine idling figure — usually 1,000 to 1,200 rpm.

Intentionally Blank

6

STRAIGHT AND LEVEL

6a

FLYING STRAIGHT AND LEVEL AT CONSTANT POWER

AIM

To fly straight and level using a constant power setting.

CONSIDERATIONS

Flying **straight** means maintaining a constant heading, and this can be achieved by holding the wings level with the ailerons, keeping the aeroplane in balance with the rudder. Flying **level** means maintaining a constant height, which can be achieved by having the correct **power** set and the nose held in the correct **attitude.**

Steady straight and level flight at a constant airspeed, in balance and properly trimmed is desirable, both for comfort and for good range. **Accurate straight and level flying is one sign of a good Pilot.**

THE FORCES THAT ACT ON AN AEROPLANE.

There are four main forces acting on an aeroplane:
- **Weight;**
- **Lift** generated by the wings;
- **Thrust** from the propeller (using engine power); and
- **Drag** (or resistance to motion of the aeroplane through the air).

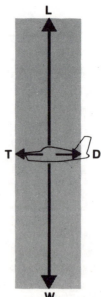

Fig.6a-1. The Four Main Forces in Steady Straight and Level Flight.

In steady straight and level flight, the aeroplane is in equilibrium with no tendency to accelerate.
- **Lift balances Weight;** and
- **Thrust balances Drag.**

It is unusual for the four main forces to counteract each other exactly. Almost always, **a balancing force, either up or down, is required from the tailplane.** This is controlled by the Pilot with the elevator. In normal flight, **continual** small adjustments of the elevator with the control column are required.

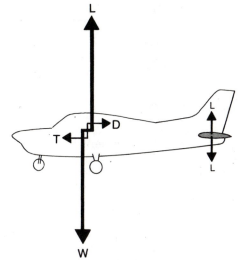

Fig.6a-2. The Tailplane Provides a Final Balancing Force.

Aeroplanes are usually designed so that **if thrust is lost** through the engine failing, **the remaining forces will automatically lower the nose** into the gliding attitude, allowing a safe flying speed to be maintained. In the situation illustrated above, this is achieved by having the Centre of Pressure (through which the Lift acts) located behind the Centre of Gravity, so that the 'Lift.Weight couple' has a nose-down effect. In normal flight, this is opposed by the 'Thrust.Drag' nose-up couple.

If thrust is lost, the nose-up couple is diminished, the L.W nose-down couple wins out, and the nose drops into the gliding attitude. The same effect occurs when the Pilot reduces power — the nose dropping unless back pressure is exerted on the control column.

THE STABILITY OF AN AEROPLANE.

Stability is the natural or in-built ability of an aeroplane to return to its original attitude following some disturbance (such as a gust) without the Pilot taking any action.

The Horizontal Stabiliser (or tailplane) provides longitudinal stability. If, for instance, a gust causes the nose to rise, then the tailplane is presented to the airflow at a greater angle of attack. It will therefore generate a greater upward (or less downward) aerodynamic force that will raise the tail and lower the nose. The tail fins of a dart, in stabilising its attitude and flight path, perform the same function as the tailplane on an aeroplane.

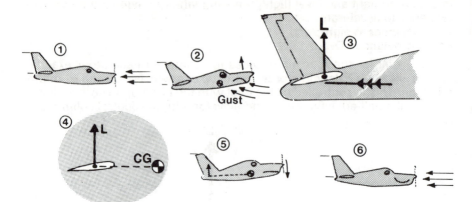

Fig.6a-3. Longitudinal Stability Following an Uninvited Nose-Up Pitch.

A forward Centre of Gravity (CG) makes the aeroplane more stable because of the greater restoring moment from the tailplane. **If the aeroplane is loaded so that the CG is too far forward:**
- the excessive stability will require stronger controlling forces from the elevator, which may become tiring for the Pilot; and
- during the landing, the elevator is less effective due to the low airspeed, and the nose-heavy moment may make it impossible to round-out.

If the aeroplane is loaded with the CG too far rearwards:
- the aeroplane will be less stable and constant attention will have to be given to maintaining the pitch attitude; and
- the tail-heavy moment may cause a stall at low speeds when the elevator is less effective.

Stability and control considerations make it imperative that an aeroplane is only flown when the **CG is within the approved range** (as stated in the Flight Manual). It is a Pilot responsibility to ensure that this is always the case.

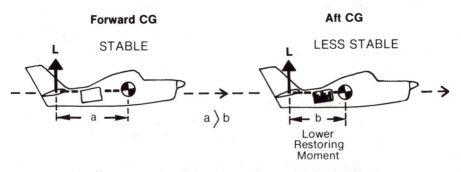

Fig.6a-4. Loading affects Longitudinal Stability and Control.

The Fin (or Vertical Stabiliser) provides directional stability. If the aeroplane is disturbed from a straight path, the fin is presented to the airflow at a greater angle of attack and generates a restoring aerodynamic force.

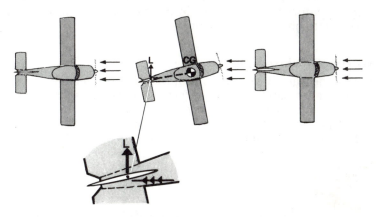

Fig.6a-5. Directional Stability Following Uninvited Yaw.

A disturbance in roll will cause one wing to drop and the other to rise. The Lift force will be tilted, causing a **sideslip** towards the lower wing. If the aeroplane has high keel surfaces, then the airflow striking them in the sideslip will tend to restore a wings-level condition.

If the wings have **dihedral** (a design feature in which each wing is inclined upwards towards the wingtips), the lower wing is presented to the airflow at a greater angle of attack in the sideslip, thereby generating a greater lift force which tends to restore a wings-level condition.

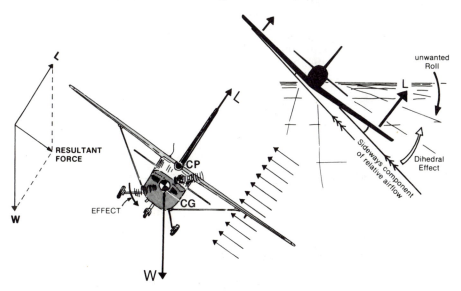

Fig.6a-6. High Keel Surfaces and Dihedral provide Lateral Stability.

Compared to stability in the pitching plane, the stability of the aeroplane is not as great in the rolling and yawing planes. The inter-relationship between roll and yaw (as seen in Chapter 4b) is such that a disturbance in either roll or yaw will eventually lead to a spiral descent unless the Pilot acts to level the wings and keep the balance ball centred. In general terms, however, the natural stability designed into the aeroplane will assist you in maintaining straight and level flight.

THE WINGS GENERATE LIFT.

The main wings are designed so that the airflow speeds-up over their upper surface, creating a lower static pressure and an upwards aerodynamic force. The vertical component is known as **Lift** and the component parallel to the flight path is called **Induced Drag** ('induced' because it is the by-product of the generation of Lift).

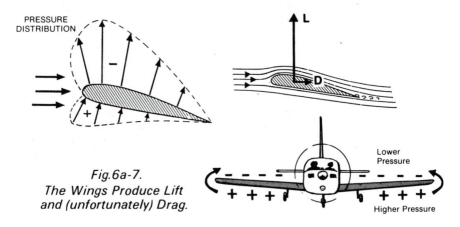

Fig.6a-7.
*The Wings Produce Lift
and (unfortunately) Drag.*

The **lifting ability** of a particular wing (known as the 'coefficient of lift' and abbreviated as C$_L$) depends upon both the **shape** of the wing and its **angle of attack** (which is the angle at which the relative airflow strikes the wing).

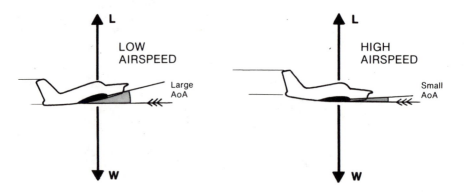

*Fig.6a-8. The Lifting Ability of the Wing depends
upon the Angle of Attack.*

Straight and level, to obtain the required Lift to balance the Weight:
- at **low speed,** a **high angle of attack** is required; and
- at **high speed,** a **low angle of attack** is required.

NOTE: The 'angle of attack', which is related to relative airflow, is not to be confused with the 'pitch attitude', which is related to the horizon.

THE PILOT CONTROLS ANGLE OF ATTACK WITH ELEVATOR.

Backward movement of the control column raises the nose. Because the aeroplane's inertia (i.e. its resistance to any change in the flight path) causes the aeroplane to continue in the same direction at the same airspeed for a brief period, the angle of attack is increased. The wing will generate increased Lift and the aeroplane will start to climb.

Conversely, moving the control column forward lowers the nose and decreases the angle of attack. Since the airspeed has not had time to alter, the wings will generate decreased Lift and the aeroplane will lose height.

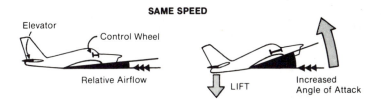

Fig.6a-9. The Elevator Controls Angle of Attack.

The Pilot cannot measure angle of attack in the cockpit but he can ensure that **suitable angles of attack** are being flown by setting:
- a suitable **power;** and
- a suitable pitch **attitude.**

PERFORMANCE.

Power plus Attitude determines the Performance of the aeroplane in terms of:
- airspeed; and
- rate of climb (which is of course zero for straight and level flight).

Flying straight and level with constant power set, there will be a particular pitch attitude for straight and level flight. If the nose is too high, the aeroplane will climb; if it is too low, the aeroplane will descend. How do you know that you have set the correct pitch attitude? The aeroplane maintains height!

FLYING THE MANOEUVRE

FLYING STRAIGHT.

The essential elements in flying straight are to **keep the wings level** with aileron and to **keep the aeroplane in balance** with rudder pressure.

The outside visual clue to the Pilot of 'wings-level' is the natural horizon being level in the windscreen. If it is not level, then rotation of the control wheel or sideways movement of the control column to operate the ailerons will remedy this.

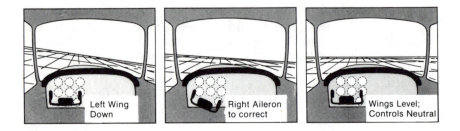

Fig.6a-10. Level the Wings with the Ailerons.

Balance is achieved by keeping the balance ball centred. If it is out to the left, more left rudder pressure is required; if it is out to the right, more right rudder pressure is required.

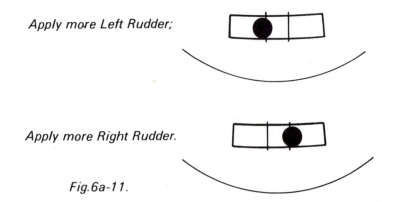

Apply more Left Rudder;

Apply more Right Rudder.

Fig.6a-11.

In straight flight, a reference point ahead on the horizon will remain in the same position relative to the nose of the aeroplane. In the cockpit, straight flight is indicated by a steady heading on the Direction Indicator and the Magnetic Compass.

If the aeroplane is deviating from straight flight, first of all stop the deviation by levelling the wings and centring the balance ball. Then make a gentle turn back onto the desired heading.

FLYING LEVEL.

The essential element in **maintaining height** is to **establish the correct nose attitude for the power set.** The external reference is the natural horizon, which should appear at a particular position in the windscreen relative to the nose cowl or the top of the instrument panel.

The relationship between the horizon and the nose cowl will differ for different Pilot eye-heights in the aeroplane, so you should **establish a comfortable seating position that you use every flight.** This will make it easier to commit to memory the correct attitude for normal cruise. Then, with cruise power set at cruise speed, you can place the aeroplane in this attitude and be reasonably certain that level flight will result. This can be confirmed on the **Altimeter** and **Vertical Speed Indicator.**

If the **pitch attitude is too high** and the aeroplane climbs, lower the nose slightly and regain the desired height. If the **pitch attitude is too low** and the aeroplane descends, raise the nose to regain the height.

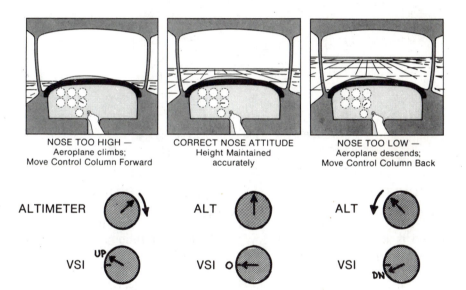

Fig.6a-12. With Cruise Power Set at Cruise Speed, Maintain Height with Elevator.

FLY AS ACCURATELY AS POSSIBLE.

Maintaining heading and height perfectly is almost impossible. There will inevitably be some deviations but these can be corrected so that the aeroplane flies very close to the target heading and height. More comfortable flight results from **continually making small corrections** than occasionally making large ones.

Keep the aeroplane in trim to make accurate level flight easier, the correct procedure being to hold the desired attitude and then trim off any steady control pressure.

Do not fly with 'crossed-controls'. It is possible to fly straight and level with one wing down and the aeroplane out of balance. For example, if the left wing is down, right rudder can be applied to stop the aeroplane turning left. This is neither comfortable nor efficient and is known as a 'sideslip' or 'flying with crossed-controls' (since the ailerons and rudder oppose each other). It degrades performance by increasing drag and results in a reduced airspeed and/or a higher fuel consumption.

'Crossed-controls' can be eliminated by levelling the wings with aileron and moving the balance ball back into the centre with rudder pressure.

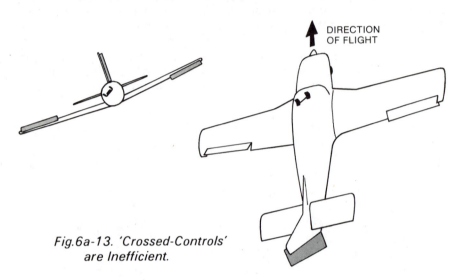

DIRECTION OF FLIGHT

*Fig.6a-13. 'Crossed-Controls'
are Inefficient.*

RECOVERING FROM SLIGHTLY UNUSUAL ATTITUDES.

If the aeroplane is banked, level the wings with the ailerons. If the nose is too high or too low, ease it into the correct attitude with the elevator. If speed is excessively high or low, or if large alterations to height are required, some adjustment of power may be necessary.

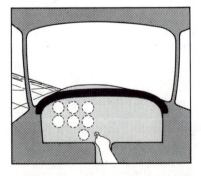

*Fig.6a-14. Nose High and Turning
Left – Lower Nose and level Wings.*

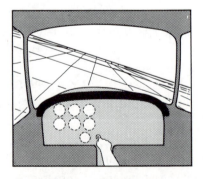

*Nose Low and Turning Left – Level
the Wings and Raise the Nose.*

AIRMANSHIP

Your eyes should be out of the cockpit most of the time to:
• check the correct nose position relative to the horizon;
• check the reference point on the horizon;
• Look Out for other aircraft above, below and to either side.

An occasional glance into the cockpit lasting only one or two seconds is sufficient to cross-check relevant instruments. Only look at the instruments from which you need information.

Maintain firm, positive and smooth control over the aeroplane and keep it well trimmed. This will decrease your workload considerably. Do not allow large deviations from the desired altitude, heading or airspeed to occur. Small and subtle movements of the controls, made sufficiently early, will avoid this, and these small movements are preferable to occasional large corrections.

Follow the basic Rules of the Air:
• Give way to airships, gliders, balloons and aircraft towing gliders or banners.
• Give way to the right and avoid passing over, under or ahead of other aircraft unless well clear.
• Turn right if there is a danger of a head-on collision.

Remain well clear of cloud.

AIRWORK 6a —

AIM: *To fly straight and level at a constant power setting.*

- *LOOK OUT:*
- Select a horizon reference point on which to keep straight;
- Keep the wings level with the ailerons;
- Maintain balance with rudder pressure.

(1) With Cruise Power Set and At Desired Height:
- Place the nose in the cruise attitude with elevator, and with constant power set:
  - cross check the Altimeter and Vertical Speed Indicator;
  - make small attitude adjustments with elevator.

- Allow the airspeed to settle:
  - check the Air Speed Indicator for airspeed information;
  - cross check the Altimeter and Vertical Speed Indicator for attitude information;
  - trim off elevator pressure, whilst holding the new pitch attitude constant.

POWER + ATTITUDE = PERFORMANCE

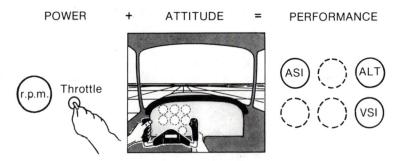

Maintain attitude with elevator.

(2) The Correct Trimming Technique is:
- Hold correct attitude with elevator pressure;
- Trim to relieve the control load.

If rudder trim is fitted, trim-off rudder pressure whilst maintaining heading and keeping the balance ball centred.

STRAIGHT AND LEVEL AT CONSTANT POWER

(3a) If the Aeroplane Tends to Climb:
- Regain desired altitude with gentle movement of elevator;
- Hold nose attitude slightly lower than previously with elevator;
  - — allow airspeed to settle:
  - — check Altimeter and Vertical Speed Indicator;
- Trim off elevator pressure for the new attitude.

Initial attitude,   Regain height.   Slightly lower attitude;
climb tendency.   re-trim.

(3b) If the Aeroplane Tends to Descend:
- Regain desired altitude with elevator (adding power if necessary);
- Hold nose attitude slightly higher than previously:
  - — allow airspeed to settle;
  - — check Altimeter and Vertical Speed Indicator;
- Trim off elevator pressure.

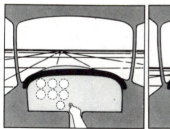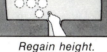

Initial attitude,   Regain height.   Slightly higher attitude;
descent tendency.   re-trim.

(3c) If the Aeroplane Wanders off Heading:
- Gently bank the aeroplane towards the desired heading using aileron, and
- Apply same-side rudder pressure;
- Maintain height with elevator (fore or aft control column pressure);

When on desired heading:
- Level the wings with aileron;
- Balance with rudder;
- Maintain height with elevator.

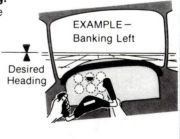

EXAMPLE—
Banking Left

Desired
Heading

6b

FLYING STRAIGHT AND LEVEL AT A SELECTED AIRSPEED

AIM

To fly the aeroplane straight and level at a selected airspeed.

CONSIDERATIONS

Straight and level flight can be maintained over a range of speeds – from a high-speed cruise to low-speed flight just above stalling speed. Whilst a normal cruise or high-speed cruise is suitable for cross-country flying, manoeuvring in the circuit in preparation for landing requires a low speed.

ACCELERATING AND DECELERATING STRAIGHT AND LEVEL.

In the cruise, **Thrust balances Drag** – the source of the Thrust being engine power. If the desired airspeed is less than that being maintained, then, by reducing power, the Thrust will not balance the Drag and consequently the aeroplane will slow down (i.e. decelerate). If, however, the desired airspeed is somewhat greater than that being maintained, then, by increasing power, the Thrust will exceed the Drag and the aeroplane will accelerate.

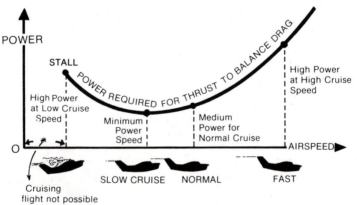

Fig.6b-1. Vary the Cruising Airspeed by altering Power.

94

POWER.

Once the aeroplane has accelerated or decelerated to the target airspeed, the power is adjusted to maintain it. Subsequent adjustments to the power may be required for the selected speed to be maintained accurately.

Fig.6b-2. Maintain Straight and Level Airspeed with Power.

ATTITUDE.

Since the Lift generated by the wings depends upon both the angle of attack and the airspeed, the Lift will increase as the airspeed increases and, unless the nose is lowered, the aeroplane will commence to climb. In other words, **as the airspeed is increased, the nose must be lowered to maintain height.**

If the speed is reducing, then the Lift will decrease and the aeroplane will lose height unless the nose is raised, i.e. **as speed is decreased, the nose must be raised for height to be maintained.**

FLYING THE MANOEUVRE

Prior to any significant power changes the Mixture Control should be in the RICH (fully in) position. Add power to increase airspeed or remove power to decrease airspeed, whilst maintaining height with elevator. Be prepared for the 'pitch/yaw' tendency that occurs with power changes ('nose-up and yaw' as power is added, 'nose-down and yaw' as power is reduced), counteracting it with control pressures. Once the desired airspeed is attained, adjust the power to maintain it. Trim.

At very low airspeeds, where high power is required, close attention must be given to maintaining the speed using power. Frequent, and sometimes large, power adjustments may be required. The reasons for this are considered in detail in Section 10 of this manual.

AIRMANSHIP

Maintain a good **Look Out.** Be positive in achieving the desired airspeed and height. Maintain them! Constant attention to power and attitude is required.

AIRWORK 6b —
STRAIGHT AND LEVEL AT A SELECTED AIRSPEED

AIM: To fly straight and level at a selected airspeed.

(1) To Increase Speed in Level Flight:
- Increase power (balance with rudder pressure);
- Lower nose gradually to maintain level flight as airspeed increases;
- Adjust power to maintain desired airspeed;
- Trim off elevator pressure (nose-down);
- Make minor adjustments of Power, Attitude and Trim as required.

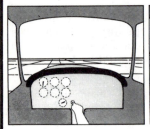 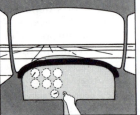 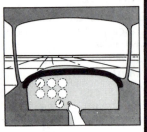

Add power.   *Lower nose attitude.*   *Adjust power and re-trim.*

(2) To Decrease Speed in Level Flight:
- Decrease power (balance with rudder pressure);
- Raise nose gradually to maintain level flight as airspeed decreases;
- Adjust power to maintain desired airspeed;
- Trim off elevator pressure (nose-up);
- Make minor adjustments of Power, Attitude and Trim as required.

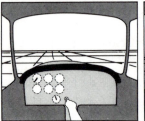 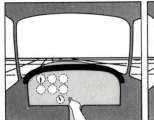 

Decrease power.   *Higher nose attitude*   *Adjust power and re-trim.*

Remember **"PAT"**: Power – Attitude – Trim

FURTHER POINTS

There are sound reasons for maintaining certain selected airspeeds; for example, when the maximum range for a given quantity of fuel is desired.

Different Airspeeds Straight and Level Require Different Power Settings. The Thrust must balance the Drag, which (like Lift) depends upon airspeed and angle of attack. **At high airspeeds the Drag is high;** at medium speeds it is somewhat less. This is because the 'Parasite Drag' decreases with airspeed – the Parasite Drag being similar to the air resistance that you feel on a bicycle.

What is different with an aeroplane, however, is that, unlike a bicycle (which is supported by the ground), an aeroplane in-flight must generate its own support, i.e. Lift. A by-product of the production of Lift by the wings is 'Induced Drag' and this is greatest at high angles of attack, i.e. at low airspeeds. As a result, **the Total Drag is high when the aeroplane is flying slowly.**

Fig.6b-3. Minimum Drag occurs at an Intermediate Airspeed.

A high power is required at both low and high airspeeds for the Drag to be balanced. At intermediate speeds, the power requirement is less. The rate at which fuel is consumed depends upon the power set, and an important aspect in operating an aeroplane efficiently is to obtain the maximum benefit from the fuel available.

THE BEST ENDURANCE SPEED.

For minimum fuel consumption, fly at the **minimum power** airspeed. This will achieve the maximum flight **time** for a given quantity of fuel. Since 'delaying' flight is sometimes required (for example, if holding near an aerodrome waiting for fog to clear), flying at the airspeed for 'maximum endurance' provides the 'minimum fuel burn for a given flight time'.

The **Best Endurance Airspeed** is nominated in the Pilot's Operating Handbook.

THE BEST RANGE AIRSPEED.

A more common requirement is to achieve the maximum **distance** for a given quantity of fuel. Since most flights are over a fixed distance, another way of expressing 'best range' is 'minimum fuel burn to cover a given distance'.

The **Best Range Airspeed** is also nominated in the Pilot's Operating Handbook and is higher than that for maximum endurance. The range distances published by the manufacturer assume **correct 'leaning' of the mixture** when cruising at powers less than 75% Maximum Continuous Power (usually occurring when cruising above 5000 ft AMSL).

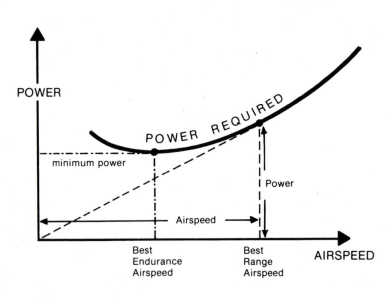

Fig.6b-4. Airspeeds for 'Best Endurance' and 'Best Range'.

Referring to the 'Best Range Airspeed' as shown on the Graph above, the 'rate of fuel consumption' depends upon power. The 'rate of covering distance' is the speed.

Therefore, the 'minimum fuel consumption for a given distance' (i.e. the best range) will occur at the airspeed where the 'power/speed' ratio is least, as illustrated above.

The line from the origin to any other point on the graph has a steeper gradient, i.e. the 'power/speed' ratio is greater and so more fuel per mile will be burned.

6c

CRUISING WITH FLAP EXTENDED

AIM

To fly the aeroplane straight and level at a selected airspeed with flap lowered.

CONSIDERATIONS

Cruising with an early stage of flap extended is desirable when you wish to fly at a low speed; for example, when inspecting a prospective precautionary landing field or when greater manoeuvrability is required.

Because the lifting ability of the wings is increased as the flaps are extended, **a lower nose attitude will be required to maintain height.** If the nose is not lowered as the flaps are extended, the aeroplane will 'balloon'.

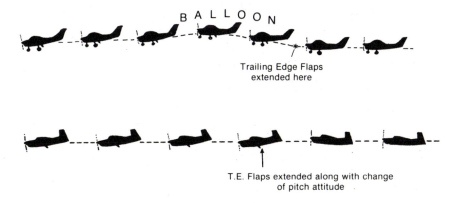

Fig.6c-1. A 'Balloon' can be avoided by Lowering the Nose as Flaps Extend.

The flaps should not be operated at high speeds, since this places unnecessary stress on the airframe. The **maximum flap extension speed** (VFE) is the high speed end of the white band on the Air Speed Indicator.

A low nose position improves the forward view from the cockpit.

Fig.6c-2. Flaps Improve the Forward View.

Lower speeds are possible with Flap Extended because of the increased lifting ability of the wings and the lower stalling speed. The stalling speed straight and level with flap extended is the low speed end of the white band on the Air Speed Indicator; the stalling speed 'clean' is the low speed end of the green band. **(See Fig.10a-2.)**

Because **extending flap increases the Drag,** power must be added if airspeed is to be maintained in straight and level flight. This increases the fuel consumption, making cruising with flap extended much less efficient than cruising 'clean'.

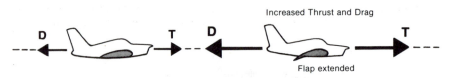

Fig.6c-3. Flap Increases Drag.

FLYING THE MANOEUVRE

As the flap position is changed, be prepared to make any necessary adjustments to power and attitude to achieve the desired performance.

Lowering flap will require a lower nose position to avoid 'ballooning' and an increase in power to maintain airspeed. Once the adjustments are made, any steady control pressure should be trimmed off.

Raising flap will require a higher nose position to avoid 'sinking' and an adjustment to power to maintain airspeed. Trim off any steady control pressures.

Do not operate the flaps at too high a speed — VFE is the limit. Do not raise the flaps below the 'clean' stalling speed.

AIRWORK 6c —
CRUISING WITH FLAP EXTENDED

AIM: To fly straight and level with flap extended.

- Reduce power;
- Establish the aeroplane in straight and level flight clean (i.e. flaps fully retracted).

(1) To Lower Flap, Maintaining Straight and Level Flight.
- Ensure airspeed is below maximum flap extension speed (VFE), i.e. in white ASI band;
- Extend flaps in stages;
- Place nose in lower attitude (to avoid 'ballooning' and maintain height);
- Adjust power to maintain desired airspeed;
- Trim off elevator pressure for each stage of flap.

(1)

(2)

(2) To Raise Flap:
- Check that the airspeed is suitable;
- Raise the flaps in stages, holding the nose in a higher attitude to prevent "sink" and maintain height;
- Adjust power to maintain desired speed;
- Trim off elevator pressure.

NOTE:
In a go-around situation, when you wish to discontinue an approach APPLY FULL POWER first, before altering the flap position.

Intentionally Blank

CLIMBING

7

CLIMBING

AIM

To enter and maintain a steady climb on a constant heading and to level-off at a particular height.

CONSIDERATIONS

THE FORCES ACTING ON THE AEROPLANE IN THE CLIMB.

For an aeroplane to climb steadily the Thrust must exceed the Drag, otherwise it would slow down and the nose would have to be lowered to maintain airspeed. The Thrust in excess of that needed to balance the Drag is called the 'excess thrust'.

In a climb, the vertical component of the 'excess thrust' supports a small part of the Weight and the Lift generated by the wings supports the remainder — hence the surprising result that **Lift is less than Weight in a steady climb.**

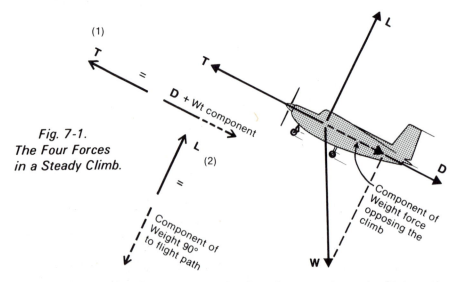

Fig. 7-1.
The Four Forces
in a Steady Climb.

A component of the Weight acts in the direction opposite to the flight path and opposes the climb.

POWER PLUS ATTITUDE EQUALS PERFORMANCE.

The **power** applied and the **attitude** of an aeroplane determine its **performance** in terms of:
• airspeed; and
• rate of climb.

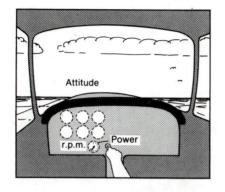

Fig.7-2. Climb Power plus Climb Attitude Provides Climb Performance.

The power in a climb is usually greater than that used for the cruise and for many training aeroplanes is in fact maximum power. The greater slipstream effect striking one side of the tail in a climb will have a yawing effect, especially at low airspeeds. **Counteract the yawing tendency with rudder pressure** and keep the aeroplane in balance.

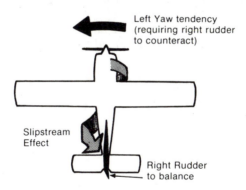

Fig.7-3. Balance the Yawing Tendency from the Slipstream with Rudder Pressure.

In a climb, the usual balance rule applies. If the ball is out to the right, for example, move it back into the centre with right rudder pressure. Most training aeroplanes have a propeller that rotates clockwise when viewed from the cockpit (as in the above diagram).

As climb power is applied, a co-ordinated increase in right rudder pressure will maintain the aeroplane in balance. Some aeroplanes have a rudder trim, which may be used to relieve steady foot pressures in the climb (and at any other time).

With climb power set, **pitch attitude controls the airspeed.** Raising the nose will decrease airspeed (and vice versa). Do not 'chase' the airspeed after altering the nose attitude – allow time for the airspeed to settle before making any further (and minor) changes in attitude. If the power and attitude are correct, then the climb performance will be as desired and reference to the Air Speed Indicator need only be made to make fine adjustments.

Fig.7-4. The Climb Attitude is Higher than the Normal Cruise Attitude.

Once established in the climb, trim-off any steady control pressures with the elevator trim, and the rudder trim (if fitted). An out-of-trim aeroplane is difficult to fly accurately.

Climb performance can be measured in the cockpit on the Flight Instruments:
- **airspeed** — primarily on the Air Speed Indicator;
- **rate of climb** — on the Vertical Speed Indicator and Altimeter.

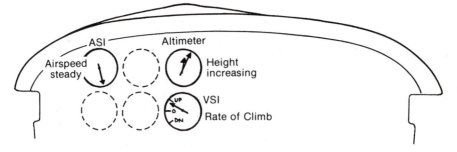

Fig.7-5. Monitor the Climb Performance Occasionally on the Flight Instruments.

THE FORWARD VIEW IN A CLIMB IS RESTRICTED BY THE NOSE COWL.

The restricted view ahead could mean danger — other aeroplanes may be hidden by your nose cowl. It is good airmanship to carry out a small turn left and right (or to lower the nose) every 500 ft or so in the climb to look ahead and 'clear' the area under the nose into which you are climbing. A reference point on the horizon will assist in returning to the original heading.

ENSURE THAT THE ENGINE IS ADEQUATELY COOLED IN THE CLIMB.

During a climb using high power the engine is producing more heat energy than at lesser power settings. The lower airspeed reduces the air cooling of the engine, so there is a risk of overheating and the Pilot must ensure that sufficient cooling is taking place.

The engine instruments should be monitored periodically in the climb and, if the engine temperature is too high, better cooling may be achieved by:
• increasing airspeed; or
• reducing power; and
• opening the cowl flaps (if fitted).

It is usual to climb with the mixture fully *RICH*, because excess fuel, as it vaporises, has a cooling effect in the cylinders.

THERE ARE VARIOUS CLIMB SPEEDS TO ACHIEVE DIFFERENT AIMS.

The Pilot can sacrifice some airspeed for a higher rate of climb (or vice versa). The choice of airspeed on the climb depends upon what the Pilot wants to achieve. It may be:
• a **steep angle of climb** to clear obstacles (best-angle climb — Vx);
• a **rapid climb** to gain height in a short time (best-rate climb — Vy);
• a **cruise-climb** (the most usual) which provides:
  – faster en route performance;
  – better aeroplane control due to greater airflow over the control surfaces;
  – better engine cooling;
  – a more comfortable aeroplane attitude.

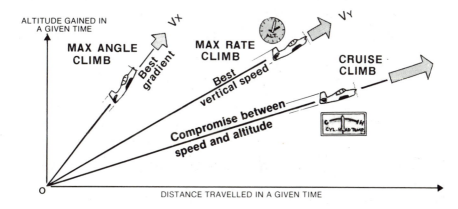

Fig. 7-6. Different Types of Climb.

The aeroplane can be made to climb at any of the above speeds. Their values may be found in your Pilot's Operating Handbook. With climb power set, simply fly the aeroplane at the appropriate Indicated Air Speed to achieve the desired type of climb – the lower the nose attitude the higher the climb airspeed. Engine cooling will be poorer at the lower airspeeds.

BEST RATE CLIMB
(e.g. 65 kt)

BEST ANGLE CLIMB
(e.g. 55 kt)

NORMAL CLIMB
(e.g. 70 kt)

Fig. 7-7. The Various Climb Attitudes.

FLYING THE MANOEUVRE

PRIOR TO ENTERING THE CLIMB.

Decide on an appropriate climb speed, select a reference point well ahead and LOOK OUT to check all clear of other aeroplanes and obstacles ahead, above, below and to either side.

TO ENTER THE CLIMB.

Increase **Power** (first ensuring mixture *RICH*) by opening the throttle to climb power. Balance the unwanted yawing effect with rudder. Raise the nose to the correct climb **Attitude,** allow the airspeed to settle and **Trim.** An easy way to remember the sequence of events when entering a climb is 'P-A-T': **Power — Attitude — Trim.**

TO MAINTAIN THE CLIMB.

Maintain the wings level with aileron and the balance ball centred with rudder pressure. Maintain the desired airspeed with elevator — the higher the nose, the lower the airspeed.

Every 500 ft or so, either lower the nose or make clearing turns left and right to clear the area ahead. Periodically check engine temperatures and pressures, taking appropriate action if the engine is overheating such as opening the cowl flaps (if fitted), increasing the airspeed and/or reducing the power.

TO LEVEL-OFF FROM A CLIMB.

Since cruise speed is higher than climb speed, it is usual to gradually adopt the cruise attitude as the intended cruise level is approached, leaving climb power set. Allow the aeroplane to accelerate until cruise speed is attained, lowering the nose as airspeed increases.

Anticipate reaching the cruise level by 20 ft or so and commence lowering the nose towards the cruise **Attitude.** This will make levelling-off a smooth manoeuvre and avoid overshooting the level.

As cruise speed is reached reduce to cruise **Power,** maintaining balance with rudder pressure. **Trim.** The sequence of events for levelling off is **'A-P-T': Attitude — Power — Trim.**

Once established in the cruise, engine operation should be considered:
- mixture leaned as required;
- carburettor heat as required;
- cowl flaps (if fitted) possibly closed;
- monitor the engine oil temperature and pressure from time to time.

AIRMANSHIP

Ensure that the engine is adequately cooled during the 'high power/low airspeed' climb. The mixture should be *RICH* before power is increased.

Maintain a continuous **LOOK OUT.** Clear the 'blind spot' under the nose every 500 ft or so in the climb. Do not climb too close to, and definitely not into, cloud.

Be aware of the nature of the airspace above you. For example, do not inadvertently climb into Controlled Airspace without a clearance to do so from ATC. Follow correct Altimetry procedures — normally Regional QNH is set during training so that the Altimeter reads height Above Mean Sea Level.

Exert firm, positive and smooth control over the aeroplane.

AIRWORK 7 —

AIM: (a) To enter and maintain a steady climb on a constant heading, and

(b) To level off at a particular height.

IN A CLIMB
MAINTAIN
AIRSPEED
WITH
ELEVATOR

(1) Prior to Entry:
- Decide on an appropriate climb speed;
- Select a reference point well-ahead, slightly to the left of the nose;
- *LOOK OUT* — clear the area ahead, above, below and to either side.

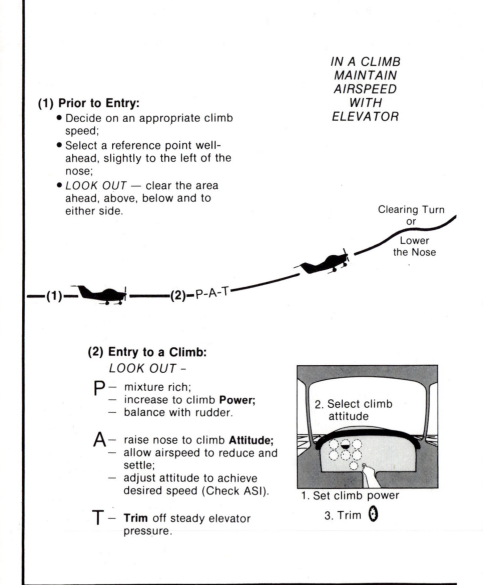

Clearing Turn
or
Lower
the Nose

—(1)— ————(2)—P-A-T

(2) Entry to a Climb:
LOOK OUT –

P – mixture rich;
 – increase to climb **Power;**
 – balance with rudder.

A – raise nose to climb **Attitude;**
 – allow airspeed to reduce and settle;
 – adjust attitude to achieve desired speed (Check ASI).

T – **Trim** off steady elevator pressure.

2. Select climb attitude

1. Set climb power

3. Trim

THE CLIMB

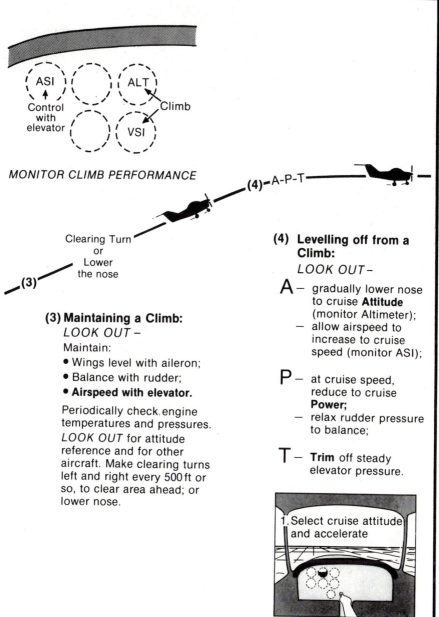

MONITOR CLIMB PERFORMANCE

ASI
Control
with
elevator

ALT
Climb

VSI

Clearing Turn
or
Lower
the nose

(3)

(4)–A-P-T

(3) Maintaining a Climb:
LOOK OUT –
Maintain:
- Wings level with aileron;
- Balance with rudder;
- **Airspeed with elevator.**

Periodically check engine temperatures and pressures.
LOOK OUT for attitude reference and for other aircraft. Make clearing turns left and right every 500 ft or so, to clear area ahead; or lower nose.

(4) Levelling off from a Climb:
LOOK OUT –

A – gradually lower nose to cruise **Attitude** (monitor Altimeter);
– allow airspeed to increase to cruise speed (monitor ASI);

P – at cruise speed, reduce to cruise **Power;**
– relax rudder pressure to balance;

T – **Trim** off steady elevator pressure.

1. Select cruise attitude and accelerate

2. Set cruise power

3. Trim

FURTHER POINTS

A BRIEF DISCUSSION OF CLIMB PERFORMANCE.

The curve below shows the power that is required for an aeroplane to maintain straight and level flight at various airspeeds. If the engine can provide power greater than this, then the aeroplane is capable of climbing at that airspeed. Power is the rate at which energy is supplied, so the best **rate of climb** will be achieved at the airspeed at which maximum 'excess power' is available.

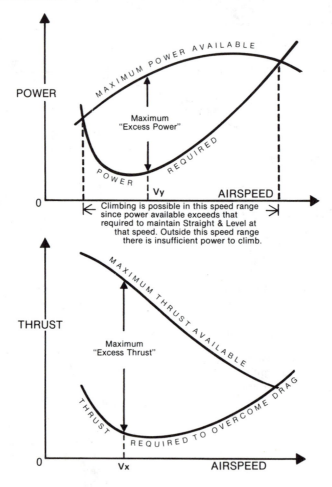

Fig.7-8. The Power Curve and the Thrust Curve (also known as the Drag Curve).

Power is defined as the product of 'thrust x velocity' so, for a given power output, the higher the velocity the lower the thrust. This explains the different shapes of the power and thrust curves in the diagrams above.

The **angle of climb** depends upon how much thrust is available over and above the drag (i.e. the 'excess thrust'), and so the steepest climb, i.e. the **best angle climb,** is achieved with maximum power set and at the airspeed where maximum 'excess thrust' occurs. This is slightly lower than the best rate speed.

NOTE: At low gross weights and low altitudes, the aeroplane will climb better than at high gross weights or high altitudes (where the air is less dense).

CLIMBING WITH FLAP EXTENDED.

Take-off is often made with some flap extended, because it:
● allows the same lift to be generated at a lower airspeed, shortening the take-off run;
● reduces the stalling speed, allowing slower flight; and
● may (depending upon the aircraft type) enable a steeper climb-out angle to be achieved.

Full flap causes a large drag increase and greatly reduces climb performance, so **always ensure that only take-off flap is set for take-off.** This is typically the first stage, or 10–15°. On some aeroplanes it is zero flap.

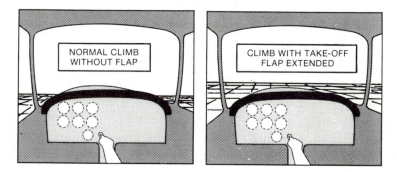

Fig. 7-9. Nose Position in the Climb is Lower with Flap Extended.

RAISING THE FLAPS IN THE CLIMB-OUT.

When climbing out after take-off, it is usual to raise the flaps when well clear of the ground (say 200 ft Above Aerodrome Level). To avoid any tendency for the nose to pitch or for the aeroplane to 'sink' as the flaps are raised:
● hold the nose in the normal attitude for a clean climb;
● allow the airspeed to settle at the desired airspeed;
● trim.

Check the Air Speed Indicator and adjust the nose attitude with the elevator if required (but do not 'chase' the airspeed).

Intentionally Blank

8

DESCENDING

8a

THE GLIDE

AIM

To enter and maintain a steady glide and to level-off at a particular height.

CONSIDERATIONS

An aeroplane may be descended in two ways:
1. In a **glide,** where engine power is not used and the Pilot accepts the resulting Rate of Descent; or
2. In a **powered descent,** where power is used by the Pilot to control the Rate of Descent.

THE FORCES IN THE GLIDE.

If power is removed when the aeroplane is in level flight, the Drag will be unbalanced and, if height is maintained, the aeroplane will decelerate. Only three forces will act on the aeroplane when the power is totally removed — **Drag** (no longer balanced by Thrust), **Lift** and **Weight.**

To maintain flying speed when the Thrust is removed, the nose must be lowered and a glide commenced. Drag (which by definition always acts in the direction opposite to the flight path) now has a component of the Weight available to balance it. A steady gliding speed will be achieved when the three forces (L, W and D) are in equilibrium.

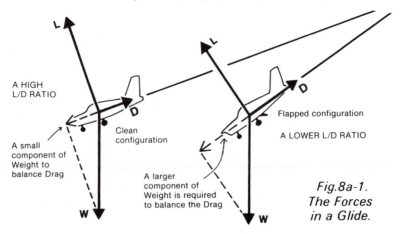

A HIGH
L/D RATIO

Clean
configuration

A small
component of
Weight to
balance Drag

Flapped configuration

A LOWER L/D RATIO

A larger
component of
Weight is required
to balance the Drag

Fig.8a-1.
The Forces
in a Glide.

STEEPNESS OF THE GLIDE DEPENDS UPON LIFT/DRAG RATIO.

If Drag is increased more than Lift (say by lowering flaps, sideslipping or flying at an incorrect airspeed), a greater component of the Weight is required to balance it and maintain airspeed. A steeper flight path is the result.

The gliding range through the air depends upon the 'Lift/Drag' ratio, e.g. if L:D is 6:1 then, for every 1000 ft lost in height, the aeroplane will glide 6000 ft (approximately 1 nm); if L:D is 10:1 then, for every 1000 ft lost in height, the aeroplane will glide 10 000 ft (1·7 nm).

THE MAXIMUM GLIDING RANGE IS ACHIEVED AT THE SPEED FOR BEST 'LIFT/DRAG'.

Changing the angle of attack with the control column changes the airspeed and the Lift/Drag ratio. This will have a significant effect on the glide path. A typical training aeroplane, flown at the best gliding speed, can achieve a Lift/Drag ratio of about 10:1. Flown at the wrong airspeed, the Lift/Drag ratio will be significantly less and consequently the glide path will be steeper.

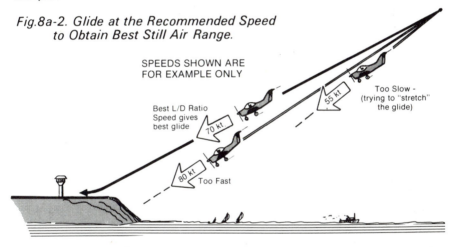

Fig.8a-2. Glide at the Recommended Speed to Obtain Best Still Air Range.

SPEEDS SHOWN ARE FOR EXAMPLE ONLY

Best L/D Ratio Speed gives best glide — 70 kt.

80 kt. — Too Fast

55 kt — Too Slow - (trying to "stretch" the glide)

NOTE: The Pilot's Operating Handbook specifies the best gliding speed when the aeroplane is at maximum weight. At lower weights, the best gliding speed is less but, since training aeroplanes do not have significant variations in gross weight, the one speed is generally acceptable at any weight.

A HEADWIND STEEPENS THE DESCENT OVER THE GROUND; A TAILWIND FLATTENS IT.

At the normal gliding speed, a headwind will retard the aeroplane's passage over the ground; a tailwind will extend it.

In a tailwind, reducing the gliding airspeed slightly below the recommended gliding speed may increase the range a little by reducing the Rate of Descent, allowing the aeroplane to remain airborne longer and be blown further by the wind.

Conversely, the effect of a headwind can be minimised by gliding at a higher airspeed. The Rate of Descent will be increased, but the higher speed will allow the aeroplane to 'penetrate' further into the wind and cover more ground. Increasing speed could be an important technique to use on an undershooting gliding approach to land in a strong headwind.

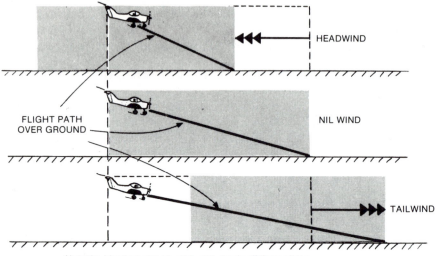

HEADWIND

FLIGHT PATH
OVER GROUND

NIL WIND

TAILWIND

Note the identical aircraft pitch attitudes in **all three** glides

Fig.8a-3. Compared to Still Air, More Ground is Covered When Gliding With a Tailwind and Less With a Headwind.

ESTIMATING THE GLIDING RANGE.

A practical means of estimating how far the aeroplane could glide **at a constant airspeed** is to note that ground feature which remains stationary in the windscreen. In the situation illustrated below, it appears that the glide will reach the trees beyond the first road, but not as far as the second road.

Raising the nose in an attempt to reach the second field may have the reverse effect. If the speed falls significantly below the best gliding speed, the glide path will steepen and fall well short of even the first road.

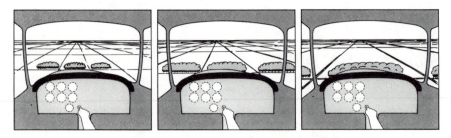

Fig.8a-4. Estimating the Gliding Distance.

THE MIXTURE CONTROL SHOULD BE MOVED TO RICH FOR A GLIDE.

It is usual to move the red Mixture Control to full rich (i.e. fully in) before commencing the descent, so that the mixture is not too lean when power is re-applied at a lower level where the air is denser. An excessively lean mixture can cause detonation that is very damaging to an engine.

SET CARBURETTOR HEAT TO HOT FOR THE GLIDE.

The usual clues of carburettor ice forming (reduced rpm and rough running) may not be evident because of the low engine speed in a glide. Power, when it is needed, may not be available. Consequently, during the glide the Carburettor Heat should be set to HOT to prevent the formation of carburettor ice (but it must be the Carburettor Heat knob that is pulled right out and not the Mixture Control!).

Selecting Carburettor Heat HOT **prior** to closing the throttle is a good practice so that some hot air passes through the induction system before the engine goes to idle. Done in the reverse sequence, there may be sufficient time after closing the throttle for ice to form before HOT air is selected. Discuss the correct technique for your aeroplane with a Flying Instructor.

REDUCE POWER AND CONTROL AIRSPEED WITH ELEVATOR AND BALANCE WITH RUDDER.

Once the mixture and carburettor heat are attended to, the power can be reduced by smoothly pulling the throttle out. Full movement of the throttle should take about the same time as a slow '1-2-3' count. The reduced slipstream effect will require rudder to balance and prevent unwanted yaw. The tendency for the nose to drop too far will require back pressure on the control column.

NOTE: Some aeroplanes have a rudder trim which may be used to relieve steady foot pressures in the descent. The tendency for the nose to drop as power is reduced is a safety feature that is designed into an aeroplane to ensure that it will adopt a safe gliding attitude without any help from the Pilot if the engine fails.

WARM THE ENGINE PERIODICALLY DURING A PROLONGED DESCENT.

Every 1000 ft or so on a prolonged descent, the Pilot should apply approximately 50% power for a few seconds to:
• keep the engine and oil warm;
• avoid carbon fouling on the spark plugs; and
• ensure that the carburettor heat is still supplying warm air.

MONITOR THE RATE OF DESCENT.

The Rate of Descent is a measure of how fast height is being lost (in ft/min) and can be monitored on either:
• the Vertical Speed Indicator; or
• the Altimeter and Clock combined.

THE BEST ENDURANCE GLIDE.

Generally, the aim in a glide is to achieve the maximum range (i.e. the greatest distance over the ground) and this is the situation that we have addressed so far. Occasionally, **time** in flight (rather than distance covered) becomes important, say if the engine has stopped at 5000 ft directly over an airfield and you want as long as possible to re-start it.

The **Best Endurance Glide** is achieved at the speed which results in the minimum Rate of Descent as indicated on the Vertical Speed Indicator. Typically, it is some 25% less than the more common gliding speed used for maximum range.

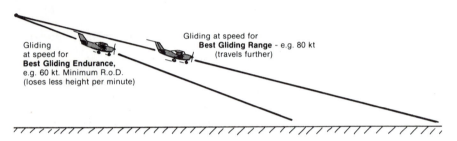

Fig.8a-5. Select the Best Gliding Speed for Range or for Endurance.

FLYING THE MANOEUVRE

Prior to commencing the descent, decide on an appropriate gliding speed, select a reference point well ahead and **Look Out** to check all clear of other aeroplanes and obstacles ahead, below and to either side. A clearing turn to view under the nose may be advisable.

TO COMMENCE THE GLIDE.

Reduce the **Power** by placing the Mixture Control to RICH (i.e. fully in), Carburettor Heat to HOT (i.e. fully out, so do not confuse it with the Mixture Control) and closing the Throttle (i.e. fully out). This removes the thrust. Back pressure on the control column and rudder pressure will be required to counteract the 'pitch/yaw' tendencies as the power is changed.

Hold the nose up and maintain height, allowing the airspeed to decrease. When at the desired gliding speed, lower the nose to the gliding **Attitude** and maintain airspeed with fore and aft pressures as required on the control column. **Trim.**

An easy way to remember the sequence of events when commencing a descent is **'P-A-T',** which stands for: **Power – Attitude – Trim.**

TO MAINTAIN THE GLIDE.

Maintain the wings level with ailerons and the Balance Ball centred with rudder pressure. Control airspeed with elevator – a higher nose attitude for a lower speed.

Maintain a good **Look Out** in the descent, possibly with clearing turns left and right every 500 ft to clear the area hidden by the nose. To enable you to maintain the original direction, select a reference point on the horizon or use the Direction Indicator and/or the Magnetic Compass. Another means of achieving a good look out, and without changing heading, is to lower the nose.

Warm the engine periodically. Also, remain very aware of your height above the ground at all times, and of the height still to be descended to your selected level. Ensure that the Altimeter subscale is set correctly.

TO LEVEL-OFF.

Anticipate by about 10% of the descent rate, e.g. at 400 ft/min RoD, commence raising the nose 40 ft above the desired level, start increasing the **power** (mixture should already be rich, throttle smoothly forward to cruise rpm, carburettor heat COLD).

Gradually allow the nose to rise to the cruise **attitude.** The yawing and pitching effects of adding power should be counteracted with rudder pressure and forward pressure on the control column to stop the nose rising too far. Once the cruise speed is achieved, **trim.**

An easy way to remember this sequence is **'P-A-T': Power — Attitude — Trim.**

TO CLIMB AWAY FROM A DESCENT (P-A-T still applies).

Climbing away hardly differs from levelling-off, except that you:
- smoothly apply **full power** (mixture RICH, a silent '1-2-3' for correct timing, carburettor heat COLD); there will be a greater 'pitch/yaw' tendency which you can counteract with pressures on the rudder and control column;
- hold the higher pitch **attitude** for climb, maintaining climb airspeed; and
- trim.

AIRMANSHIP

Maintain a high visual awareness and clear the area under the nose every 500 ft or so in the descent. Maintain a listening watch on the radio if appropriate.

Remain very conscious of your height above the ground when descending. Set the Altimeter subscale correctly so that you can level off exactly at the desired altitude. QNH will normally be set in training so that height AMSL is displayed.

AIRWORK 8a —

> **AIM:** *To enter and maintain a steady glide on a constant heading and to level-off at a particular height.*

(1) Prior to Descent;
- Decide on a gliding speed;
- Select a reference point.
- *LOOK OUT*

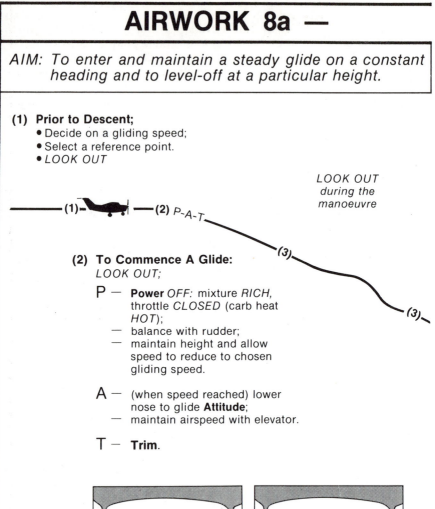

LOOK OUT
during the
manoeuvre

(2) To Commence A Glide:
LOOK OUT;

P — **Power** *OFF:* mixture *RICH,* throttle *CLOSED* (carb heat *HOT*);
— balance with rudder;
— maintain height and allow speed to reduce to chosen gliding speed.

A — (when speed reached) lower nose to glide **Attitude**;
— maintain airspeed with elevator.

T — **Trim**.

1. Reduce power, maintain height.

2. Select glide attitude.

3. Trim.

THE GLIDE

(3) To Maintain the Glide:
- *LOOK OUT* — make clearing turns if necessary.
  Maintain:
    - — wings level with ailerons;
    - — balance with rudder pressure;
    - — airspeed with elevator;
- Monitor engine instruments and warm engine periodically.

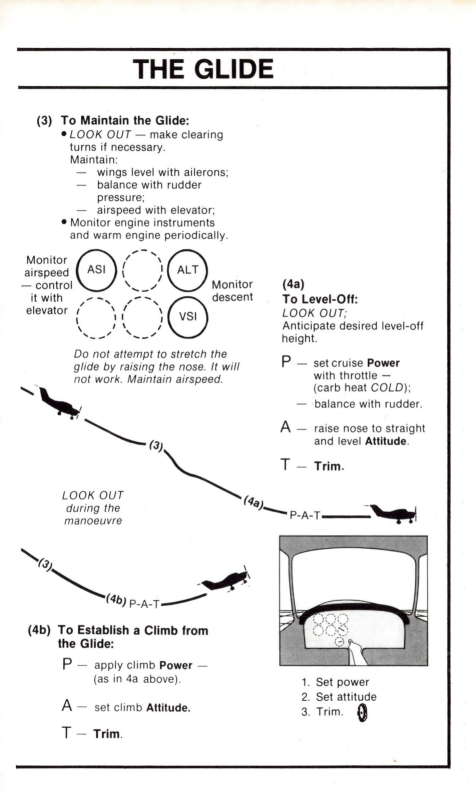

Monitor airspeed — control it with elevator

ASI   ALT

VSI   Monitor descent

Do not attempt to stretch the glide by raising the nose. It will not work. Maintain airspeed.

LOOK OUT during the manoeuvre

(3)

(4a) P-A-T

(3)

(4b) P-A-T

(4a)
To Level-Off:
LOOK OUT;
Anticipate desired level-off height.

P — set cruise **Power** with throttle — (carb heat *COLD*);
  — balance with rudder.

A — raise nose to straight and level **Attitude**.

T — **Trim**.

(4b) To Establish a Climb from the Glide:

P — apply climb **Power** — (as in 4a above).

A — set climb **Attitude**.

T — **Trim**.

1. Set power
2. Set attitude
3. Trim.

8b

THE
POWERED DESCENT

To control the rate of descent and the flight path using power, whilst maintaining a constant airspeed.

CONSIDERATIONS

THE FORCES IN A POWERED DESCENT.

If power is applied in a descent, the resulting Thrust will balance some of the Drag. Consequently, the component of Weight acting along the flight path need not be as great for the same airspeed to be maintained. The pitch attitude will be higher and the rate of descent less, resulting in the descent being shallower.

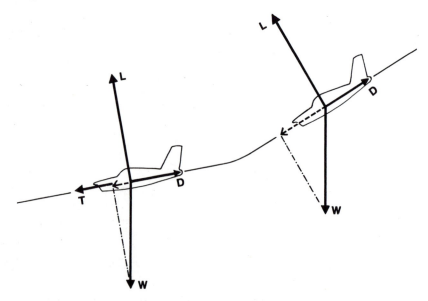

Fig.8b-1. Adding Power Flattens the Descent.

POWER PLUS ATTITUDE EQUALS PERFORMANCE.

The performance achieved by an aeroplane depends both on the **power** selected and the **attitude.** To alter the rate of descent and the flight path, whilst maintaining a constant airspeed, both power and attitude must be adjusted — power with the throttle and attitude with the control column. This is precisely what happens on a normal approach to land and on a cruise-descent.

The **cruise-descent** is used to save time, say at the end of a long cross-country flight, by commencing descent to the destination airfield from the cruise level some miles out by reducing the power slightly and lowering the nose to maintain the same speed as on the cruise.

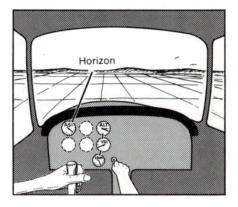

Fig.8b-2. Control Airspeed with Elevator and Rate of Descent with Power.

THE 'AIMING POINT' ON THE GROUND DURING DESCENT STAYS FIXED IN THE WINDSCREEN.

A practical means of estimating where the descent would reach ground level is to note the particular ground feature which remains 'stationary' in the cockpit windscreen whilst a constant nose attitude is maintained. This becomes particularly important when you are on an approach to land, adjusting your flight path to arrive at the chosen aiming point on the runway.

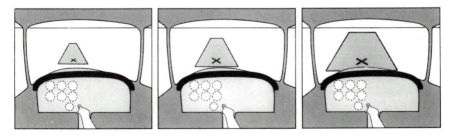

Fig.8b-3. The Aiming Point Stays 'Fixed' in the Windscreen.

FLYING THE MANOEUVRE

If desired, the **rate of descent** can be monitored on:
- the Vertical Speed Indicator; or with
- the Altimeter and a Clock.

To decrease the rate of descent and flatten the descent flight path:
- increase power;
- raise the nose to maintain airspeed;
- trim.

To increase the rate of descent and steepen the descent path:
- decrease power;
- lower the nose to maintain airspeed;
- trim.

The pitch/yaw tendency as power is altered should be balanced with appropriate pressures on the rudder and control column.

On an approach to land, the Pilot monitors the descent by constantly referencing the aiming point on the runway and estimating whether his flight path will take him there. If not, he takes positive action with power and attitude to ensure that it does.

AIRMANSHIP

Take positive action to achieve the desired airspeed and rate of descent. If on approach to land, firmly control the airspeed and the flight path.

Consider the engine. Warm it periodically on a prolonged descent and use the Carburettor Heat as required.

Maintain a good visual awareness.

AIRWORK 8b —
THE POWERED DESCENT

AIM: *To control the rate of descent and the flight path using power, whilst maintaining a constant airspeed.*

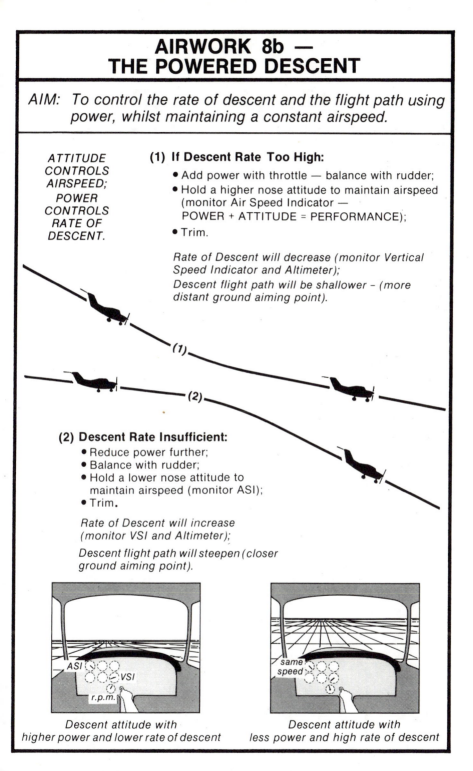

ATTITUDE CONTROLS AIRSPEED; POWER CONTROLS RATE OF DESCENT.

(1) If Descent Rate Too High:

- Add power with throttle — balance with rudder;
- Hold a higher nose attitude to maintain airspeed (monitor Air Speed Indicator —
  POWER + ATTITUDE = PERFORMANCE);
- Trim.

Rate of Descent will decrease (monitor Vertical Speed Indicator and Altimeter);
Descent flight path will be shallower – (more distant ground aiming point).

(1)

(2)

(2) Descent Rate Insufficient:

- Reduce power further;
- Balance with rudder;
- Hold a lower nose attitude to maintain airspeed (monitor ASI);
- Trim.

Rate of Descent will increase (monitor VSI and Altimeter);

Descent flight path will steepen (closer ground aiming point).

ASI   VSI   r.p.m.

same speed

Descent attitude with higher power and lower rate of descent

Descent attitude with less power and high rate of descent

8c

USE OF FLAP
IN THE DESCENT

To use flap to steepen the descent.

CONSIDERATIONS

FLAPS INCREASE DRAG AND STEEPEN THE GLIDE PATH.

Extending the flaps causes a small increase in lift and a greater proportional increase in drag, i.e. the L/D ratio is decreased. If maintaining a constant airspeed in the glide, the flight path will be progressively steeper following the extension of each stage of flap.

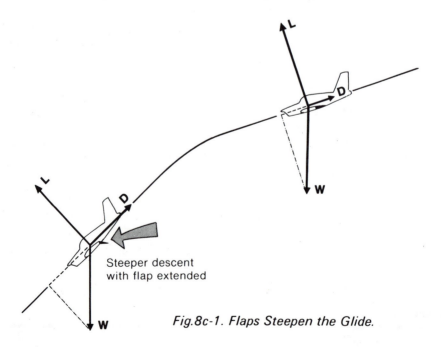

Steeper descent
with flap extended

Fig.8c-1. Flaps Steepen the Glide.

WITH FLAP EXTENDED, A LOWER NOSE ATTITUDE IS REQUIRED.

The increased drag as the flaps extend requires a lower pitch attitude if airspeed is to be maintained. The lower nose position affords a better view through the windscreen in a flapped descent. This is a significant advantage, especially on an approach to land. The greater the flap extension, the lower the nose position.

The desired airspeed is maintained by adjusting the pitch attitude with elevator, trimming-off any steady control column pressure.

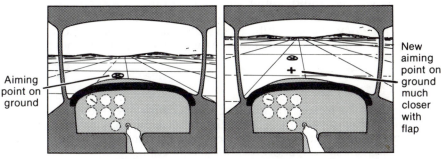

Aiming point on ground

New aiming point on ground much closer with flap

CLEAN   WITH FLAP

Fig.8c-2. A Lower Nose Attitude is Required to Maintain Speed with Flaps Extended.

FLAP LOWERS THE STALLING SPEED.

Extending the flaps alters the shape of the wing and increases its lifting ability. The stalling speed is reduced and so safe flight at a (slightly) lower airspeed is possible, retaining an adequate safety margin above the stall.

OPERATE THE FLAPS AT A SUITABLE AIRSPEED AND BE PREPARED FOR A PITCH CHANGE.

As flap is lowered, the changing shape of the wing and the different aerodynamic forces produce extra stress on the airframe structure. For this reason, flap should only be extended when the airspeed does not exceed the maximum flap operating speed (known as VFE).

The flap range is shown on the Air Speed Indicator as a white band. VFE is at the high speed end of this white arc; stalling speed with full flap extended and wings level is at the low speed end. (See Fig.10a-2.)

There may be a pitching tendency as the flaps are lowered due to the Centre of Pressure (through which Lift acts) moving its position fore or aft on the wing. This can be counteracted with movements of the control column to hold the desired nose attitude.

FLYING THE MANOEUVRE

EXTENDING THE FLAPS.

With the aircraft established in a normal descent, check that the airspeed is below VFE (i.e. in the white band). Extend the flaps in stages as required, holding the desired pitch attitude for each stage of flap and controlling the airspeed with elevator. Trim.

The more flap that is extended, the lower the required nose position. Re-trimming will be required after each stage of flap is extended to relieve control column pressures. If the original airspeed is maintained, a higher rate of descent will occur. If the airspeed is reduced slightly (e.g. as on an approach to land), then the increase in the rate of descent will not be quite as much.

RAISING THE FLAPS.

As the flaps are raised, the loss of Lift will cause the aeroplane to 'sink' unless a higher nose attitude is set. Do not raise the flaps at speeds below the green band on the Air Speed Indicator; the lower end of the green arc is the stalling speed wings-level with a 'clean' wing.

To raise the flaps, retract them in stages, holding the desired nose attitude for each configuration and controlling the airspeed with elevator. Trim.

The flaps are generally used on an approach to land, so it is not a common procedure to raise flap in a continued descent once having lowered it if the landing is to proceed. It is, however, necessary to raise the landing flap in a 'go-around' from a discontinued approach because the high drag would compromise the ability to climb out.

There is a very strong pitch-up tendency as maximum power is applied to go-around and this has to be resisted with forward pressure on the control column.

Full flap generates too much drag for a good climb-away and should be retracted in stages at a safe speed. This very important manoeuvre (the go-around) is covered in detail in a later chapter.

AIRMANSHIP

Do not exceed the maximum speed for flap extension (VFE) and do not raise flap at airspeeds below the 'clean' stalling speed.

AIRWORK 8c —
USE OF FLAPS IN THE DESCENT

AIM: To extend the flaps in a descent.

(a) Check at desired speed — speed must be definitely below maximum flap extension speed — **V**FE (high speed end of white band on ASI);

(b) Lower the flaps in stages;

(c) Hold a lower nose attitude and control airspeed with elevator);

(d) Trim off any steady elevator pressure.

Note the increased rate of descent resulting from the flap extension in the descent.

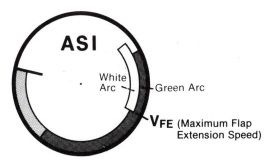

ASI

White Arc

Green Arc

VFE (Maximum Flap Extension Speed)

8d

THE SIDESLIP

To increase the rate of descent and steepen the descent flight path at a constant airspeed by sideslipping using 'crossed controls' and without using flap.

CONSIDERATIONS

WHAT IS A SIDESLIP?

The sideslip is an out-of-balance flight condition. In days gone by, it was mainly used to steepen the glide without gaining airspeed in aeroplanes not fitted with flaps. A sideslip is an especially valuable manoeuvre when too high on an approach to land in such aeroplanes. Nowadays, of course, flap is generally used to increase the steepness of the flight path.

When an aeroplane is banked using the ailerons alone, it will slip towards the lower wing and (due to its large keel surfaces, especially the fin) the nose will yaw towards the lowered wing. This yaw can be prevented by applying opposite rudder (sometimes referred to as 'top rudder'). If the bank is to the left, right rudder would be applied – the greater the bank angle, the greater the opposite rudder.

The aeroplane will be out of balance with the balance ball on the low wing side. You will have 'crossed-controls' – the control column one way and the rudder the other. This is a sideslip.

Pitch attitude and airspeed control can be maintained with back pressure on the control column, but do not rely heavily on the Air Speed Indicator since it may not give a reliable reading due to the unusual airflow around the pitot tube and static vent(s) in a sideslip.

A SIDESLIP STEEPENS THE DESCENT.

Presenting the wing-down side of the aeroplane to the airflow causes a large increase in drag and therefore the L/D ratio is significantly decreased. This causes the rate of descent to increase, resulting in a steeper flight path. The greater the bank angle and top rudder used, the steeper the descent.

SIDESLIPPING IS NOT AN APPROVED PROCEDURE FOR ALL AEROPLANES.

The sideslipping manoeuvre is restricted for some aeroplanes when flap is extended. This is to avoid high rates of descent developing and situations where the elevator and rudder, which are used in the sideslip, lose their effectiveness through 'blanketting' of the airflow over them. The Aeroplane Flight Manual or the Pilot's Operating Handbook will contain this restriction if it applies. There may also be a placard in the aeroplane itself.

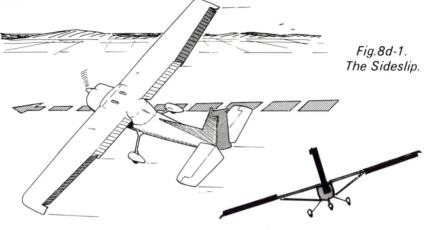

Fig.8d-1.
The Sideslip.

FLYING THE MANOEUVRE

To Enter A Sideslip, ensure that you have adequate height above the ground to recover, since a high rate of descent can be achieved in a sideslip. Close the throttle, bank the aeroplane and apply opposite rudder to stop the yaw. The nose may want to drop and back pressure on the control column may be required. Do not trim, since sideslipping is a transient manoeuvre.

To Maintain The Sideslip, maintain the bank angle with ailerons and control the heading with opposite rudder. The greater the bank angle and rudder used, the steeper the flight path. Airspeed is controlled with the elevator, but bear in mind that the Air Speed Indicator may be unreliable.

To Recover From A Sideslip, level the wings with ailerons and centralise the balance ball by removing the excess rudder pressure. Resume a normal, in-balance descent.

AIRMANSHIP

Maintain a good visual awareness of other aircraft and your proximity to the ground due to the very high descent rates. Do not sideslip in non-approved configurations.

AIRWORK 8d —
THE SIDESLIP

AIM: *To increase rate of descent and steepen the descent flight path at a constant airspeed by sideslipping using "crossed-controls" and without using flap.*

(1) To Enter the Sideslip:
From a Normal Descent:
- Apply bank with ailerons;
- Maintain heading with coarse use of opposite rudder;
- **Hold** nose attitude and maintain airspeed with elevator.

(2) To Maintain the Sideslip:
- Maintain bank angle with ailerons — (the steeper the bank, the greater the rate of descent);
- Control heading with opposite rudder;
- Maintain airspeed with elevator.

IMPORTANT
Throughout the manoeuvre —
LOOK OUT
for other aircraft.

(3) To Remove the Sideslip:
- Level wings with ailerons;
- Remove opposite rudder — balance normally;

- Maintain desired airspeed with elevator.

134

9

TURNING

9a

THE MEDIUM LEVEL TURN

AIM

To enter, maintain and roll out of a medium level turn, using constant power.

CONSIDERATIONS

WHAT IS A MEDIUM LEVEL TURN?

A medium level turn is a turn performed:
- at a constant height; with
- a medium angle of bank (30° or less);
- at constant power; and
- in balance.

Apart from the medium level turn, other turns which you will master in the course of your training are:

- climbing turns;
- descending turns;
- Rate 1 turns (a rate of turn to achieve 360° in 2 minutes);
- steep turns (bank angle 45° or greater).

A TURN IS ACCOMPLISHED BY BANKING THE AEROPLANE.

Banking the aeroplane tilts the Lift which provides a horizontal turning force (known as the centripetal force). Since there is no other horizontal force to counteract it, the aeroplane is no longer in equilibrium and will be pulled into a turn. The greater the bank angle, the greater the turning force.

IN A LEVEL TURN, BACK PRESSURE IS APPLIED TO INCREASE LIFT AND MAINTAIN HEIGHT.

Tilting the Lift reduces its vertical component which will result in a height loss unless the Pilot increases the Lift generated by the wings. By applying the correct amount of back pressure on the control column as the aeroplane is banked, a vertical component of the Lift sufficient to balance the Weight can be retained.

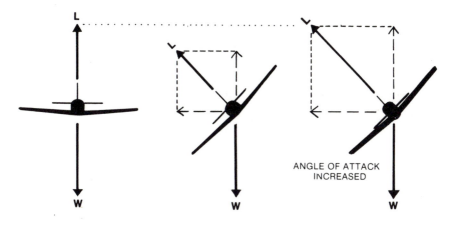

Fig.9a-1. Banking an Aeroplane Creates a Turning Force.

AIRSPEED TENDS TO DECREASE IN A TURN.

The Lift is increased by increasing the angle of attack, which also results in increased Induced Drag. As a consequence of this **increased Drag,** the aeroplane will tend to slow down, usually by 5 kt or so in a medium level turn. At normal flight speeds, this small airspeed loss at medium bank angles is acceptable.

STALLING SPEED INCREASES IN A TURN.

The wings are at a higher angle of attack in a turn than when the aeroplane is flying straight at the same speed. They carry an extra load (i.e. they generate increased Lift) and so experience a **higher Load Factor.** The stalling angle will therefore be reached at a higher speed in a turn than when straight and level. It is about 7% higher in a 30° banked turn, increasing a stall speed of 50 kt to 54 kt.

For medium level turns at normal flight speeds, the small drop in airspeed (due to the increased drag) still allows an adequate speed range for safe flight above the new and slightly increased stalling speed.

Fig.9a-2. Airspeed Decreases and Stalling Speed Increases in a Level Turn.

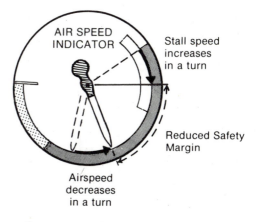

ESTIMATE THE BANK ANGLE USING THE NATURAL HORIZON.

A specific bank angle can be flown quite accurately by the Pilot estimating the angle between the nose cowl of the aeroplane and the natural horizon. This is referred to as the **bank attitude.** It can be verified in the cockpit on the Attitude Indicator using either the angle between the index aeroplane and the artificial horizon, or by using the 'sky pointer'.

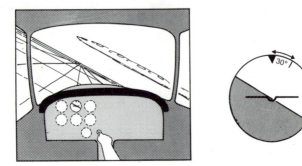

Fig.9a-3. Estimate the Bank Angle.

THE PITCH ATTITUDE IS HIGHER IN A LEVEL TURN.

Lift is increased in a turn with back pressure on the control column to increase the angle of attack. For this reason, the nose attitude of the aeroplane will be higher in a level turn than when flying straight and level.

Estimating the correct pitch attitude against the natural horizon requires a little experience, especially if you are flying in a side-by-side cockpit, as is the case in most modern training aeroplanes. The pitch attitude for a given bank angle and airspeed will be correct if the aeroplane neither gains nor loses height.

THE NOSE-COWL/HORIZON RELATIONSHIP APPEARS DIFFERENT IN LEFT AND RIGHT TURNS.

These remarks apply to a side-by-side cockpit. **In a left turn,** the Pilot in the left seat will be on the low side of the aeroplane's longitudinal axis and the position of the centre of the nose-cowl will appear to be higher relative to the natural horizon. Conversely, **when turning right,** the centre of the nose cowl should appear lower against the horizon. After one or two turns left and right, you should have these attitudes fixed in your mind.

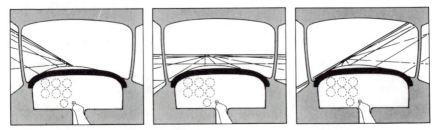

Fig.9a-4. Different Nose Positions for Left and Right Turns.

TURNING PERFORMANCE.

The two aspects of turning performance are:
- the rate at which the heading changes; and
- the tightness of the turn (i.e. its radius).

Turning Performance Increases at Steeper Bank Angles. The steeper the bank angle (for a constant airspeed), the better the turning performance – the rate of heading change increasing and the radius of turn decreasing as bank angle is increased.

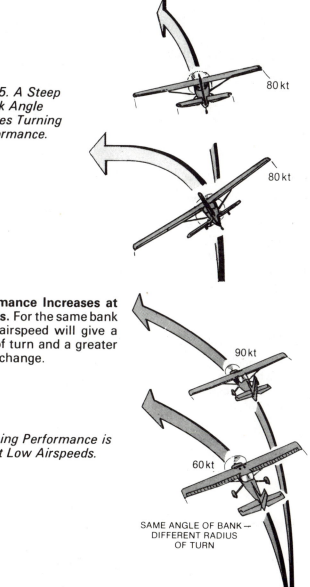

Fig.9a-5. A Steep Bank Angle Increases Turning Performance.

80 kt

80 kt

Turning Performance Increases at Lower Airspeeds. For the same bank angle, a lower airspeed will give a smaller radius of turn and a greater rate of heading change.

90 kt

Fig.9a-6. Turning Performance is Increased at Low Airspeeds.

60 kt

SAME ANGLE OF BANK –
DIFFERENT RADIUS
OF TURN

RATE ONE (1) TURNS.

Changing heading at 3°/sec is known as a Rate 1 turn and is marked on the Turn Co-ordinator (or Turn Indicator). It is the 'Standard Rate of Turn' commonly used in Instrument Flying (IF) and will achieve a turn of 180° in 1 minute or 360° in 2 minutes (hence the label '2 MIN' shown on many Turn Co-ordinators).

Fig.9a-7. Rate 1 Turn Indications.

To achieve Rate One turning performance at different airspeeds, different bank angles will be required. These are easily estimated using the simple formula:

Rate 1 bank angles = airspeed/10 + 7
e.g. at 120 kt, Rate 1 bank angle = 120/10 + 7 = 12 + 7 = 19°
at 80 kt, Rate 1 bank angle = 80/10 + 7 = 8 + 7 = 15°

The estimate gives you a target bank angle to achieve a Rate 1 turn, which can be verified in the turn by checking either:
• the Turn Co-ordinator (or Turn Indicator); or
• the Direction Indicator and Clock combined.

THERE IS A TENDENCY TO OVERBANK IN A LEVEL TURN.

The higher speed of the outer wing in a level turn will create extra Lift on that wing, which tends to increase the bank angle. There is no need for you to be particularly conscious of this — simply maintain the desired bank angle using the control column.

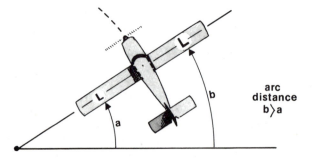

arc
distance
b > a

Fig.9a-8. There is a Tendency to Overbank in a Level Turn.

FLYING THE MANOEUVRE

TRIM THE AEROPLANE FOR STEADY STRAIGHT AND LEVEL FLIGHT.

Unless an immediate turn is necessary, trimming the aeroplane properly for steady straight and level flight makes it easier to maintain height before and after the turn. **Do not trim in the turn** since it is only a transient manoeuvre.

Prior to applying bank, glance at the cockpit instruments and ensure that you are flying at the desired:
- Indicated Air Speed; and
- Altitude (altimeter reading desired height; VSI zero, or fluctuating about zero, indicating no tendency to climb or descend).

ALWAYS LOOK OUT FOR OTHER AIRCRAFT.

Develop a thorough scanning technique from side to side and both up and down before turning, remembering that aeroplanes move in three dimensions. A good sky-scanning technique is:
- first look in the direction of turn, raising/lowering the wing to give you a view above and below;
- look in the direction opposite to the turn and as far behind as cockpit vision allows; then
- commence a steady scan from that side of the windscreen both up and down until you are again looking in the direction of turn.

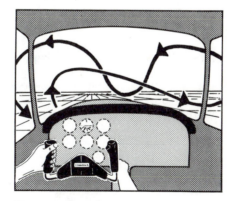

Fig.9a-9. A Suitable Scan Before a Left Turn.

SELECT A REFERENCE POINT ON WHICH TO ROLL-OUT.

Whilst scanning for other aircraft, you can note visible landmarks helpful for orientation (i.e. knowing where you are). Select a landmark as a reference point on which to roll out following the turn. Anticipate the desired heading by commencing the roll-out about 10° prior to reaching it, since the aeroplane will continue turning (although at a decreasing rate) until the wings are level.

USING THE CONTROLS IN A MEDIUM LEVEL TURN.

Roll into the turn with a co-ordinated use of 'stick and rudder'. Apply bank with ailerons and balance with same-side rudder pressure (keeping the ball in the centre). Back pressure on the control column will be needed to maintain height, which can be checked on the Altimeter and VSI. Estimate the bank angle against the horizon, checking it on the Attitude Indicator if desired.

To maintain the turn, control the bank angle with ailerons, balance with rudder and height with elevator. Do not forget to **look out** for other aircraft. **If gaining height,** either the bank angle is too shallow or the back pressure is too great – increase bank angle and/or lower the nose. **If losing height,** either the bank angle is too steep or the back pressure is insufficient – decrease bank angle and/or raise the nose.

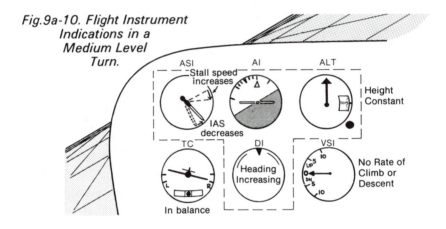

Fig.9a-10. Flight Instrument Indications in a Medium Level Turn.

Keep in balance using rudder pressure. Rolling right requires more right rudder pressure, rolling left requires more left rudder pressure. The balance ball indicates the precise balance of the aeroplane – if the ball is out to the right, more right rudder is needed (and vice versa). Aim to keep the ball centred throughout the turning manoeuvre.

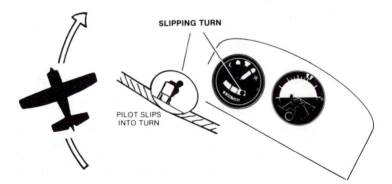

Fig.9a-11. Slipping Turn: More Right Rudder is Required.

142

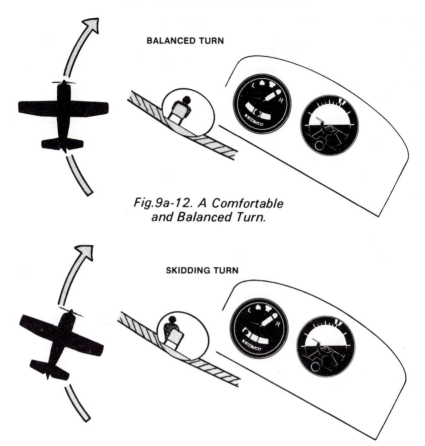

Fig.9a-12. A Comfortable
and Balanced Turn.

Fig.9a-13. A Skidding Turn: Too Much Right Rudder has been Applied.

To roll out of a medium level turn, anticipate reaching the reference point by about 10° and commence removing bank with aileron, balancing with same-side rudder pressure. Gradually release the back pressure and lower the nose to the straight and level position. Adjust the heading and height as required.

AIRMANSHIP

Remain aware of landmarks and keep yourself orientated with respect to the airfield. Your aeroplane will be changing heading in a turn, so maintain a good **Look Out.**

Since a constant power will be set, you can concentrate on placing the nose just exactly where you want it on the horizon. Become familiar with these attitudes for both left and right turns. Do not trim in the turn since it is only a transient manoeuvre. Develop an awareness of balance and use rudder pressure to keep the ball in the centre at all times. Aim for smoothly co-ordinated use of controls.

AIRWORK 9a —
THE MEDIUM LEVEL TURN

AIM: *To enter, maintain and roll out of a medium level turn, using constant power.*

(4) Rolling Out of the Turn:
- *LOOK OUT;*
- Anticipate reference point;
- Roll-off bank with ailerons;
- Balance with rudder pressure;
- Release back pressure.

MAINTAIN HEIGHT
WITH ELEVATOR AND
ACCEPT THE SLIGHT LOSS
OF AIRSPEED

(3) Maintaining the Turn:
- *LOOK OUT;*
- Maintain bank angle with ailerons;
- Maintain balance with rudder;
- Maintain height with elevator — (back pressure on the control column).

(2) Entry to a Medium Level Turn:
- *LOOK OUT;*
- Roll on bank with aileron;
- Balance with rudder pressure (right rudder in this example);
- Exert back pressure on control column to maintain height.

START HERE

(1) Prior to Entry:
- At desired height and airspeed;
- In trim;
- *LOOK OUT* for other aircraft;
- Select reference point for roll-out.

NOTE:
TRIM IS NOT USED
DURING THIS MANOEUVRE

144

9b

THE
CLIMBING TURN

AIM

To change heading whilst climbing at a **constant airspeed**.

CONSIDERATIONS

THE FORCES IN A CLIMBING TURN.

The forces in a climbing turn are similar to those in a straight climb except that, because the Lift is tilted to turn the aeroplane, its contribution to supporting the Weight is reduced. The result is a decreased climb performance (i.e. a reduced rate of climb) if airspeed is maintained.

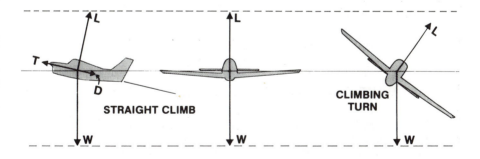

Fig.9b-1. A Straight Climb and a Climbing Turn.

THE RATE OF CLIMB DECREASES IN A CLIMBING TURN.

The **rate of climb** depends upon the 'excess power', i.e. the amount of power available in excess of that required to overcome the Drag. Tilting of the Lift and the increased Drag in a climbing turn reduces the excess power available for climb performance. The result is a decreased rate of climb in a turn, as indicated on the Vertical Speed Indicator and the Altimeter.

The steeper the bank angle in a climbing turn, the poorer the rate of climb. To retain a reasonable rate of climb, the bank angle in climbing turns should be limited to 15° or 20°.

MAINTAIN AIRSPEED IN A CLIMBING TURN BY LOWERING THE NOSE ATTITUDE.

Climb performance depends upon the correct climb speed being flown with climb power set. For many training aeroplanes, climb power is maximum power, so the tendency to lose airspeed cannot be overcome by adding extra power (since there is no more). To maintain the correct climb speed in a turn it is therefore necessary to lower the nose.

There is a natural tendency for the nose to drop too far as bank is applied in a climbing turn, but this can be checked with slight back pressure on the control column. Hold the desired pitch attitude with elevator and monitor the airspeed with an occasional glance at the Air Speed Indicator.

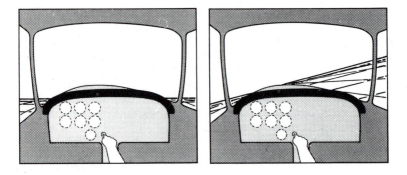

Fig.9b-2. Maintain Airspeed in a Climbing Turn by Lowering the Nose.

BALANCE THE SLIPSTREAM EFFECT WITH RUDDER.

Most aeroplanes are designed so that slipstream effect is balanced at cruise speed with cruise power set. Climbs are carried out with high power at an airspeed less than the cruise, with the result that steady rudder pressure is usually required to balance the slipstream effect on the tail.

The usual rules for maintaining balance apply, no matter what the manoeuvre involved, i.e. move the balance ball back into the centre with same-side rudder pressure. The balance ball tells you which rudder pressure is needed.

THERE IS A TENDENCY TO OVERBANK IN A CLIMBING TURN.

The higher speed and greater angle of attack of the outer wing in a climbing turn creates a tendency for the bank angle to increase. Bank may have to be held-off in a climbing turn, but this will occur naturally as you monitor the bank angle against the horizon.

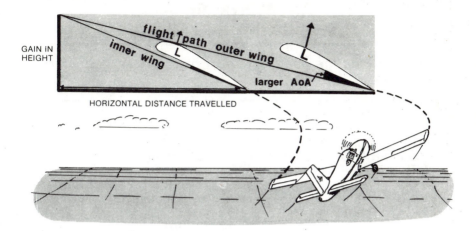

Fig.9b-3. There is an Overbanking Tendency in a Climbing Turn.

FLYING THE MANOEUVRE

To enter a climbing turn, establish the aeroplane in a straight climb at the desired airspeed and in trim. **Look Out** and select a reference point on which to roll out. Roll into the turn by applying bank in the direction of turn, using sufficient rudder to keep the ball in the centre. Limit the turn to 15 – 20° bank angle and hold the nose in a slightly lower position to **maintain airspeed.**

To maintain the climbing turn, control bank angle with ailerons, balance with rudder pressure and maintain the desired airspeed with nose attitude. Keep a constant airspeed throughout the climbing turn even though the rate of climb will decrease. Continue a steady **Look Out.**

To roll-out of a climbing turn, commence removing the bank some 10° before reaching your reference point. Roll-off bank with aileron, balance with rudder pressure and raise the nose to the normal climb attitude. Level the wings and keep the balance ball centred, adjusting the heading and airspeed as required.

AIRMANSHIP

Limit the bank to 15 – 20° and maintain a constant airspeed with elevator. Exert firm, positive and smooth control over the aeroplane. Maintain a **Look Out.**

AIRWORK 9b —
THE CLIMBING TURN

AIM: *To change heading whilst climbing at a constant airspeed.*

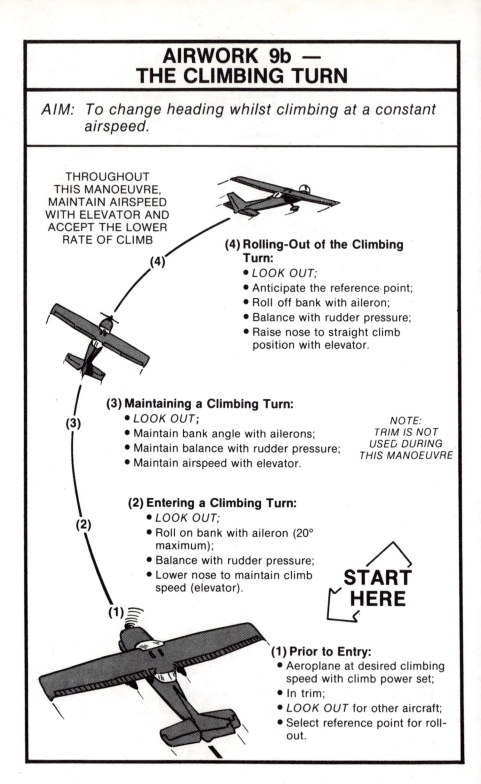

THROUGHOUT THIS MANOEUVRE, MAINTAIN AIRSPEED WITH ELEVATOR AND ACCEPT THE LOWER RATE OF CLIMB

(4) Rolling-Out of the Climbing Turn:
- *LOOK OUT;*
- Anticipate the reference point;
- Roll off bank with aileron;
- Balance with rudder pressure;
- Raise nose to straight climb position with elevator.

(3) Maintaining a Climbing Turn:
- *LOOK OUT;*
- Maintain bank angle with ailerons;
- Maintain balance with rudder pressure;
- Maintain airspeed with elevator.

NOTE: TRIM IS NOT USED DURING THIS MANOEUVRE

(2) Entering a Climbing Turn:
- *LOOK OUT;*
- Roll on bank with aileron (20° maximum);
- Balance with rudder pressure;
- Lower nose to maintain climb speed (elevator).

START HERE

(1) Prior to Entry:
- Aeroplane at desired climbing speed with climb power set;
- In trim;
- *LOOK OUT* for other aircraft;
- Select reference point for roll-out.

9c

DESCENDING TURNS

The four types of descending turn covered are:
- The Gliding Turn.
- The Descending Turn Using Power.
- The Descending Turn with Flap Extended.
- Sideslipping in a Descending Turn.

Part (i) – THE GLIDING TURN

AIM

To enter, maintain and roll out of a gliding turn, whilst maintaining airspeed.

CONSIDERATIONS

THE FORCES IN A GLIDING TURN.

The forces acting on an aeroplane in a gliding turn are similar to those in a straight glide, except that the aeroplane is banked and the Lift is tilted.

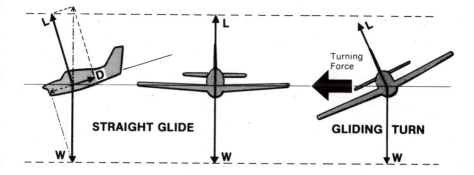

Fig.9c-1. The Forces in a Straight Glide and in a Gliding Turn.

Banking the aeroplane to create a turning force:
- reduces the amount of Lift available to oppose the Weight force – resulting in an **increased rate of descent** and a steeper glide; and
- increases the Drag – resulting in **a tendency to decrease the airspeed** (which is not desirable since an aeroplane's stalling speed increases in a turn).

MAINTAIN AIRSPEED IN A GLIDING TURN BY LOWERING THE NOSE.

The increased Drag in a turn will tend to decrease airspeed so, to maintain the desired airspeed in a gliding turn, the nose should be held in a lower attitude.

As in all turns, there will be a tendency for the nose to drop, requiring back pressure to stop it dropping too far. Simply hold the attitude that gives the desired airspeed. For side-by-side cockpits, the position of the nose-cowl relative to the horizon will differ for left and right turns.

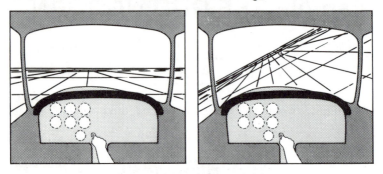

Fig.9c-2. Entering a Gliding Turn, Lower the Nose to Maintain Airspeed.

THE RATE OF DESCENT IN A GLIDE INCREASES IN A TURN.

Tilting of the Lift in a gliding turn, and the lower nose position to maintain airspeed, result in an increased rate of descent and a steeper flight path. The steeper the turn, the greater the effect, so be careful near the ground!

Limit the rate of descent in a gliding turn by restricting the bank angle. In a gliding approach to land, the turn to join final 500 ft Above Aerodrome Level should be flown at about 20° and certainly should not exceed 30°.

THERE IS LESS TENDENCY TO OVERBANK IN A DESCENDING TURN.

Two effects tend to cancel each other out in descending turns, both when gliding and when using power. They are:
1. An overbanking tendency due to the outer wing travelling faster; and
2. An underbanking tendency due to the inner wing in a descending turn having a higher angle of attack.

There is no need to be conscious of this when flying – simply maintain the desired bank angle with aileron.

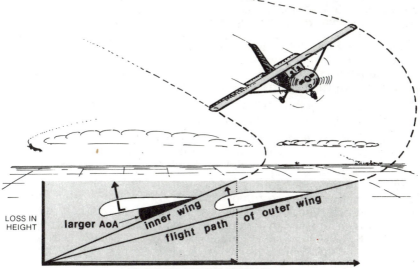

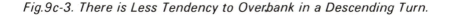

Fig.9c-3. There is Less Tendency to Overbank in a Descending Turn.

BALANCE THE LACK OF SLIPSTREAM EFFECT IN A GLIDE WITH RUDDER PRESSURE.

Most aeroplanes are designed to be in balance and require no rudder pressure when cruising. In a glide (in which there is no slipstream effect) rudder pressure may be required for balance, i.e. to keep the balance ball in the centre.

For an aeroplane fitted with a propeller that rotates clockwise as seen from the cockpit, the lack of slipstream effect in the glide will require steady left rudder pressure. If the aeroplane has a rudder trim, then make use of it to relieve this steady pressure. Normal balance rules apply. If the ball is out to the left, apply left rudder pressure. Left rudder pressure should be increased when rolling left in a descent and decreased when rolling right.

KEEP THE ENGINE WARM IN A PROLONGED GLIDE.

As in a normal straight glide, apply power from time to time if the gliding turn is prolonged. This will keep the engine and its oil supply warm and clear any spark plug fouling that may have built-up while the engine was idling in the glide.

FLYING THE MANOEUVRE (i)

To enter a gliding turn, establish the aeroplane in a straight glide at the desired airspeed and in-trim. **Look Out** for other aircraft and select a reference point on which to roll-out. Roll into the turn with aileron and apply sufficient rudder pressure to keep the balance ball centred.

Lower the nose slightly to maintain airspeed (back pressure may be required to stop it dropping too far). Do not exceed a bank angle of 30°.

To maintain the gliding turn, control bank angle with aileron, balance with rudder pressure and airspeed with elevator. Accept the higher rate of descent and maintain the desired airspeed. Keep a good **Look Out.**

To roll-out of the gliding turn, anticipate reaching the reference point by 10° or so and commence removing bank with aileron, balancing with rudder pressure. Hold the nose in the straight glide attitude (slightly higher than in the turn). Level the wings and then make minor adjustments to maintain the desired heading and airspeed.

AIRMANSHIP

Maintain airspeed with elevator and exert firm, positive and smooth control over the aeroplane.

Do not trim, since the turn is a transient manoeuvre.

AIRWORK 9c, Part (i) — THE GLIDING TURN

AIM: *To enter, maintain and roll-out of a gliding turn, whilst maintaining airspeed.*

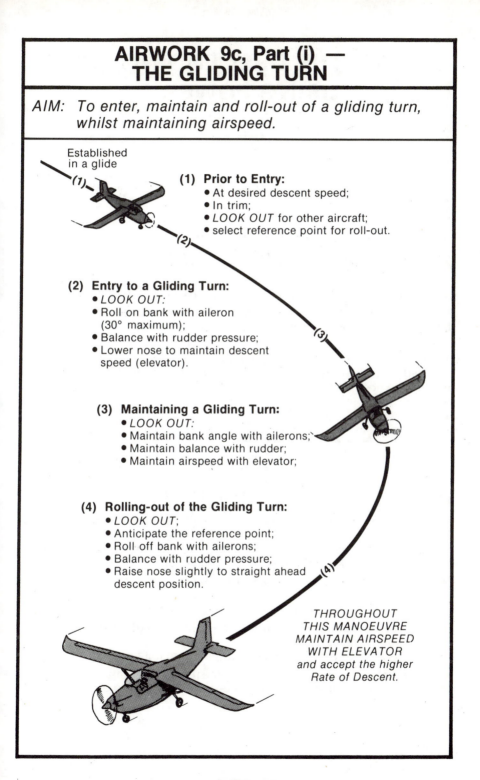

Established in a glide

(1) Prior to Entry:
- At desired descent speed;
- In trim;
- *LOOK OUT* for other aircraft;
- select reference point for roll-out.

(2) Entry to a Gliding Turn:
- *LOOK OUT:*
- Roll on bank with aileron (30° maximum);
- Balance with rudder pressure;
- Lower nose to maintain descent speed (elevator).

(3) Maintaining a Gliding Turn:
- *LOOK OUT:*
- Maintain bank angle with ailerons;
- Maintain balance with rudder;
- Maintain airspeed with elevator;

(4) Rolling-out of the Gliding Turn:
- *LOOK OUT;*
- Anticipate the reference point;
- Roll off bank with ailerons;
- Balance with rudder pressure;
- Raise nose slightly to straight ahead descent position.

THROUGHOUT THIS MANOEUVRE MAINTAIN AIRSPEED WITH ELEVATOR and accept the higher Rate of Descent.

Part (ii) – THE DESCENDING TURN USING POWER

AIM

To alter heading in a descent at a constant airspeed with a controlled rate of descent.

CONSIDERATIONS

THE RATE OF DESCENT CAN BE CONTROLLED WITH POWER.

A descent may be either a 'glide' with the throttle closed, or a 'powered descent' in which power is used to control both the rate of descent and the flight path.

Descent performance is controlled by power and attitude – **control' airspeed with the elevator** and the **rate of descent and flight path with power.** The nose attitude in a powered descent is higher compared to that in a glide at the same airspeed.

FLYING THE MANOEUVRE (ii)

Establish the aircraft in a powered descent at a steady airspeed and a specific rate of descent (e.g. 300 ft/min) using power as required, with the wings level and in-trim. Enter the turn normally, adding power to maintain the desired rate of descent and controlling airspeed with elevator. The steeper the bank angle in a descending turn, the greater the additional power required to keep the rate of descent constant.

To reduce the rate of descent and flatten the descent path:
• add power; and
• raise the nose to a slightly higher attitude to maintain airspeed.

To increase the rate of descent and steepen the flight path:
• reduce power; and
• lower the nose to a slightly lower attitude to maintain airspeed.

Rolling out of the turn, gradually reduce the power to maintain the desired descent rate and adjust the pitch attitude to maintain the airspeed.

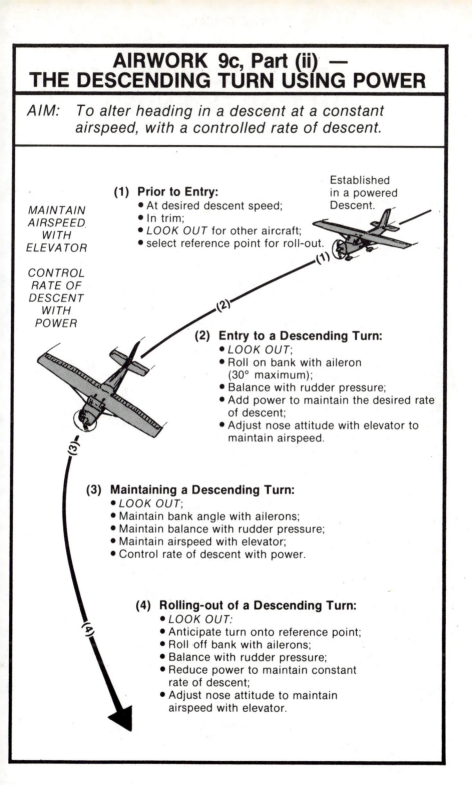

AIRWORK 9c, Part (ii) —
THE DESCENDING TURN USING POWER

AIM: *To alter heading in a descent at a constant airspeed, with a controlled rate of descent.*

MAINTAIN AIRSPEED WITH ELEVATOR

CONTROL RATE OF DESCENT WITH POWER

Established in a powered Descent.

(1) Prior to Entry:
- At desired descent speed;
- In trim;
- *LOOK OUT* for other aircraft;
- select reference point for roll-out.

(2) Entry to a Descending Turn:
- *LOOK OUT*;
- Roll on bank with aileron (30° maximum);
- Balance with rudder pressure;
- Add power to maintain the desired rate of descent;
- Adjust nose attitude with elevator to maintain airspeed.

(3) Maintaining a Descending Turn:
- *LOOK OUT*;
- Maintain bank angle with ailerons;
- Maintain balance with rudder pressure;
- Maintain airspeed with elevator;
- Control rate of descent with power.

(4) Rolling-out of a Descending Turn:
- *LOOK OUT:*
- Anticipate turn onto reference point;
- Roll off bank with ailerons;
- Balance with rudder pressure;
- Reduce power to maintain constant rate of descent;
- Adjust nose attitude to maintain airspeed with elevator.

Part (iii) – THE DESCENDING TURN WITH FLAP EXTENDED

AIM

To alter heading in a descending turn with flap extended.

CONSIDERATIONS AND FLYING THE MANOEUVRE (iii)

Turning with flap extended is a very common manoeuvre when making an approach to land. Flying with flap extended:
- allows the required Lift to be generated at a lower airspeed;
- reduces the stalling speed, making slower flight and shorter landing distances possible;
- requires a lower nose attitude for the same airspeed.

A descending turn with flaps extended is flown exactly the same as a clean descending turn except that the **nose position is lower.** Because such manoeuvres are made during the approach to land it is important that suitable airspeeds and rates of descent are maintained. In general, do not exceed 30° bank angle.

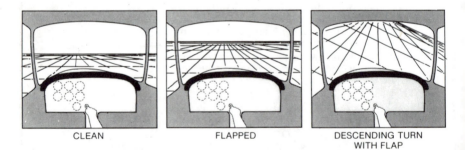

CLEAN   FLAPPED   DESCENDING TURN
                            WITH FLAP

Fig.9c-4. With Flap Extended, the Nose Position is Lower.

As in all turns:
- **maintain the bank angle with ailerons;**
- **maintain balance with rudder pressure;**
- **maintain airspeed with elevator;** and
- (if desired) **control rate of descent with power.**

AIRWORK 9c, Part (iii) — THE DESCENDING TURN WITH FLAP EXTENDED

The same procedure as in the previous exercise (9c, Part Two), applies, except that the nose attitude is lower with flap extended.

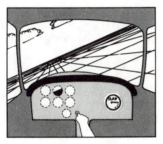

Typical horizon view in a descending turn clean.

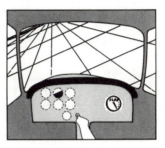

Typical horizon view in a descending turn with full flap extended.

Part (iv) – SIDESLIPPING IN A DESCENDING TURN

AIM

To lose excess height in a gliding turn at a constant airspeed by sideslipping the aeroplane in the turn using 'crossed-controls'.

NOTE: Refer to the Pilot's Operating Handbook to determine if sideslipping is an approved manoeuvre for your particular aeroplane type and, if so, in which configurations. Some aeroplanes are not to be sideslipped with flap extended because of the disturbed airflow around the wings, for example.

CONSIDERATIONS

SIDESLIPPING IS NOT AS IMPORTANT AS IT ONCE WAS.

The rate of descent and the steepness of the flight path can be increased dramatically by sideslipping, whilst the airspeed is kept constant. This manoeuvre is especially useful in an aeroplane not fitted with flaps when too high on approach to land. (The modern means of steepening the glide is to use the flaps).

THE FORCES IN A GLIDING TURN WHEN SIDESLIPPING.

These are similar to the forces in a normal gliding turn, except that Drag is increased dramatically to steepen the descent. This is achieved by applying significant rudder pressure opposite to the turn, i.e. 'top rudder', causing the large keel surfaces of the aeroplane to be presented to the airflow. The sideslip can only occur in the direction of the turn, e.g. if turning to the left, apply right rudder to sideslip to the left.

The aeroplane will be out of balance in the sideslipping turn and this is indicated by the balance ball being on the 'downside' of the slip, i.e. to the inside of the slipping turn. The imbalance can also be felt by the occupants of the aeroplane. The rudder actually opposes the turn and so the rate of turn will decrease unless the bank angle is increased.

To maintain airspeed, the nose attitude must be lower than in a straight descent. With a large keel surface presented to the airflow, there may be a tendency for the nose to drop and so back pressure on the control column may be required to stop the nose dropping too far. Do not rely too greatly on the Air Speed Indicator, as the sideways airflow over the pitot tube and static vent may cause indication errors. A safe airspeed must still be maintained.

The result of a sideslip is an increased rate of descent at a constant airspeed and a steeper descent angle. The greater the bank angle and rudder pressure, the steeper the flight path. It is not usual to use power during this manoeuvre since the purpose of a sideslip is to increase the steepness of the flight-path.

Since a sideslip, and especially a sideslipping turn, are transient manoeuvres, **do not trim.**

FLYING THE MANOEUVRE (iv)

Establish the aeroplane in a gliding turn.

To commence a sideslip in the gliding turn apply 'top rudder' and control bank angle with aileron and airspeed with the nose position. The rate of descent and the steepness of the flight path can be increased by using a greater bank angle and more top rudder.

To stop the sideslip in the turn, centralise the balance ball with the rudder, maintain the desired bank angle with aileron and the airspeed with elevator.

AIRMANSHIP

Only sideslip in approved aeroplanes and configurations.

Be aware that high rates of descent and steep flight paths can result from sideslipping, so allow sufficient height to recover balanced flight at the end of the manoeuvre.

AIRWORK 9c, Part (iv) —
SIDESLIPPING IN A GLIDING TURN

AIM: *To lose excess height in a gliding turn at a constant airspeed by sideslipping the aeroplane in the turn using crossed-controls.*

Note: *Refer to the Pilot's Operating Handbook to determine if sideslipping is an approved manoeuvre for your particular aircraft type.*

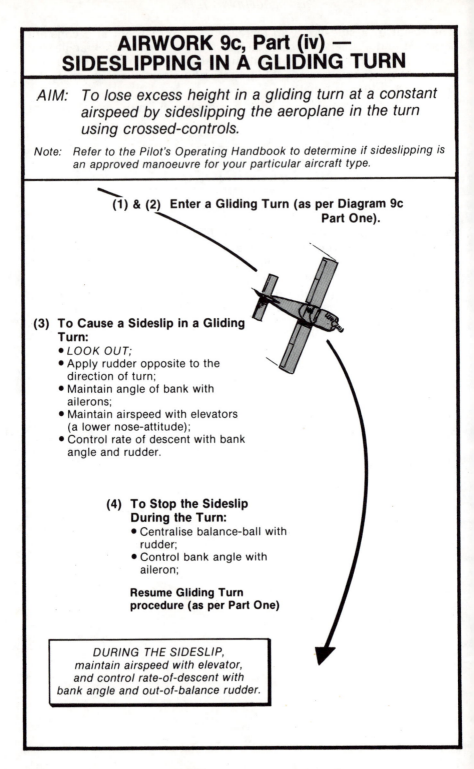

(1) & (2) Enter a Gliding Turn (as per Diagram 9c Part One).

(3) To Cause a Sideslip in a Gliding Turn:
- *LOOK OUT;*
- Apply rudder opposite to the direction of turn;
- Maintain angle of bank with ailerons;
- Maintain airspeed with elevators (a lower nose-attitude);
- Control rate of descent with bank angle and rudder.

(4) To Stop the Sideslip During the Turn:
- Centralise balance-ball with rudder;
- Control bank angle with aileron;

Resume Gliding Turn procedure (as per Part One)

DURING THE SIDESLIP,
maintain airspeed with elevator,
and control rate-of-descent with
bank angle and out-of-balance rudder.

9d

TURNING ONTO SELECTED HEADINGS

AIM

To turn onto a selected magnetic heading using:
1. The Direction Indicator; or
2. The Clock and the Turn Co-ordinator; or
3. The Magnetic Compass.

CONSIDERATIONS AND FLYING THE MANOEUVRES

SELECT A VISUAL REFERENCE POINT AS A GUIDE.

Whenever possible, select a distant reference point onto which to turn. This acts as a back-up to the instrument indications as well as aiding you in orientation.

(1) USING THE DIRECTION INDICATOR (DI) TO TURN ONTO A SELECTED HEADING.

The Direction Indicator is easier to use and more accurate in a turn than a Magnetic Compass because it is a gyroscopic instrument and consequently does not suffer acceleration and turning errors. It must, however, be correctly aligned with the Magnetic Compass in steady flight.

Fig.9d-1. The Direction Indicator.

To turn onto a specific Heading using the 'DI':
- fly steady, straight and level;
- align the DI with the Magnetic Compass (uncaging the DI if necessary);
- decide the shorter way to turn (i.e. left or right) to reach the desired heading (e.g. from 090°M to 240°M, turn right 150°);
- **Look Out;**
- carry out a normal turn with occasional reference to the DI;
- commence the roll-out approximately 10° prior to reaching the desired heading on the DI;
- make minor adjustments to maintain the desired heading.

(2) USING THE CLOCK AND THE TURN CO-ORDINATOR TO TURN ONTO A SELECTED HEADING.

The Turn Co-ordinator allows you to turn at a constant Rate and the Clock can be used to time the turn. A Rate 1 turn (3°/sec) for 30 seconds will alter the heading by 90°.

To turn onto a specific heading using a Rate 1 timed turn;
- divide the change in heading by 3 to obtain the number of seconds (e.g. from 090°M to 240°M is 150° to the right which, at 3°/sec, will take 50 seconds);
- carry out a normal Rate 1 turn with reference to the Turn Co-ordinator (at say 120 kt, this will require an angle of bank of 120/10 + 7 = 19°);
- time the turn using the second hand on the Clock.

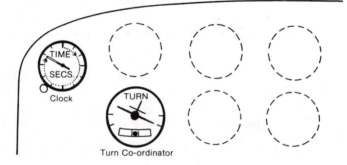

EXAMPLE — From 090°M to 240°M is 150°;
at Rate 1 (3°/sec) = 50 sec.

Fig.9d-2. A Timed Turn Using the Clock and Turn Co-ordinator.

(3) USING THE MAGNETIC COMPASS TO TURN ONTO A SELECTED HEADING.

This is the least-preferred method since the Magnetic Compass suffers considerable indication errors in a turn. It can, however, be used to verify heading once the aeroplane has settled into steady wings-level flight and the compass oscillations have ceased.

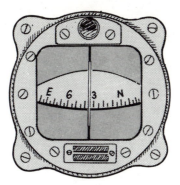

Heading 035° M

Fig.9d-3. The Magnetic Compass.

The construction of a Magnetic Compass is such that, when an aeroplane is turning (especially through North or South), it will give false indications of magnetic heading. To allow for this **in the Northern Hemisphere** observe the following:

(a) When turning onto Northerly headings, roll out when the Magnetic Compass indicates approximately 30° **before** your desired heading.

(b) When turning onto Southerly headings, roll out when the Magnetic Compass has passed approximately 30° **past** your desired heading.

The above allowances should be reduced:
• when turning with bank angles less than 30°; and
• when turning onto headings well removed from North and South (in fact, when turning onto due East or due West, no allowances need be made).

NOTE: The allowances described above only apply to the Magnetic Compass because of the turning and acceleration errors associated with it. They do not apply to the Direction Indicator because it is a gyroscopic device which does not suffer from these errors and hence is easier to use.

If the aeroplane has an unserviceable Direction Indicator, perform a timed Rate 1 turn (using the Turn Co-ordinator and the Clock), using the Magnetic Compass as a back-up.

In the Southern Hemisphere, the **allowances** required when turning onto particular headings using the Magnetic Compass are **reversed.**

• When turning onto Northerly headings, roll out when the Magnetic Compass indicates approximately 30° past your desired heading.

• When turning onto Southerly headings, roll out when the Magnetic Compass indicates approximately 30° before your desired heading.

Intentionally Blank

10

STALLING
AND
SLOW FLIGHT

10a

STALLING

AIM

To recognise the stall and to recover from it as efficiently as possible.

CONSIDERATIONS

STALLING OCCURS WHEN STREAMLINE FLOW BECOMES TURBULENT.

Streamline flow over the wings breaks down and becomes turbulent when the critical angle of attack is exceeded. This causes:

- buffeting (shaking or shuddering) of the airframe, felt through the controls;
- a marked decrease in Lift, resulting in sinking;
- rearward movement of the Centre of Pressure (through which the Lift acts), resulting in the nose dropping;
- a marked Drag increase.

Stalling will occur whenever the critical angle of attack is exceeded, irrespective of airspeed. The only way to recover is to decrease the angle of attack (i.e. relax the back pressure and/or move the control column forward).

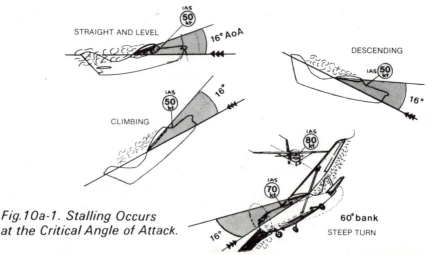

Fig.10a-1. Stalling Occurs at the Critical Angle of Attack.

166

The Pilot can increase the angle of attack (and reduce airspeed) by pulling the control column back. This happens in many manoeuvres such as:
- establishing slow flight;
- turning (especially steep turns);
- pulling out of a dive; and
- landing.

Also, an upward gust of wind encountering the wing will increase its angle of attack.

WHAT IS 'STALLING SPEED'?

The 'basic stalling speed' is considered to be the speed at which the aeroplane stalls when it is at maximum weight, with the wings 'clean' (i.e. no flap) and flying straight and level with the power removed. The stall is made to occur by the Pilot progressively raising the nose.

The basic stalling speed is called 'Vs1'. It is published in the Pilot's Operating Handbook and shown on the Air Speed Indicator as the lower end of the green arc. Vs1 for your aeroplane should be memorised as it is a valuable guide.

The stalling speed with full flap extended (at maximum weight, straight and level, and idle power) is called Vso. It is also found in the Pilot's Operating Handbook and at the lower end of the white arc on the Air Speed Indicator. The Vso speed should also be memorised.

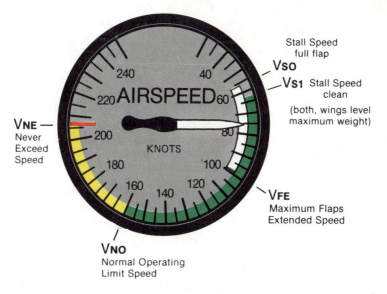

Fig.10a-2. Colour-Coding on the ASI.

The published stalling speeds are only a guide, since stalling always happens at the same angle of attack and not the same Indicated Air Speed. Turns, pulling out of dives and contaminated wing surfaces (e.g. frost or snow) will increase the stalling speed; high power and decreased weight will reduce it.

THE FLIGHT CONTROLS ARE LESS EFFECTIVE NEAR THE STALL.

A reduced airflow over the controls will cause them to become less effective as speed reduces and the stall is approached. Control pressures will decrease and larger movements of the elevator and rudder will be required.

It is the main wing that stalls. The fin and the tailplane remain unstalled (by design) so that during the stall the elevator and rudder remain effective. The ailerons may or may not remain effective during a stall depending upon the aeroplane type.

BE CAREFUL USING AILERONS NEAR THE STALL.

A dropping wing can normally be 'picked-up' by moving the control column in the opposite direction. This causes the aileron on the dropping wing to deflect downwards, increasing the angle of attack, and producing more Lift on that wing. **If the wing is near the stalling angle,** the aileron deflection could cause the critical angle to be exceeded on that wing and, instead of rising, the loss of Lift would cause the wing to drop further. **With any yaw, a spin could develop.**

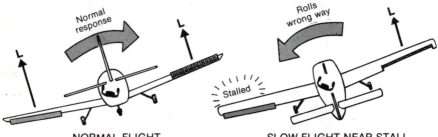

NORMAL FLIGHT   SLOW FLIGHT NEAR STALL

Fig.10a-3. Near the Stall, Use of Aileron May Not Pick-up the Wing.

The ailerons on some more recently designed aeroplanes are effective right through the stall and their use, co-ordinated with rudder, may be possible. This point should be discussed with your Flying Instructor.

PREVENT FURTHER YAW AND WING DROP BY USING COARSE OPPOSITE RUDDER.

Near the stall, any tendency for a wing to drop or for the aeroplane to yaw can be prevented with opposite rudder.

Fig.10a-4. Near the Stall, Prevent Wing Drop and Further Yaw with Opposite Rudder.

168

FLYING THE MANOEUVRE

THE STALL IN STRAIGHT AND LEVEL FLIGHT.

Stalling is first practised in straight and level flight by reducing power and raising the nose to maintain height. The angle of attack will gradually increase.

Warnings of an impending stall include:
- a reducing airspeed and air noise level, decreasing control effectiveness and a 'sloppy' feel;
- operation of a pre-stall warning (such as a horn, buzzer, light or whistle);
- the onset of buffet, felt in the airframe and through the control column;
- a high nose attitude for the manoeuvre being flown.

The **actual stall** may be recognised by:
- the nose dropping (caused by the Centre of Pressure moving rearwards);
- a high sink rate.

Stall Recovery requires decreasing the angle of attack. To recover from a stall:
- reduce the angle of attack by releasing the back pressure on the control column, positively lowering the nose.

Once the wings are unstalled buffetting ceases, the airspeed increases, and the aeroplane can be eased out of the slight dive back into normal flight. The height loss will be of the order of 200 ft. Power can be added to regain or maintain height, otherwise flying speed should be maintained in a glide.

Height loss during the stall can be minimised with power. Adding power is not required to recover from the stall, however **height loss will be minimised if full power is applied as back pressure is released** and the nose is lowered. Recovery can be achieved with a height loss of less than 50 ft.

Fig.10a-5. Stall and Recovery Attitudes.

HAVING RECOVERED FROM A STALL, DO NOT STALL AGAIN!

Following stall recovery, ease the aeroplane into normal flight by gently raising the nose and applying power as the nose passes through the horizon.

The inertia of an aeroplane causes it to follow the original flight path for a brief time before the change in attitude and resulting change in forces move it into a new flight path. Pulling the nose up too sharply during the stall recovery may not give the aeroplane time enough to react and ease out of the dive, but may merely increase the angle of attack beyond the stalling angle again. A **secondary stall** will be induced, and a second recovery from the stall will be necessary.

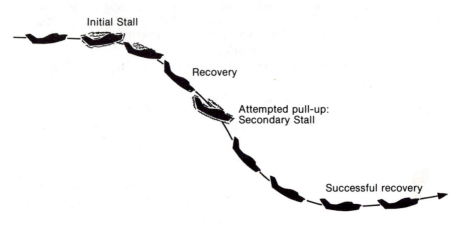

Initial Stall

Recovery

Attempted pull-up:
Secondary Stall

Successful recovery

Fig.10a-6. Raising the Nose Too Sharply During Recovery May Induce A Secondary Stall.

AIRMANSHIP

Unexpected stalls should **never** occur.

Carry out the 'HASELL' check (see next page) prior to practising stalls and stall recovery.

Exert smooth, but firm and positive control over the aeroplane.

Be particularly conscious of any other aircraft in the vicinity, your height Above Ground Level and the area over which you are flying. Ensure that stalling is only practised at altitude. Note landmarks and the direction to the airfield. Maintain a high visual awareness.

THE PRE-AEROBATIC 'HASELL' CHECK LIST

Stalling is the first aerobatic-type manoeuvre that you will perform.

Prior to doing any aerobatics, it is usual to carry out a series of checks to ensure safe operation. The Pilot's Operating Handbook will contain a suitable check covering items such as those in the 'HASELL' check below. The items it contains start with these letters.

H – Height sufficient to recover by 3000 ft Above Ground Level.

A – Airframe (flaps and landing gear as desired, brakes off, in trim).

S – Security – hatches and harnesses secure;
- no loose articles in the cockpit (such as fire extinguishers, tie-down kits, mallet, etc.);
- gyros caged (if necessary).

E – Engine – normal engine operation;
- fuel contents and selection checked (fullest tank selected, fuel pump on if appropriate);
- Mixture and Carburettor Heat as required.

L – Location satisfactory – away from controlled airspace, towns, active aerodromes and other aircraft, and in visual conditions.

L – LOOK OUT – make an inspection turn (of at least 180°, preferably 360°) to clear the area around and below you. Commence the manoeuvre immediately upon completion of the clearing turn.

NOTE: Re-align the Direction Indicator with the Magnetic Compass once the manoeuvre is completed.

AIRWORK 10a —

AIM: To fully stall the aeroplane and then recover with a minimum loss of height.

Standard Stall and Recovery Procedure:

(1) Prior to Entry:

* Pre-Aerobatic Check

H — Height sufficient to recover by 3000 ft AGL.

A — Airframe (flaps *AS DESIRED*, brakes *OFF*, in-trim).

S — Security:
- Hatches and harnesses secure;
- No loose articles;
- Gyros *CAGED* (if applicable).

E — Engine:
- Operating normally;
- Fuel contents and selection checked;
- Mixture and carb heat as required.

L — Location satisfactory.

L — *LOOK OUT*- clearing turn to check for any other aircraft.

Commence the manoeuvre as soon as area is clear.

(2) Stall Entry:
- Power OFF — throttle *CLOSED*, (carb heat *HOT);*
- Maintain height with elevator;
- Use rudder to keep straight and wings level;
- Ailerons neutral;
- Continue bringing control column fully-back.

(3) Symptoms of an Approaching Stall:
- Decreasing airspeed and noise level;
- Controls less firm and less effective;
- Pre-stall warning (light, horn or buzzer);
- Shuddering air-frame;
- A relatively high nose-up attitude.

DURING THE STALL USE RUDDER ONLY TO PREVENT FURTHER YAW.

(1)— ——— (2)— ——— (3)

Recognise the Actual Stall:
- Nose drop;
- Sink rate.

LOOK OUT

PRACTISING THE BASIC STALL

**Practise Stalls in
Various Configurations:**

- **Clean, Power-off;**
- **Clean, Power-on;**
- **Flapped, Power-off;**
- **Flapped, Power-on;**
- **Climbing, Descending
  and Turning.**

**(4a) Stall Recovery
with Power:**

Simultaneously:
- Release back pressure
  to lower the nose —
  (see cockpit diagram);
  and
- Add full power —
  throttle *FULLY OPEN*
  (carb heat *COLD)*;

- Regain flying speed;
- Resume normal flight
  (desired attitude,
  power and airspeed).

*HEIGHT LOSS
APPROX. 50 ft.*

STALL

RECOVERY WITH POWER

**(4b) Stall Recovery
without Power.**

- Release back pressure
  and lower nose (see
  cockpit diagram);
- Regain flying speed;
- Resume normal flight
  — (desired attitude,
  power and airspeed).

*HEIGHT LOSS
APPROX 200 ft.*

*RECOVERY WITHOUT
POWER*

VARIATIONS ON THE BASIC STALL

RECOVERY AT THE INCIPIENT STALL STAGE.

The term 'Incipient Stall' means the beginning stages of a stall. It precedes the actual stall. If ever an unwanted stall appears imminent, then recover at the incipient stage. This is especially applicable if the aeroplane is near the ground, say during take-off, approach to land, going-around or low level flying.

The recovery from an incipient stall is simply:
- relax the back pressure (or move the control column forward); and simultaneously;
- apply power smoothly; and
- use the controls normally (i.e. the ailerons), since the wing is not stalled.

CONTAMINATED OR DAMAGED WINGS INCREASE STALLING SPEED.

If ice, frost, insects or any other contaminant is on a wing or if the wing is damaged (especially its upper leading edge), the airflow could become turbulent at a lesser angle of attack than normal. Stalling will then occur sooner and at a higher airspeed. **Always check the surface condition of the wings (especially the upper leading edges) in your pre-flight inspection.**

STALLING SPEED INCREASES IN MANOEUVRES.

To turn or pull out of a dive, the wings must produce more Lift. This is achieved by the Pilot using back pressure on the control column to increase the angle of attack. The relative air flow striking the wings at a greater angle causes the **stalling angle** to be reached at a higher Indicated Air Speed. For example, the stalling speed increases by 7% at 30° bank angle and by 40% when pulling '2g' in a 60° banked turn or dive recovery.

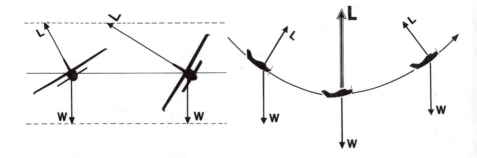

*Fig.10a-7. Increased Wing Loading (g-factor)
means Increased Stall Speed.*

The Pilot physically recognises an increased load factor by the increased g-loading, so any time the Pilot's 'apparent weight' is increased in manoeuvres, the stall speed is increased.

When the aeroplane approaches a stall in manoeuvres (say in a steep turn or pulling out of a dive), releasing back pressure is usually sufficient to prevent the stall occurring.

IF THE AEROPLANE STALLS IN A TURN.

Back pressure on the control column increases the angle of attack and may cause a stall. Since the Load Factor is increased in a turn, the stall will occur at a higher speed than in straight and level flight – by how much depends upon the g-loading. Stalls at a higher speed than normal are called 'accelerated stalls'.

Follow the standard recovery of releasing the back pressure and, when the wings are unstalled, use co-ordinated rudder and ailerons to roll the wings level. Apply power as required and resume the desired flight path.

EXTENDING FLAP LOWERS THE STALLING SPEED AND AFFECTS THE STALL CHARACTERISTICS.

The stall with flaps extended will differ somewhat from the clean stall. For a start, flaps increase the lifting capability of the wings, allowing the required Lift to be generated at a lower speed. The stalling speed will be lower. The increased Drag will cause the aeroplane to decelerate more rapidly when power is reduced and the lower speed may make the controls feel very 'sloppy'. Also, the changed distribution of Lift on the wings may cause a greater tendency for a wing to drop.

With flaps extended, the nose attitude will be lower in each phase of flight, therefore stalling will occur at a lower pitch attitude than when 'clean'.

The **recovery from a stall with flaps extended** is standard. Height loss can be minimised by applying full power as the nose is lowered, but be prepared to hold forward pressure on the control column so that the nose does not rise too far with the strong pitch-up moment that full power produces. Do not use ailerons to roll the wings level until the wings are unstalled. If full flap is used, a climb-away may be difficult unless some flap is raised once a safe speed is attained.

STALLING ON FINAL APPROACH (DON'T LET IT HAPPEN!)

Initiate a recovery immediately you suspect an impending stall on approach. Lower the nose and apply power to minimise height loss.

It is worthwhile practising the developed stall in the approach configuration at altitude so as to familiarise yourself with it. This should ensure that you never allow a stall to occur near the ground.

A situation in which a stall might occur could be an approach that has got out of hand; for example, full flap extended and a tendency to undershoot, with the Pilot raising the nose (instead of adding power). The airspeed will decrease and the undershoot will worsen. If the Pilot continues to pull the control column back, a stall could occur. With full flap and possibly high power applied, the stall could be fairly sudden and with a wing drop.

The standard recovery technique would be used. The control column may have to be moved well forward to unstall the wings, and care should be taken to avoid using ailerons until the wing is unstalled. The substantial drag from full flap may make a climb-away difficult; gain speed in level flight or a slight climb, reduce the flap in stages and then climb away as desired.

POWER DECREASES THE STALLING SPEED.

With power on, the propeller creates a slipstream over the inner sections of the wings which may delay the stall. This will occur at a higher nose position. The slipstream makes the elevator and rudder more effective, but not the ailerons. The increased airflow may delay the stall on the inner sections of the wing – the stall occurring first on the outer sections, perhaps leading to a greater wing-dropping tendency. Standard recovery technique is used, any further yaw being prevented with opposite rudder to prevent a spin developing.

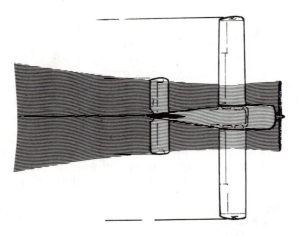

Fig.10a-8. Power Reduces Stalling Speed.

RECOVERY FROM AN INCIPIENT SPIN.

The recovery from a stall with a wing drop (i.e. the initial stages of a spin) is really the same as for an incipient stall with a wing drop. Simultaneously:
- ease the control column forward sufficiently to unstall the wings;
- apply sufficient rudder to prevent further yaw;
- apply maximum power;

- when the airspeed increases as the wings become unstalled, level the wings with co-ordinated use of rudder and ailerons, ease out of the descent and resume the desired flight path.

STALLING SPEED DECREASES AS WEIGHT DECREASES.

The lighter the aeroplane is, the less Lift the wings must generate for straight and level flight, and so the smaller the required angle of attack at a given speed. Therefore a light aeroplane can be flown at a slower airspeed before the stalling angle of attack is reached.

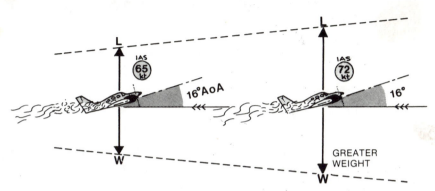

Fig.10a-9. Stalling Speed is Less at Lower Weights.

A FORWARD CENTRE OF GRAVITY INCREASES THE STALLING SPEED.

In many aircraft, the tailplane generates a small downwards force to balance the four main forces and prevent the aeroplane pitching. The Lift from the main wings in straight and level flight will therefore have to support both the Weight **plus** this downwards aerodynamic force on the tail.

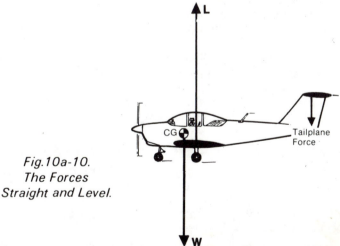

*Fig.10a-10.
The Forces
Straight and Level.*

The further forward the CG, the greater the downwards tailplane force and so the greater is the Lift required from the main wings. This requires a greater angle of attack at a given airspeed, therefore the stalling angle will be reached at a higher airspeed. This is one very good reason why the aeroplane must be correctly loaded with the CG within approved limits.

10b

SLOW FLYING

To develop an awareness of the aeroplane's handling characteristics at **abnormally** low airspeeds, and to return the aeroplane to a safe flying speed.

CONSIDERATIONS

"SLOW FLYING" IS AN AWARENESS EXERCISE.

This Exercise is designed to provide exposure to flight at abnormally low airspeeds so that the Pilot can:
- recognise an inadvertent approach to the stall;
- experience how the aeroplane handles at an abnormally low airspeed; and
- take recovery action by returning the aeroplane to a safe flying speed.

The Exercise also provides handling practice for those brief periods of low airspeed that do occur in normal flight, when the aeroplane is accelerating to climbing speed immediately after lift-off, and during the landing flare as the airspeed decreases prior to touchdown.

THE POWER REQUIRED FOR STEADY FLIGHT.

To maintain a steady airspeed, engine power must produce enough Thrust from the propeller to balance the Total Drag. The 'Power Required' curve is therefore similar in shape to the 'Drag Curve'. It shows that high power is required for steady flight at both high and low speeds, with 'minimum power' occurring at a specific speed in between.

'Minimum power' will give minimum fuel consumption and consequently maximum endurance, so this speed is often listed as the *'Endurance Speed'* in the Pilot's Operating Handbook.

Flight at speeds less than the best endurance speed is slow flight.

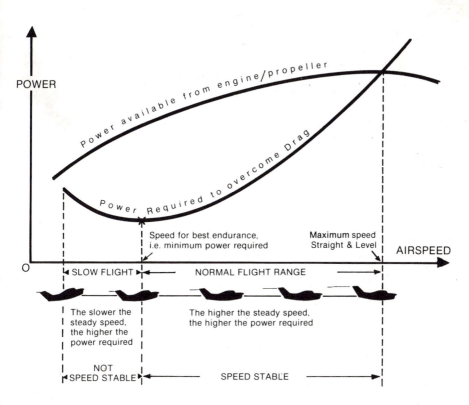

Fig.10b-1. The Power Curve.

POWER HANDLING.

At **normal cruising speeds,** higher speeds require higher power settings. Also, any minor speed variations due to gusts will automatically correct themselves in the **normal flight range** – a slight increase in speed causing a Drag increase that will slow the aeroplane down. Conversely, a slight decrease in speed reduces Drag, allowing the aeroplane to regain speed. **An aeroplane is 'speed-stable' in the 'normal flight range'.**

In the **slow flight range** the situation is reversed, i.e. the lower the speed the higher the power required. This is because at low speeds a high angle of attack is needed to produce the required Lift, greatly increasing the Induced Drag. The increase in Total Drag will slow the aeroplane down unless power is applied. The lowest steady speed that can be maintained by an aeroplane may be limited either by the maximum power that the engine/propeller can deliver, or by the stall.

In the **slow speed range, the aeroplane is not 'speed-stable'** because an airspeed loss due to a gust will result in an increase in Total Drag which will slow the aeroplane down even further (and continue to do so) unless the Pilot takes corrective action by adding power. An airspeed gain, conversely, will reduce the Total Drag and the aeroplane will accelerate unless the Pilot reduces power.

CONTROL EFFECTIVENESS IN SLOW FLIGHT.

The effectiveness of the flight controls depends upon the airflow over them. At low airspeeds, they will feel 'sloppy' and less effective. Large control movements may be required to obtain the desired response. Since the elevator and rudder are in the propeller slipstream, they may be somewhat more effective when high power is set. The ailerons will not be affected by the slipstream.

A high power and a low airspeed will lead to a strong slipstream effect, which may require significant rudder deflection to balance the yawing tendency. At very low speeds and high power, the large rudder deflection might require extra aileron movement to hold the wings level, i.e. 'crossed-controls'.

The 'Feel' of the aeroplane becomes very important in slow flight. The low speed, the less-effective controls, the high nose attitude, the high power required and the large rudder deflection are all clues that the stalling angle is not far away. Slow flight at 10 kt above the stall (and then possibly only 5 kt above) will be practised. Stalling speeds straight and level at maximum weight are delineated on the Air Speed Indicator: V_{S1} at the lower end of the green band for a clean wing and V_{S0} at the lower end of the white band for full flap.

The **airspeed needs to be monitored closely in slow flight.** It should be controlled accurately with power and attitude changes due to the proximity of the stall. The tendency to lose speed in a turn should be counteracted with additional power. Do **not** attempt steep turns at slow speeds near the stall – the stalling speed will increase to meet your actual airspeed!

FLYING THE MANOEUVRE

TO ATTAIN SLOW FLIGHT.

To reduce airspeed to the selected value (5 or 10 kt above the stall):
- reduce power and gradually raise the nose to maintain height;
- when the desired airspeed is reached, increase power and continually adjust both power and attitude to maintain that speed;
- re trim and check the Balance Ball for correct balance.

ATTENTION TO POWER AND ATTITUDE IS REQUIRED TO MAINTAIN A LOW SPEED.

To maintain speed and height, be prepared to work the throttle vigorously and to re-adjust the attitude as necessary. The longer you leave corrections, the greater they will have to be. As always: **power + attitude = performance.**

To correct speed variations:
- if speed increases – raise the nose and reduce power;
- if speed decreases – lower the nose and add power;

To correct height variations:
- if the aeroplane climbs – reduce power and lower the nose.
- if the aeroplane sinks – add power and raise the nose.

The use of elevator, power and rudder must be co-ordinated. Every time power changes there will be a 'pitch/yaw' tendency that you will have to counteract. Slow flight is very good practice for your co-ordination.

To enter a slow speed climb:
- increase power;
- slowly adjust attitude to maintain airspeed;
- trim.

To level off from a slow speed climb:
- lower the nose;
- slowly reduce power;
- trim.

To commence a descent:
- reduce power;
- lower the pitch attitude to maintain airspeed;
- trim.

To level-off from a descent:
- add power;
- gradually raise the nose to the cruise attitude to maintain airspeed;
- trim.

To turn at a low airspeed:
- add power to maintain speed as bank angle is applied.

A maximum performance climb away from a descent:
- open the throttle fully (and balance with rudder);
- allow the nose to rise and hold it in the climb attitude;
- control airspeed with elevator;
- trim.

To approach the stall:
- raise the nose until a stall is imminent;
- recover by easing the control column forward and applying power.

To return to normal cruise speed:
- increase power;
- lower the pitch attitude to maintain height;
- adjust power as desired speed is attained;
- trim.

These manoeuvres should be practised both clean and with flap extended.

AIRMANSHIP

Exert firm, positive and smooth control over the aeroplane, being prepared to make large and prompt power changes when required.

Maintain airspeed in level turns at a low airspeed with the use of additional power. Co-ordinate the use of power/elevator/rudder.

Monitor the engine instruments to confirm adequate cooling of the engine at the high power and low airspeed.

Maintain a safe height above ground level and obstacles if the slow flying is associated with low flying.

Remember that a continuing **Look Out** is important in all phases of visual flight.

AIRWORK 10b — SLOW FLYING

AIM: *To develop an awareness of the aeroplane's handling characteristics at **abnormally** low airspeeds, and to return the aeroplane to a safe flying speed.*

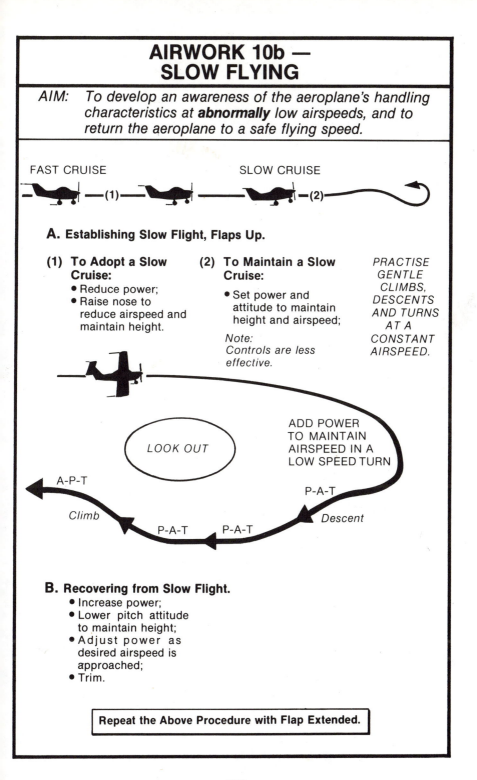

FAST CRUISE   SLOW CRUISE

—(1)—   —(2)—

A. Establishing Slow Flight, Flaps Up.

(1) To Adopt a Slow Cruise:
- Reduce power;
- Raise nose to reduce airspeed and maintain height.

(2) To Maintain a Slow Cruise:
- Set power and attitude to maintain height and airspeed;

Note: Controls are less effective.

PRACTISE GENTLE CLIMBS, DESCENTS AND TURNS AT A CONSTANT AIRSPEED.

LOOK OUT

ADD POWER TO MAINTAIN AIRSPEED IN A LOW SPEED TURN

A-P-T

P-A-T

Climb

P-A-T   P-A-T

Descent

B. Recovering from Slow Flight.
- Increase power;
- Lower pitch attitude to maintain height;
- Adjust power as desired airspeed is approached;
- Trim.

Repeat the Above Procedure with Flap Extended.

Intentionally Blank

11

SPINNING

11a

FULL SPINS

AIM

To enter, maintain and recover from a fully-developed spin (provided it is an approved manoeuvre for the aeroplane).

NOTE: Spinning is an optional instructional exercise.

CONSIDERATIONS

WHAT IS A SPIN?

A spin is a condition of stalled flight in which the aeroplane describes a spiral descent.

As well as the aeroplane being in a stalled condition, one wing is producing more lift than the other (caused by yaw) and this results in a roll. Greater drag from the stalled lower wing results in further yaw, further roll, etc., etc.

Pitching of the nose may also occur.

The aeroplane is in motion about all three axes. In other words, lots of things are happening!

In a spin, the aeroplane is:
- stalled;
- rolling;
- yawing;
- pitching;
- sideslipping; and
- rapidly losing height, even though the airspeed may not be increasing.

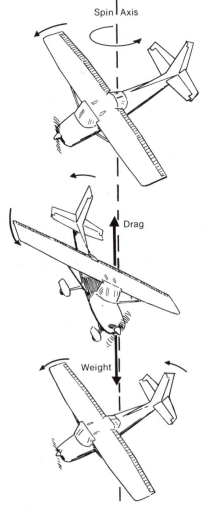

Fig.11a-1. The Spin.

In a spin the wings will not produce much Lift, since they are stalled. The aeroplane will accelerate downwards until it reaches a vertical rate of descent where the greatly increased Drag balances the Weight. The height loss will be rapid as the aeroplane spins downwards about the vertical spin axis.

Characteristics of a developed spin include a low Indicated Air Speed (which does not increase until recovery action is initiated) and a high rate of descent. A vital part of the spin recovery is to unstall the wings by lowering the nose (which reduces the angle of attack), and to build up flying speed.

THE 'FLATNESS' OF THE SPIN DETERMINES THE RATE OF ROTATION.

If the aeroplane adopts a higher nose attitude and the spin flattens:
- the rate of rotation will decrease; and
- the rate of descent will reduce (due to increased drag from the higher angle of attack).

A spinning ice-skater moves her arms in and out from her body to alter the rate of rotation. The same effect occurs in an aeroplane. In a steep nose-down attitude, the mass of the aeroplane is close to the spin axis and the rate of rotation is high. If the spin flattens, some of the aeroplane's mass is distributed further from the spin axis and the rate of rotation decreases.

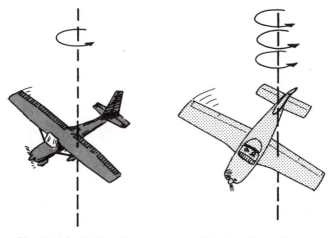

Fig.11a-2. A Flat Spin.   *Fig.11a-3. A Steep Spin.*

If the nose pitches up and down in the spin, the rate of rotation will vary – becoming slower when the spin is flatter and faster when the nose position is steeper. Since the nose is purposely lowered in the recovery from a spin, you can expect a temporary increase in the rate of rotation until the recovery is complete.

A rearwards CG will encourage a flatter spin and it will be more difficult to lower the nose in the recovery. This is one (very important) reason for ensuring that you never fly an aeroplane loaded outside its approved weight and balance limits.

Conversely, a forward CG normally results in a steeper spin with a higher rate of descent and a higher rate of rotation. It may make recovery much easier and, in fact, may even prevent a spin occurring.

DO NOT CONFUSE A SPIN WITH A SPIRAL DIVE.

A manoeuvre that must not be confused with a spin is the spiral dive, which can be thought of as a steep turn that has gone wrong. In a spiral dive the nose attitude is low, the wing is not stalled, the airspeed is high and rapidly increasing and the rate of descent is high. Because the wing is not stalled, there is no need, in the recovery from a spiral dive, to move the nose forward. Spiral dives are considered in Section 15 on Advanced Turning.

YOU WILL SOON BECOME COMFORTABLE WHEN PRACTISING SPINS.

During your first spin, you will probably be a little overcome by the sensations and not really know exactly what is happening. After a few practice spins, however, you will become reasonably comfortable and the whole manoeuvre will seem to slow down enough for you to recognise the characteristics, count the turns, recognise landmarks and so on.

Fig.11a-4. The Spin As You First See It ...... and As You Will See It.

THE THREE STAGES IN A SPIN MANOEUVRE.

The spin manoeuvre can be considered in three stages:

1. The **incipient spin** (or the beginning of the spin), which is an unsteady manoeuvre in which the entry path of the aeroplane is combined with a phenomenon called 'autorotation'.

2. The **fully-developed spin,** in which the aeroplane has settled into a comparatively steady rate of rotation and a steady rate of descent at a low airspeed and a high angle of attack.

3. The **recovery from the spin,** initiated by the Pilot who:
   - opposes the autorotation with rudder;
   - unstalls the wings with forward control column; and
   - eases out of the ensuing dive.

HOW A SPIN DEVELOPS.

A Spin is a condition of stalled flight, so the first prerequisite is that the wings be at a high angle of attack. This is achieved by moving the control column progressively back, as in a normal stall entry.

A wing drop is essential to enter a spin and this may occur by itself or (more likely) be induced by the Pilot yawing the aeroplane with rudder or 'misusing' the ailerons just prior to the aeroplane stalling.

'Autorotation' will commence through the dropping wing becoming further stalled, with a consequent decrease in lift and increase in drag. The aeroplane will roll, a sideslip will develop and the nose will drop. If no corrective action is taken, the rate of rotation will increase and a spin will develop. It will be an unsteady manoeuvre with the aeroplane appearing to be very nose-down. The rate of rotation may increase quite quickly and the Pilot will experience a change of g-loading.

An aeroplane will not usually go straight from the stall into a spin. There is usually a transition period which may vary from aeroplane to aeroplane, typically taking two or three turns in the unsteady and steep autorotation mode, before settling into a fully-developed and stable spin.

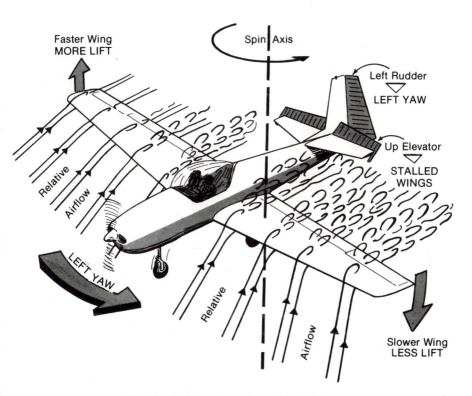

Fig.11a-5. The Aeroplane In A Spin.

ON SOME AEROPLANES, 'MISUSE' OF AILERONS CAN CAUSE A SPIN.

Trying to raise a dropped wing with opposite aileron may have the reverse effect when the aeroplane is near the stall. If, as the aileron goes down, the stalling angle of attack is exceeded, instead of the wing rising it may drop quickly, resulting in a spin. This is the spin entry technique on some aircraft types.

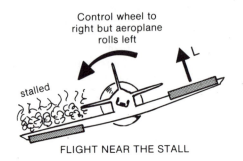

Control wheel to
right but aeroplane
rolls left

stalled

FLIGHT NEAR THE STALL

Fig.11 a-6. Inducing A Spin With Opposite Aileron.

POWER MAY DESTABILISE AN AEROPLANE BEFORE AND DURING THE SPIN.

At the incipient (early) stage of a stall, having power on may cause a greater tendency for a wing to drop, which could lead to a spin. Once the aeroplane is in a spin, power may destabilise it as the slipstream will tend to flow across the outer wing, increasing its lift and consequently increasing the rate of roll. If power is applied, the entire spin manoeuvre will be speeded up.

It is essential, therefore, to remove power by closing the throttle either before or during the spin recovery.

THE FLAPS SHOULD BE RAISED FOR SPINNING.

The flaps tend to decrease the control effectiveness of the elevator and rudder and so should be raised either before or during the spin recovery. For many aircraft, practising spinning with flaps down is not permitted, since the aerodynamic loads on the flap structure may cause damage.

FLYING THE MANOEUVRE

IT IS USUAL TO ENTER A SPIN BY YAWING WITH RUDDER JUST PRIOR TO THE AEROPLANE STALLING.

5-10 kt prior to the aeroplane stalling, with the control column being progressively moved back, a smooth and firm large-deflection of the rudder will speed up one wing and cause it to generate more Lift. The aeroplane will commence to roll and a spin will develop.

The spin entry may require full travel of the rudder. If the left rudder pedal is pushed fully forward, the aeroplane will yaw and roll to the left and a spin to the left will develop. If the right rudder is pushed fully forward, the aeroplane will yaw and roll to the right and a spin to the right will develop.

MAINTAINING THE SPIN.

To allow a steady spin to develop and be maintained, continue to:
• hold the control column fully back;
• hold on full rudder;
• keep ailerons neutral.

RECOGNITION OF A SPIN.

The Pilot can recognise a spin by the following characteristics:
• a steep nose-down attitude;
• continuous rotation;
• buffeting (possibly);
• an almost constant low airspeed;
• a rapid loss of height at a steady rate of descent.

The gyroscopes may topple in a spin, so information from the Attitude Indicator will be of no value. Some aircraft have gyroscopic instruments (e.g. the AI) which should be caged (locked) prior to performing any aerobatic manoeuvre in order to protect them.

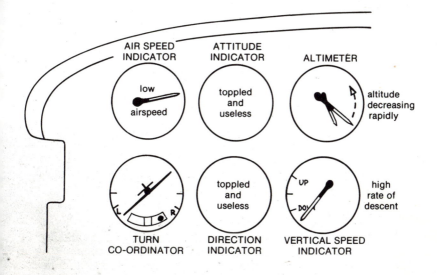

Fig.11a-7. The Flight Instruments in a Spin.

The precise spin recovery depends upon the **spin direction.** In practice, of course, you will know the direction of the spin that you have induced. In an inadvertent spin, however, where the direction of spin may not be obvious, it can be obtained from the Turn Co-ordinator indicating Left or Right. Pay no attention to the Balance Ball in a spin. Your outside view of the ground may also assist you, **but the Turn Co-ordinator is the best clue to spin direction.**

RECOVERY FROM A SPIN.
The technique is:
- check throttle closed and flaps up;
- verify direction of spin on the turn co-ordinator;
- apply full opposite rudder;
- pause (to allow the rudder to become effective and stop the yaw, which turns a stall into a spin);
- ease the control column forward to unstall the wings (full forward if necessary);
- as soon as the rotation stops, centralise the rudder (it may take one, two or more complete turns for the rotation to stop);
- level the wings and ease out of the ensuing dive;
- as the nose comes up through the horizon add power and climb away to regain height.

In the process of unstalling the wings, the nose attitude will become steeper and the mass of the aeroplane will move closer to the spin axis. The result may be a noticeable increase in the rate of rotation just before recovery.

AIRMANSHIP

Ensure that your aeroplane is certified for spins and that Weight and Balance aspects are correct.

Ensure that you know the correct spin recovery technique for your aeroplane type (found in the Pilot's Operating Handbook).

The spin is an aerobatic manoeuvre and so the pre-aerobatic 'HASELL' check should be performed prior to practising. A proper aerobatic harness should be worn. A thorough **Look Out** is essential as a spin and recovery will consume a lot of height (possibly 500 ft per rotation). Commence your practice at a height that will allow you to recover by 3000 ft AGL.

Exert firm control over the spin entry and recovery. You should fly the aeroplane – not vice versa. Never spin inadvertently! When climbing away after each spin recovery, reorientate yourself using familiar landmarks.

AIRWORK 11a —
FULL SPINS

AIM: *To enter, maintain and recover from a fully-developed spin, (provided that it is an approved manoeuvre for the aeroplane).*

Note: recovery should be made by 3000 ft AGL.

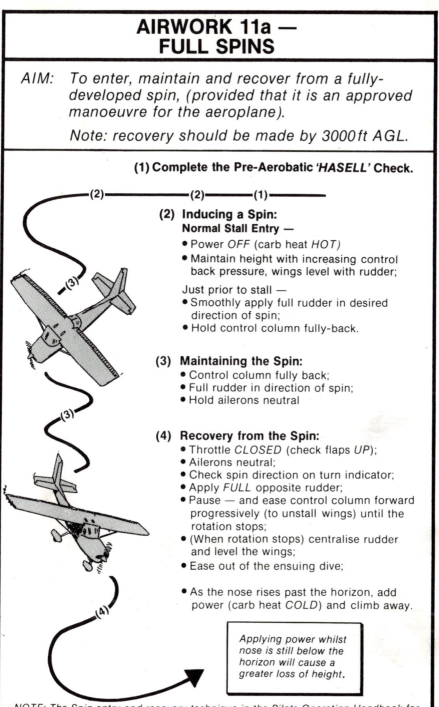

(1) Complete the Pre-Aerobatic *'HASELL'* Check.

(2)————————(2)———————(1)—————

(2) Inducing a Spin:
Normal Stall Entry —
- Power *OFF* (carb heat *HOT)*
- Maintain height with increasing control back pressure, wings level with rudder;

Just prior to stall —
- Smoothly apply full rudder in desired direction of spin;
- Hold control column fully-back.

(3) Maintaining the Spin:
- Control column fully back;
- Full rudder in direction of spin;
- Hold ailerons neutral

(4) Recovery from the Spin:
- Throttle *CLOSED* (check flaps *UP*);
- Ailerons neutral;
- Check spin direction on turn indicator;
- Apply *FULL* opposite rudder;
- Pause — and ease control column forward progressively (to unstall wings) until the rotation stops;
- (When rotation stops) centralise rudder and level the wings;
- Ease out of the ensuing dive;

- As the nose rises past the horizon, add power (carb heat *COLD*) and climb away.

> *Applying power whilst nose is still below the horizon will cause a greater loss of height.*

NOTE: The Spin entry and recovery technique in the Pilots Operating Handbook for your aircraft may differ slightly from this procedure.

11b

INCIPIENT SPINS

AIM

To recognise the onset of a spin and recover before a full-spin develops.

CONSIDERATIONS

'Incipient Spin' means the 'beginning' or 'onset' of a spin. It is, if you like, a recovery from a spin before the spin actually occurs – and with a minimum loss of height.

Whilst spinning is not permitted in many training aeroplanes, the incipient spin is. Recovery should be made before the wings go through a bank angle exceeding 90°.

FLYING THE MANOEUVRE

An Incipient Spin can be induced from almost any flight condition by flying slowly, continually bringing the control column back and then, when almost at the stall, applying full rudder to generate yaw in the desired spin direction.

To recover from an Incipient Spin, simultaneously:
- ease the control column forward sufficiently to unstall the wings;
- apply sufficient rudder to prevent further yaw;
- apply maximum power (see note below);
  and
- as airspeed increases, level the wings with co-ordinated use of rudder and ailerons, ease out of the descent and resume desired flight path.

NOTE: If the nose has dropped below the horizon, do not apply power until after the recovery is complete and the nose rises above the horizon.

AIRWORK 11b —
THE INCIPIENT SPIN

AIM: *To recognise the onset of a spin and recover before a full-spin develops.*

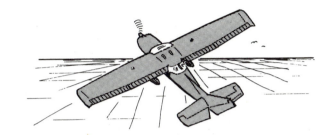

Fly slowly, bringing the control column progressively back, maintaining height as the speed reduces.

Just prior to the stall:
- Apply full rudder in the desired spin direction.

Recovery Procedure —

As the spin commences, simultaneously:
- ease the control column forward sufficiently to unstall the wings;
- apply sufficient rudder to prevent further yaw;
- apply maximum power (see note below);

- as the airspeed increases when the wings are unstalled, level the wings with co-ordinated use of rudder and ailerons, ease out of the descent and resume desired flight path.

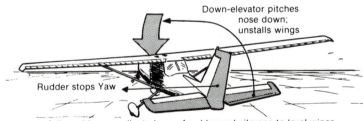

Down-elevator pitches nose down; unstalls wings

Rudder stops Yaw

— followed by co-ordinated use of rudder and ailerons to level wings.

NOTE: If the nose has dropped below the horizon, do not apply power until after the recovery is complete and the nose rises above the horizon as you ease out of the dive.

Intentionally Blank

12

THE STANDARD TAKE-OFF AND CLIMB TO DOWNWIND LEG

NOTE: The Crosswind Take-Off, the Short-Field Take-Off and the Soft-Field Take-Off are covered in the relevant Chapters of Section 13.

12

THE
STANDARD TAKE-OFF
AND CLIMB TO
DOWNWIND LEG

AIM

To take-off into-wind and climb-out in the circuit pattern to downwind leg.

CONSIDERATIONS

This manoeuvre involves:
- flying the aeroplane off the ground and clearing any obstacles;
- a climb to circuit altitude; and
- positioning the aeroplane on downwind leg.

TAKE-OFF INTO-WIND IF POSSIBLE.

During the take-off, the aeroplane must be accelerated to an airspeed at which it is capable of flying. Having a headwind component on a runway 'gives' you airspeed even before you have started rolling. For example, a 10 knot headwind component gives you 10 kt of airspeed on line-up for take-off.

Taking-off into wind is good airmanship because it gives:
- the shortest ground run;
- the lowest ground speed for the required take-off airspeed;
- the best directional control, especially at the start of the ground run, (when there is not much airflow over the control surfaces);
- no side forces on the undercarriage (like there are in a crosswind);
- the best obstacle clearance because of the shorter ground run and the steeper flight path over ground;
- the best position in the climb-out from which to make an into-wind landing straight ahead (or slightly to one side) in the case of engine-failure immediately after take-off.

Fig.12-1. Take-Off Into Wind.

ALWAYS BE AWARE OF THE SURFACE WIND DIRECTION.

The circuit direction will normally be into wind, since this benefits both take-offs and landings. Knowing the wind, you can choose the most suitable runway and work out what the circuit pattern will be. You can determine the wind direction:
- as you walk out to the aeroplane;
- from the wind direction indicator (i.e. the windsock);
- from other clues such as smoke being blown away from a chimney;
- by asking Air Traffic Control (ATC), who will advise you of the (magnetic) direction from which the wind is blowing and its strength, e.g. 360/25 is a North wind at 25 kt.

ENSURE THAT THE RUNWAY IS ADEQUATE.

The Take-Off Performance Chart should be consulted if you are not certain that the runway is adequate in all respects. High elevation aerodromes and high temperatures will increase the runway distances required, because of the decreased air density which degrades both engine and aerodynamic performance. Runway downslope and a tail wind component will also degrade the take-off.

USE OF TAKE-OFF FLAPS SHORTENS THE TAKE-OFF RUN.

Most training aircraft use either zero flap or an early stage of flap for take-off. Extending **take-off flap** increases the lifting ability of the wings, enabling the aeroplane to take-off at a lower airspeed and with a shorter ground run.

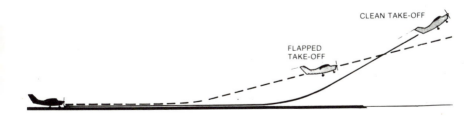

Fig.12-2. Flap Allows a Shorter Take-Off Ground Run.

Do not use landing flap for take-off, because the significant increase in drag will degrade the take-off and climb-out performance. **Do not exceed the recommended flap settings for take-off!**

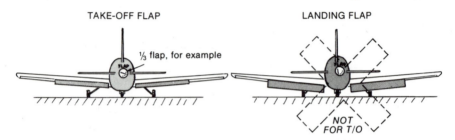

TAKE-OFF FLAP

⅓ flap, for example

LANDING FLAP

NOT
FOR T/O

Fig.12-3. Flap for Take-Off is Less Than That Used for Landing.

THE STANDARD CIRCUIT.

To maintain some form of safe and orderly flow of traffic at an aerodrome, and to allow easy and safe access to the active runway, aircraft are flown in the standard circuit pattern. For good operational reasons, the preferred direction of take-off and landing is into-wind, hence the same direction will generally be used by aircraft both taking-off and landing.

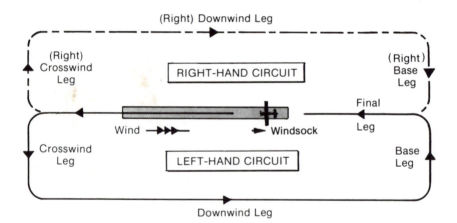

(Right) Downwind Leg

(Right) Crosswind Leg

RIGHT-HAND CIRCUIT

(Right) Base Leg

Final Leg

Wind ➤➤➤   ➤ Windsock

Crosswind Leg

LEFT-HAND CIRCUIT

Base Leg

Downwind Leg

Fig.12-4. The Circuit Pattern is Rectangular.

The circuit is a rectangular pattern based on the runway in use. The standard circuit is left-handed, with all turns being made to the left. This gives a better view from the Captain's seat than turns to the right. At some aerodromes and on some particular runways, however, the circuits are right-handed to avoid built-up areas, high terrain, restricted airspace, etc.

The circuit is referred to the runway on which it is based, e.g. "join the circuit for 36" refers to the circuit based on Runway 36. The '36' indicates that the runway heading is somewhere in the range 355°–360°–005°M.

THE LEGS OF A CIRCUIT.

Following take-off, climb straight ahead on the upwind leg to at least 500 ft Above Aerodrome Level (AAL).

At 500 ft, commence a turn onto the crosswind leg and continue the climb to circuit height, which for most aerodromes is 1000 ft AAL, and level out. Circuit height at some aerodromes may be different for various reasons (to avoid high terrain or remain beneath certain airspace), but will almost certainly lie in the range of 750 ft to 1250 ft AAL.

A turn is made onto **downwind leg** and the aeroplane is flown at circuit height parallel to the runway. A 'downwind' radio call as you fly abeam the upwind (i.e. take-off) end of the runway is often made to alert other aircraft and Air Traffic Control to your position.

At a suitable point on downwind a turn onto **base leg** is made and a descent commenced. Ideally, a turn onto **final approach** should be completed by 500 ft Above Aerodrome Level (AAL).

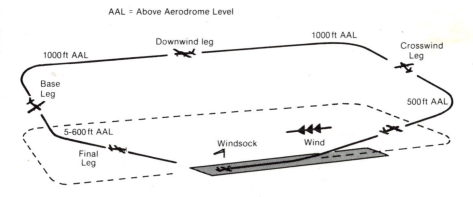

Fig.12-5. The Normal Circuit Pattern is Flown at 1000 ft AAL.

ALLOW FOR WIND EFFECT IN THE CIRCUIT.

Whilst flying in the circuit, a Pilot should aim to fly a rectangular pattern over the ground. This means that, on any leg where there is a crosswind component, drift should be laid off to compensate for the wind effect. This is most easily achieved by selecting a reference point on the ground well ahead of the aeroplane and making sure that the aeroplane tracks directly towards it.

The wind at circuit height may differ to that on the ground – simply adjust your heading so that the track over the ground is correct.

FLYING THE MANOEUVRE

TAXI TO A SUITABLE POSITION FOR THE PRE-TAKE-OFF CHECKS.

Taxi towards the runway and position the aircraft clear of the runway (or in a run-up bay if provided) to carry out your engine run-up and pre take-off checks. Ensure that:
- the slipstream will not affect other aircraft;
- a brake failure will not cause you to run into other aircraft or obstacles;
- loose stones will not damage the propeller or be blown rearwards.

A suitable position is usually at 90° to the runway, giving you a good view in either direction although, in strong winds, it is better to face into wind. This ensures adequate cooling of the engine and avoids spurious rpm fluctuations due to wind gusts during the run-up.

Set the Brakes to PARK and set idling rpm (typically 1,000 to 1,200 rpm). This allows the engine to continue warming-up, yet be adequately cooled.

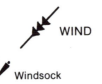

WIND

Windsock

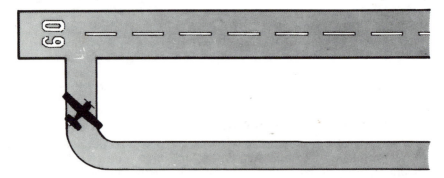

Fig.12-6. Position Aircraft for Pre Take-Off Check,
Preferably Into-Wind.

THE PRE TAKE-OFF CHECK CONTAINS VITAL ACTIONS.

Set the brakes to PARK and complete the Pre Take-Off Vital Actions. You are just about to take the aeroplane off the ground and into the air, so it is vital that everything is as it should be. The Pre Take-Off Check should confirm this.

A TYPICAL PRE TAKE-OFF CHECK.

Use the Pre Take-Off Check in your Pilot's Operating Handbook. It will probably contain such items as:

T –**Trim:** set for take-off.

–**Throttle friction nut:** sufficiently tight (to prevent the throttle slipping once it has been set), but not so tight that the throttle is difficult to move.

M –**Mixture:** *RICH.*

–**Magnetos:** confirm that there are no aircraft behind you and run the engine up (typically to 1,800 or 2,000 rpm).

• whilst at high rpm, the carburettor heat can be tested at *HOT,* which should cause the rpm to drop by about 100 rpm. This indicates that the system is working, the warm air entering the engine being less dense and causing a drop in the power produced. An rpm increase during the 10 seconds or so you leave the carburettor heat *HOT* indicates that carburettor ice was present and has been melted. At the end of this test, return carburettor heat to *COLD.* The magnetos can now be checked knowing that the carburettor is free of ice. If you think carburettor ice may reform prior to take-off, take appropriate action (see later).

• switch from *BOTH* to *LEFT* (and note an rpm drop, typically between 75–175 rpm drop, due to the right magneto sytem being earthed and only the left spark plug in each cylinder firing, then back to *BOTH,* when the rpm should return to that set);

• switch from *BOTH* to *RIGHT* (and note an rpm drop, typically between 75–175 rpm drop, due to the left magneto sytem being earthed and only the right spark plug in each cylinder firing, then back to *BOTH,* when the rpm should return to that set);

• no rpm drop, a 'dead cut' (i.e. the engine stops firing) or an imbalance in the two rpm drops (exceeding 75–100 rpm) indicates a problem.

NOTE: If you inadvertently go to *OFF* when testing the magnetos, allow the engine to stop. An experienced Pilot will be able to keep the engine going, but quick action is needed, otherwise backfiring and possible damage could occur. It is no problem to stop the engine and then restart it again normally.

• close the throttle and check rpm (typically 600–700 rpm), then return to 1,000 or 1,200 rpm.

P –**Primer:** fuel primer in and locked.

F –**Fuel:** correct fuel tank selected and contents sufficient for flight.

–**Fuel pump** on (if fitted – most likely in low-wing aeroplanes) and fuel pressure adequate.

–**Flaps:** set for take-off.

I - **Instruments**: Flight Instruments checked for correct settings and indications and engine instruments checked for correct indications. Follow a systematic scan around the instrument panel.

Flight Instruments:
- **Air Speed Indicator**: indicating zero or well below the stalling speed;
- **Attitude Indicator**: set the model aeroplane against the artificial horizon;
- **Altimeter**: set Aerodrome QNH and check that correct elevation is indicated (or vice versa, i.e. set the known aerodrome elevation and confirm that a reasonable QNH is displayed in the subscale); or set QFE so that the Altimeter indicates zero;
- **Vertical Speed Indicator**: showing zero (neither a climb nor a descent);
- **Direction Indicator**: align with the Magnetic Compass (which you also check);
- **Turn Co-ordinator**: previously checked with left and right turns during the taxi (if it is driven electrically or by an engine-driven vacuum pump – if venturi-driven, it cannot be tested prior to flight);
- **Balance Ball**: tested during the taxi with left and right turns.
- **Clock**: wound (yes, the clock is a flight instrument!), check that the correct time is set.

Engine and Other Instruments:
- **Tachometer**: rpm remaining steady as set (at idling rpm, typically 1,000 to 1,200 rpm);
- **Oil Pressure**: normal;
- **Oil Temperature**: normal;
- **Fuel Pressure**: already checked if a fuel pump (or boost pump or auxiliary pump) is fitted;
- **Ammeter**: to indicate that the electrical system is charging;
- **Suction Gauge**: for correct 'suction' from engine-driven vacuum pumps (if a vacuum-driven gyroscopic Attitude Indicator and/or Direction Indicator is fitted);
  NOTE: This seems a lot but, if you work your way around the panel systematically, you will cover them all.

S - **Switches**: as required (including Pitot Heaters, Rotating Beacon, if fitted);
C - **Controls**: full and free movement;
   - **Carburettor heat**: 'COLD' (or as advised by the Pilot's Operating Handbook if you are in conditions where the formation of carburettor ice is likely).
   - **Cowl Flaps**: set for take-off (if fitted);
H - **Hatches**: doors secure, and no loose articles in the cockpit;
   - **Harness**: secure, seat firmly locked in place on the floor, passengers briefed;
   - **Hydraulics**: as required (if appropriate).
NOTE: 'TMPFISCH' is only one mnemonic to help Pilots remember the items in the Pre Take-Off Check. There are others such as 'TTMFGHH' and so on. The important thing is that you learn the check as described in your own Pilot's Operating Handbook. **Checks are a vital part of safe flying.**

CONSIDER AIR TRAFFIC CONTROL (ATC) AND RADIO PROCEDURES BEFORE LINING UP ON THE RUNWAY.

The category of the aerodrome will determine whether take-off clearances are required. Consider this and other ATC aspects before entering the runway, checking "all clear left" and "all clear right" along the runway and on final approach before you do. Aircraft already taking-off or landing have right-of-way over a taxying aeroplane.

LINE-UP AND ENSURE THAT THE NOSE-WHEEL IS STRAIGHT.

Make full use of the runway length available (within reason). One of the most useless things in aviation is runway behind you!

The take-off run should be along the centreline of the runway and the easiest way to achieve this is to line-up with one mainwheel either side of the centreline markings (if the runway has them). Roll forward a metre or two, thereby ensuring that the nose-wheel is straight (before applying brakes if used); but do not waste runway length.

Have a good **Look Out.** Scan the runway and circuit area for other aircraft that could conflict with you. Maintain an awareness of other circuit traffic, both visually and aurally (by listening to the radio). It is a good habit to check the windsock at this time, just before you roll.

RELEASE THE BRAKES AND OPEN THE THROTTLE SMOOTHLY.

Select a reference point at the end of the runway (or beyond) on which to keep straight. Release the brakes and smoothly apply full power. A mental count of "one-two-three" will occupy the time required to advance the throttle to full power. Glance at the tachometer early in the take-off run to confirm that the correct rpm has been achieved. Have your heels on the floor with the balls of your feet on the rudder pedals to control steering (and **not** high enough to apply the toe brakes).

Using Rudder

On Take-off

CORRECT

INCORRECT

Fig.12-7. Heels on the Floor (and No Pressure on Brakes).

KEEP STRAIGHT WITH RUDDER.

Use your reference point at or beyond the far end of the runway centreline to assist you in keeping straight. Even though you are focussing well ahead, the edges of the runway in your peripheral vision and the runway centreline disappearing under the nose provide supporting guidance.

With the application of power, there may be a tendency to yaw because of the:
- slipstream effect on the tail-fin; and
- torque reaction pressing one wheel down.

For an aeroplane whose propeller rotates clockwise as seen from the cockpit, the tendency is to yaw left on take-off. If the propeller rotates anti-clockwise, the tendency is to yaw right.

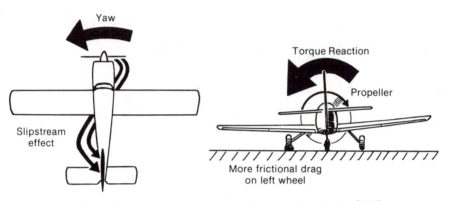

Fig.12-8. There is a Tendency to Yaw on the Take-Off Run.

Any yawing tendency should be counteracted with rudder. If yawing left, apply right rudder (and vice versa). Large rudder pedal movements may be required early in the take-off run but, as the airflow over the rudder increases, smaller movements will be sufficient. Just look ahead and keep the aeroplane tracking straight down the centreline. Steer the aeroplane with your feet (and not your hands). **Keep straight with rudder.**

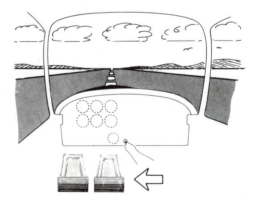

Fig.12-9.
Keep Straight
Using Your Feet.

NOTE: A brief mention of crosswinds (which are covered more fully in a later chapter) in case an into-wind runway is not available. Any significant crosswind will tend to lift one wing. The wings can be kept level by holding the control column sufficiently into-wind (by a large amount at the start of the take-off run, reducing the amount as speed is gained and the ailerons become more effective). **Keep the wings level with aileron.**

PROTECT THE NOSE-WHEEL BY HOLDING THE WEIGHT OFF IT.

On the ground, the nose-wheel carries a fair load, especially if the take-off surface is rough or soft. During the normal take-off roll of a tricycle gear aeroplane, the Pilot should hold a little back pressure on the control column. This takes some of the weight off the nose-wheel and protects it somewhat.

Back pressure also prevents 'wheel-barrowing' – a situation where the nose-wheel is held on the ground after sufficient Lift has been generated for flight. 'Wheel-barrowing' is bad news for the nose-wheel!

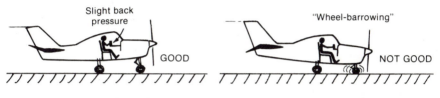

Fig.12-10. Protect The Nose-wheel.

CHECK THE POWER EARLY IN THE TAKE-OFF RUN.

After maximum power has been set and tracking down the runway centreline is under control, glance at the engine instruments to check that full power is indeed being delivered. Engine rpm should be as expected. Oil pressure and temperature should both be within limits. This glance should take no more than one or two seconds.

WHEN FLYING SPEED IS REACHED, TAKE THE AEROPLANE OFF THE GROUND WITH ELEVATOR.

A gradual backward movement of the control column will allow the aeroplane to become airborne when flying speed is reached.

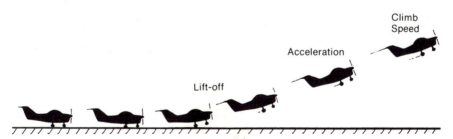

Fig.12-11. When Flying Speed is Reached, Lift-Off Gently with Elevator.

If you lift-off too soon, the aeroplane may not fly and will settle back onto the ground; if you lift-off too late, the wheels and tyres will have been subjected to extra stress, the airspeed will be excessive and the take-off will have been unnecessarily lengthened. Obstacle clearance might also be a problem.

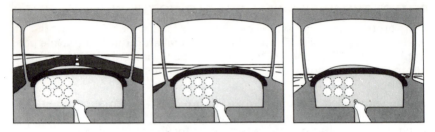

Fig.12-12. Gradually Assume the Climb Attitude with Elevator.

The 'cushioning' of ground effect when the aeroplane is flying close to the ground allows flight at lower speeds than when the aeroplane is well clear of the ground. It is important that the aeroplane accelerates to the correct climbing speed soon after lift-off to avoid 'sink'.

WHEN AIRBORNE AND CLIMBING AWAY.

- **Look Out,** both at the horizon to check your attitude and your tracking, and to look for other aircraft;
- keep the wings level with ailerons; and
- maintain balance with rudder pressure;

- with the elevator, hold the nose attitude in the correct position relative to the horizon for the climb-out, glancing at the Air Speed Indicator to confirm that climb speed has been achieved;
- Trim.

At a safe height (say 200 or 300 ft AAL) raise the take-off flaps (if used). During the climb following take-off, **Look Out** to check your attitude and to check for other aircraft. Confirm that you have achieved the desired climb speed and adjust the attitude if necessary. After the aeroplane has settled into a steady climb, trim-off any steady control pressure.

The procedure for aircraft that have a fuel pump switched on for take-off is to switch it off at a safe height (say 500 ft AAL). The Pilot checks that fuel pressure remains satisfactory.

NOTE: In more advanced aeroplanes with a retractable undercarriage the wheels will be raised once a positive climb is established after lift-off. Most training aeroplanes have fixed-undercarriages and so this is not a consideration.

If your Pilot's Operating Handbook calls for an After Take-Off Check (with respect to flaps and fuel pump for instance), then it would be appropriate to perform this check when you are established in the climb-out (say at about 600 ft AAL).

THE CLIMB-OUT TO CIRCUIT HEIGHT.

As you climb-out following take-off:
- **Look Out** to check your attitude and scan ahead, above and to either side. Check your reference point to confirm that you are tracking on the extended centreline of the runway and not drifting to one side.

- At 500 ft AAL, first scan the area into which you will be turning and then turn (usually left) onto the crosswind leg using a normal climbing turn (bank angle 20° or less). Balance with rudder pressure and maintain climbing speed with elevator. Selecting a new reference point will assist you to track correctly on this crosswind leg. Allow for any drift due to wind effect.
- Complete the After Take-Off Check (if required).

Anticipate reaching Circuit-Height and, as you approach it, start lowering the nose to the cruise attitude. To level-off from a climb, use 'A-P-T':

A: **Attitude** – lower the nose to the straight and level attitude;
　　　　　　　 – allow the speed to increase to the desired airspeed;
P: **Power** – reduce power to maintain the desired airspeed.
T: **Trim.**

DOWNWIND LEG.

At (or approaching) circuit height, check 'all clear' and turn onto downwind leg, selecting a reference point well ahead on which to parallel the runway. You may be required to call 'Downwind' on the radio as you pass abeam the upwind end of the runway (i.e. the climb-out end of the runway).

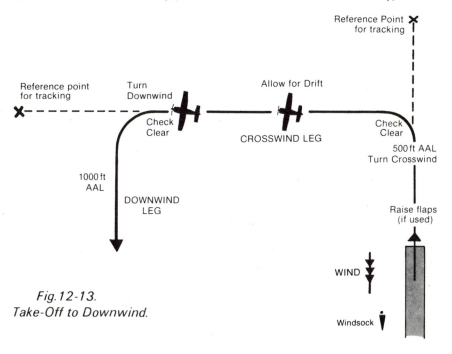

Fig. 12-13.
Take-Off to Downwind.

AIRMANSHIP

Maintain a good **Look Out** prior to entering the runway and in the circuit area. Fly an accurate circuit and follow the basic Rules of the Air.

AIRWORK 12 —

AIM: To take-off into wind and climb-out in the circuit pattern to downwind leg.

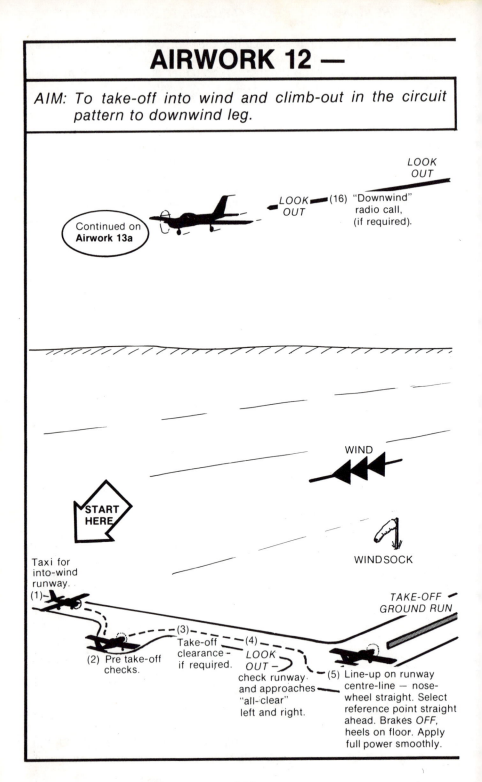

LOOK OUT

(16) "Downwind" radio call, (if required).

LOOK OUT

Continued on **Airwork 13a**

WIND

START HERE

WINDSOCK

Taxi for into-wind runway.

(1)

(2) Pre take-off checks.

(3) Take-off clearance – if required.

(4) *LOOK OUT –* check runway and approaches "all-clear" left and right.

TAKE-OFF GROUND RUN

(5) Line-up on runway centre-line — nose-wheel straight. Select reference point straight ahead. Brakes *OFF*, heels on floor. Apply full power smoothly.

THE STANDARD TAKE-OFF AND CLIMB TO DOWNWIND

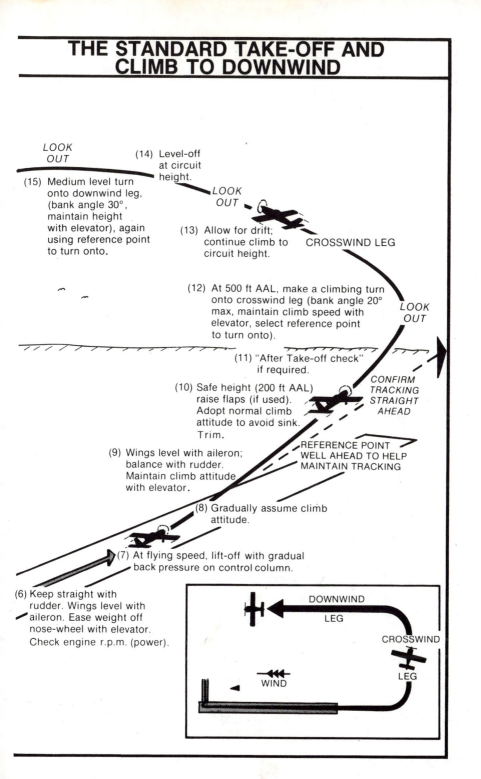

LOOK OUT

(14) Level-off at circuit height.

LOOK OUT

(15) Medium level turn onto downwind leg, (bank angle 30°, maintain height with elevator), again using reference point to turn onto.

(13) Allow for drift; continue climb to circuit height.

CROSSWIND LEG

(12) At 500 ft AAL, make a climbing turn onto crosswind leg (bank angle 20° max, maintain climb speed with elevator, select reference point to turn onto).

LOOK OUT

(11) "After Take-off check" if required.

CONFIRM TRACKING STRAIGHT AHEAD

(10) Safe height (200 ft AAL) raise flaps (if used). Adopt normal climb attitude to avoid sink. Trim.

REFERENCE POINT WELL AHEAD TO HELP MAINTAIN TRACKING

(9) Wings level with aileron; balance with rudder. Maintain climb attitude with elevator.

(8) Gradually assume climb attitude.

(7) At flying speed, lift-off with gradual back pressure on control column.

(6) Keep straight with rudder. Wings level with aileron. Ease weight off nose-wheel with elevator. Check engine r.p.m. (power).

DOWNWIND LEG

CROSSWIND LEG

WIND

211

EMERGENCIES DURING THE TAKE-OFF

There are two emergencies in the take-off for which you should be prepared (even though they may never happen):

(1) Engine failure after take-off (fortunately not as common these days as it once was!).

(2) The discontinued take-off whilst still on the ground (Pilot-initiated).

Prior to opening the throttle on each take-off, it is a good idea to run through both of these procedures in your mind.

ENGINE FAILURE AFTER TAKE-OFF.

If engine power is lost in the climb-out following take-off, the options open to the Pilot will vary according to how high the aeroplane is, the nature of the terrain ahead, the wind conditions and so on. An event such as engine failure close to the ground requires prompt and decisive action by the Pilot.

No matter when the engine fails in flight, the first priority is to **maintain flying speed. Immediately lower the nose** to the gliding attitude to maintain flying speed.

A controlled descent and landing, even on an unprepared surface, is preferable by far to an unwanted stall in the attempted climb-out. Close the throttle, in case the engine comes back to life at an inopportune time.

Do Not Turn Back to the Field.

The height at which the failure occurs determines how you manoeuvre but, in general, you should plan to land fairly well straight ahead. Height is rapidly lost in descending turns and, from less than 500 ft AAL, it is doubtful if you would make the runway. **Look For a Landing Area Ahead and Within Range.**

Make yourself familiar with suitable emergency landing areas in the vicinity of your aerodrome, so that in the unlikely event of engine failure you already have a plan of action in mind.

Following engine failure, and having established the glide, **quickly select the best landing area** from the fields available ahead and within approximately ±30° if possible, otherwise ±60°. Make only gentle turns (say 15° angle of bank maximum).

Gliding turns at low level can be dangerous due to:
- high rates of descent; and
- a tendency for the Pilot to raise the nose to stop a high rate of descent and **inadvertently** stalling or spinning the aeroplane.

Complete checks and make a *MAYDAY* call if time permits. Any attempt to switch fuel tanks and/or to restart the engine depends on time being available.

Maintaining flying speed is vital, more important than any radio call or even starting the engine. If the selected field looks rough and you feel that damage could ensue then, when committed to carrying out the landing:
- ignition *OFF;*
- fuel *OFF;*

- doors – unlocked (or as advised in the Pilot's Operating Handbook) in anticipation of a quick evacuation.

After landing:
- stop the aeroplane and set the brakes to park;
- stop the engine (if it is still running);
- check: fuel *OFF* / ignition *OFF* / electrics *OFF;*
- evacuate.

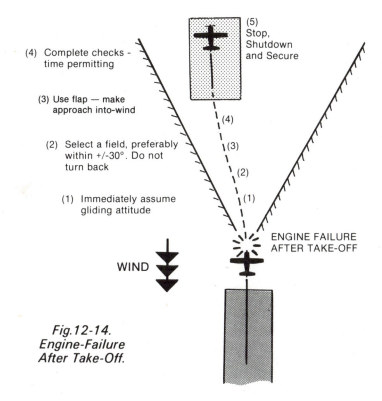

(5) Stop, Shutdown and Secure

(4) Complete checks - time permitting

(3) Use flap — make approach into-wind

(2) Select a field, preferably within +/-30°. Do not turn back

(1) Immediately assume gliding attitude

ENGINE FAILURE AFTER TAKE-OFF

WIND

Fig.12-14.
Engine-Failure
After Take-Off.

THE DISCONTINUED TAKE-OFF.

A Pilot may decide to abort a take-off during the ground run for many reasons, such as:
- an obstruction on the runway;
- engine failure or loss of power;
- engine or fuel problems;
- faulty instrument indications (e.g. Air Speed Indicator zero);
- a doubt that the aeroplane is capable of flying;
- an insecure seat that feels like it might slip backwards; or
- any other condition that may, in your opinion, make the take-off inadvisable.

This 'accelerating-and-then-stopping' manoeuvre is known by various names, including *'accelerate-stop'*, the *'discontinued take-off'*, the *'aborted take-off'* or the *'abandoned take-off'*.

Procedure to Abort the Take-Off:
- close the throttle fully;
- keep straight with rudder;
- brake firmly (immediate maximum braking if required), avoiding skidding or slipping, whilst maintaining directional control;
- stop the aeroplane, set the brakes to *PARK,* and establish the problem;
- if necessary, shut down the engine (preferably clear of the runway);
- notify the ATS Unit and seek assistance if required.

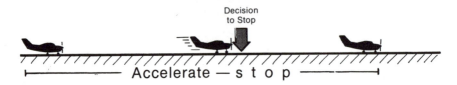

Decision
to Stop

Accelerate — s t o p

Fig.12-15. The Aborted Take-Off.

VARIATIONS ON THE STANDARD TAKE-OFF

A restricted runway length, a soft surface, and a runway crosswind component, are all variables which require the Pilot to adopt a slightly different technique on take-off, compared to the basic technique covered in this Chapter.

To avoid interrupting the flow of learning to fly a Standard Circuit by describing these variations now, they are covered in the next Section (13), within the relevant Chapters:

- **The Crosswind Take-Off** – **in Chapter 13f,** (Crosswind Operations);
- **The Short-Field Take-Off** – **in Chapter 13g,** (Short-Field Operations);
- **The Soft-Field Take-Off** – **in Chapter 13h,** (Soft-Field Operations).

However, in the UK these Take-Offs actually form part of Exercise 12 for the purpose of standard Flying Training Records.

13

CIRCUIT OPERATIONS, APPROACHES AND LANDINGS

Intentionally Blank

13a

THE CIRCUIT, POWERED APPROACH AND NORMAL LANDING

AIM

To continue a normal circuit for a powered approach and landing into-wind.

CONSIDERATIONS

Continuing from the previous chapter, this manoeuvre involves:
- flying an accurate circuit based on the runway used;
- making a powered descent, an approach; and
- an into-wind landing.

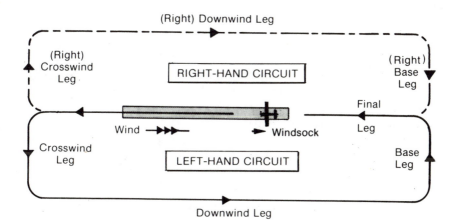

Fig.13a-1. The Circuit Pattern.

LAND INTO-WIND IF POSSIBLE.

Landing into-wind is desirable because:
- for a given airspeed on approach, a headwind gives the lowest ground speed;
- there is no tendency to drift sideways;
- it allows the best directional control both in-flight and on the ground; and
- the landing distance required is least.

ENSURE THAT THE LANDING DISTANCE AVAILABLE IS ADEQUATE.

If necessary, consult the Landing Chart to confirm that the runway is adequate for the conditions and aeroplane weight. High elevations and high temperatures decrease air density and increase the landing distance required, as does a tailwind component, a downslope, or a contaminated runway.

USING POWER IN THE APPROACH AND LANDING.

An engine-assisted approach is the normal procedure, since:
- the Pilot can control the rate of descent and approach flight path in varying winds;
- the engine is kept warm (ensuring power is available for a go-around); and
- the change of attitude in the round-out from a powered approach to the landing attitude is less compared with that for a glide approach.

USING FLAP IN THE APPROACH AND LANDING.

Using flap provides:
- a lower stalling speed, thus permitting a lower approach speed whilst retaining an adequate margin over the stall;
- a steeper flight path at a given airspeed, because of the increased drag;
- a lower nose attitude at a given airspeed, providing a better view of the approach and landing path;
- a shorter hold-off and a shorter landing run because of the increased drag and the lower airspeed.

NOTE: The amount of flap used will depend upon the aeroplane and the wind conditions actually prevailing. In strong and gusty winds it may be preferable to use less than full flap (possibly no flap at all) for better controllability and power response. Your flying instructor will advise you.

POSITIONING IN THE CIRCUIT.

A good landing is most likely following a good approach. Fly an accurate circuit and get set-up early. Make a 'downwind' call abeam the take-off end of the runway, complete the pre-landing drills and keep a good **Look Out,** both for other aircraft and to check your position relative to the runway.

THE PRE-LANDING CHECK SHOULD BE COMPLETED ON DOWNWIND LEG.

Completing the Pre-Landing Check by about the mid-point on the downwind leg allows you to concentrate fully on your base turn, approach and landing.

Know the Pre-Landing Drill for your aeroplane. It will include such items as:
- Brakes *OFF;*
- Mixture *RICH;*
- Fuel: correct tank(s) selected, contents sufficient, fuel pump on (if fitted) and fuel pressure normal, fuel primer locked;
- Flaps as required (and consider what flap you will use on approach, since this may affect where you turn onto base leg);
- Hatches (doors) and Harnesses (seat belts): *SECURE.*

TURNING BASE.

A medium level turn from downwind onto base leg is made when the touchdown point on the runway lies approximately 30° behind. This is the 8 o'clock position from the track of the aeroplane. In a strong wind, the turn should be commenced earlier to keep base leg closer to the aerodrome boundary.

Allow for drift on base leg so that the wind does not carry the aeroplane too far from the field and to maintain the rectangular circuit pattern. The amount of drift can assist the Pilot in estimating wind-strength – the greater the drift angle on base, the stronger the headwind on final.

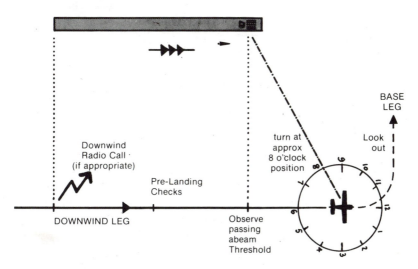

Fig.13a-2. Positioning in the Circuit and Turning Base.

COMMENCING DESCENT ON BASE LEG.

An approximate descent point for a normal engine-assisted approach to the aiming point on the runway lies at 45° to the aeroplane's track on base leg. In strong winds, when base is usually flown closer to the aerodrome boundary, the descent point at 45° will still be suitable.

The descent should be judged so that you roll-out on final no lower than 500 ft Above Aerodrome Level (AAL). This means that the turn onto final should be commenced not below 600 ft AAL. With a little experience, you will get a 'feel' for just where to commence descent to achieve this. Judgement develops with experience. The availability of power and flap also gives you the ability to control your descent flight path as you wish.

Flap for the approach and landing should be used as recommended in the Pilot's Operating Handbook and as advised by your Flying Instructor.

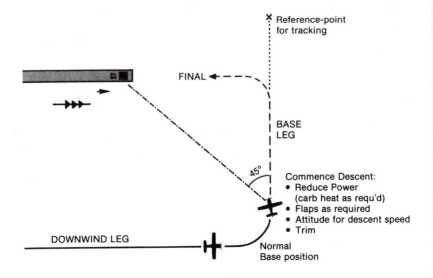

Fig. 13a-3. Commencing Descent on Base Leg.

The turn onto final is a medium descending turn in which the Pilot should:
- limit the bank angle to 30° or less (ideally about 15–20°), maintaining balance with rudder pressure;
- aim to be lined-up on final at or above 500 ft AAL;
- maintain airspeed with elevator.

The runway perspective as seen from the cockpit will indicate whether you are in line with the runway or not. If not, then do something about it!

  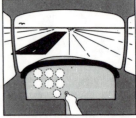

Left of	*On*	*Right of*
Runway Centreline	*Runway Centreline*	*Runway Centreline*

Fig. 13a-4. Runway Perspective on Final Approach.

Steep turns near the ground should be avoided. If you overshoot the turn onto final, rather than steepen the turn, fly through final and rejoin it from the other side without exceeding a medium bank angle.

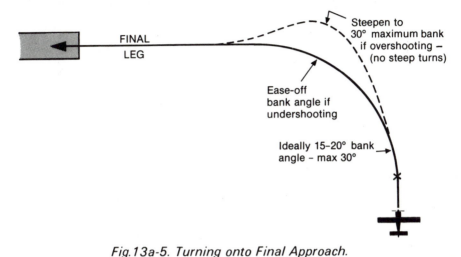

Fig.13a-5. Turning onto Final Approach.

ALLOW FOR THE WIND EFFECT WHEN TURNING FINAL.

A **tailwind on base** will increase the aeroplane's speed over the ground and the turn should be commenced a little early to avoid flying through final. Conversely, if there is a **headwind on base,** the turn onto final can be delayed. If any crosswind exists on final, then lay-off drift so that the aeroplane tracks along the extended centreline of the runway, ensuring that the aeroplane is in balance.

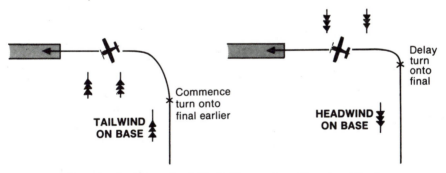

Fig.13a-6. Allow for Wind Effect when Turning Final.

WINDSHEAR AND TURBULENCE ON FINAL.

It is usual for the wind to change in strength and direction near the ground due to friction and other causes. A sudden reduction in the headwind component will cause a reduction in Indicated Air Speed, which can result in an increased sink rate. Turbulence on final also causes airspeed and descent rate fluctuations.

If a strong wind gradient is suspected, then the Pilot should consider flying the approach using a lower flap setting (or no flap at all) and a higher approach speed than normal. The aeroplane will be more stable and more responsive compared to when full flap is lowered and a slow airspeed flown.

HOW SHOULD THE RUNWAY APPEAR ON APPROACH?

The perspective of the runway seen on approach will depend upon the position of the aeroplane. If it is too high, then the runway will appear longer and narrower than usual and a steep flight path will be required to arrive near the aiming point for round-out. If the aeroplane is too low, then the runway will appear shorter and wider than usual and the aeroplane will have to be 'dragged in' with power.

Either of these situations can be remedied and the earlier the better! Adjust the rate of descent and the flight path (using power and attitude) so that the runway assumes its normal perspective as soon as possible. This may require firm and positive action, but the sooner you do it, the more likely you are to make a good landing.

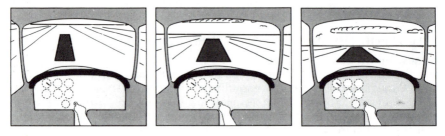

Too High.   *Just Right.*   *Too Low.*

Fig.13a-7. Runway Perspective on Approach.

FLY A STABILISED APPROACH.

The approach path to the runway is three-dimensional. A good approach requires tight control of the flight path and of the airspeed (i.e. a stabilised approach) and this will set the scene for a good landing. Landing flap should be selected by at least 300 ft AAL and the aeroplane re-trimmed.

Approach at the selected Indicated Air Speed (IAS) on a suitable slope and remain aligned with the extended runway centreline. This will require positive and firm action on your part. The approach speed chosen will depend upon the flap selected and the prevailing conditions (wind strength and direction, or the suspected presence of gustiness, windshear, turbulence or wake turbulence).

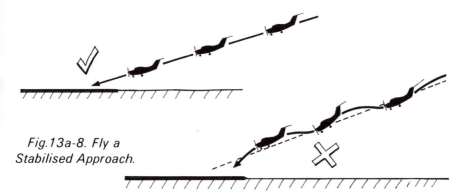

Fig.13a-8. Fly a Stabilised Approach.

THE AIMING POINT SHOULD STAY FIXED IN THE WINDSCREEN.

Ideally, the aiming point should remain fixed in the windscreen – the runway appearing larger and larger as it is approached, without its perspective changing.

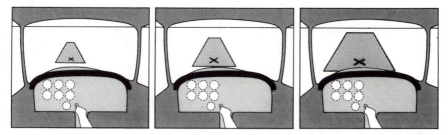

Fig.13a-9. Ideally, the Aiming Point Remains Fixed in the Windscreen.

If the aiming point moves progressively up the windscreen, then the aeroplane is 'undershooting'. Conversely, if the aiming point moves progressively down the windscreen, then the aeroplane is 'overshooting'. In each case, the Pilot must take positive action to modify the approach path.

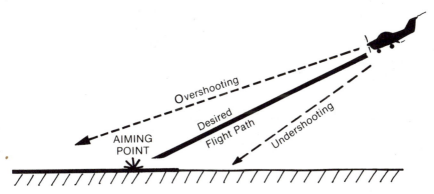

Fig.13a-10. Fly the Aeroplane Down the Desired Approach Path.

CONTROL AIRSPEED WITH ELEVATOR AND FLIGHT PATH WITH POWER.

Power plus attitude equals performance. Any change in power will require a change in pitch attitude if the same airspeed is to be maintained.

- If power is added, raise the nose to maintain airspeed.
- If power is reduced, lower the nose to maintain airspeed.

Keeping the aeroplane in trim during the approach will make your task considerably easier.

If 'Undershooting', Regain the Desired Flight Path.

If the actual approach path projects to a point short of the aiming point (indicated by the aiming point moving up the windscreen and the runway appearing shorter and wider), then regain the desired flight path by adding power and raising the nose to maintain airspeed.

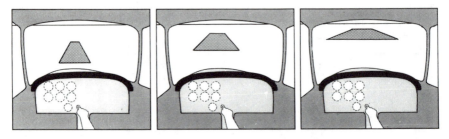

Fig.13a-11. Add Power if Undershooting.

If 'Overshooting', Steepen the Descent.

If the actual approach path projects beyond the aiming point (indicated by the aiming point moving down the windscreen and the runway appearing longer and narrower), steepen the descent by:

- increasing flap and adjusting the pitch attitude; or
- reducing power and lowering the nose to maintain airspeed.

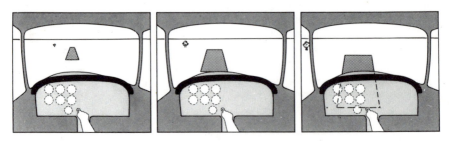

Fig.13a-12. If 'Overshooting', Reduce Power (or Increase Flap).

YOU WILL MAKE MANY CORRECTIONS TO THE APPROACH FLIGHT PATH.

Most flight paths fluctuate between a slight overshoot and a slight undershoot and continual minor corrections are required. Ideally, of course, a Pilot will always be on the perfect slope.

SHORT FINAL.

A good landing is most likely following a good approach, so aim to be well established in a stabilised approach by the time you reach short final. 'Short Final' for a training aeroplane may be thought of as the last 200 ft. Do not allow significant deviations in flight path, tracking or airspeed to develop and de-stabilise the approach.

Carburettor heat will normally be returned to COLD on short final in case maximum power is required for a go-around, however, if icing conditions exist, follow the guidance provided in your Pilot's Operating Handbook.

Throughout the final approach and landing, have your:
- left hand on the control column to control attitude; and
- right hand on the throttle to control power.

THE LANDING.

The landing starts with a round-out commencing at about 20 feet above the runway and does not finish until the end of the landing run. Once you reach the round-out height, forget the aiming point because you will fly over and well past it before the wheels actually touch down. It has served its purpose and you should now look well ahead.

A normal landing is similar to a power-off stall, with touchdown just prior to the moment of stall. This method of landing allows the lowest possible touchdown speed (significantly less than the approach speed), with the Pilot still having full control.

The landing consists of four phases:
- The flare (or round-out);
- The hold-off;
- The touchdown; and
- The landing run.

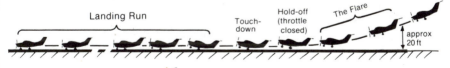

Fig.13a-13. The Landing.

- During the **Flare** (or Round-Out) the power is reduced and the nose is gradually raised to break the rate of descent. The rate of sink is checked with the control column – a high rate of sink requiring a greater backward movement to check it.

- The **Hold-Off** should occur with the aeroplane close to the ground (within a foot or so). The throttle is closed and the control column progressively brought back to keep the aeroplane flying level with the wheels just off the ground. If sinking, apply more back pressure; if moving away from the ground, relax the back pressure. The airspeed will be decreasing to a very low figure, but this is of no concern to you. You should be looking well ahead from the commencement of round-out until touchdown. Any sideways drift caused by a slight crosswind can be counteracted by lowering the into-wind wing a few degrees and keeping straight with rudder.

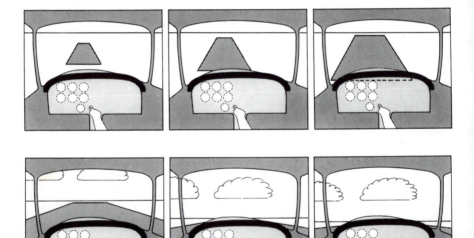

Fig.13a-14. Some Typical Attitudes in the Approach and Round-Out.

- In the **Touchdown,** the main wheels should make first contact with the ground (which will be the case following a correct hold-off). The nose-wheel is kept off the ground using the control column whilst the speed decreases.

- During the **Landing Run** the aeroplane is kept rolling straight down the centreline using rudder and the wings kept level with aileron. The nose-wheel is finally lowered to the ground before elevator control is lost. **Brakes** (if required) may be used once the nose-wheel is on the ground. Remember that the landing is not complete until the end of the landing run when the aeroplane is stationary or at taxying speed.

Judgement in the Flare and Landing.

To assist in judging the height of the wheels above the ground and the rate at which the aeroplane is 'sinking', your eyes should remain 'outside the cockpit' from shortly before commencing the flare (when airspeed is no longer important) until the end of the landing run.

To achieve the best depth perception and develop a 'feel' for just where the main wheels are in relation to the ground, it is best to look ahead and to the left of the aeroplane's nose. If you look too close, the ground will be blurred as it passes by; too far and your depth perception will suffer.

Avoid looking directly over the nose. This makes it difficult to raise the nose in the flare and still retain depth perception, as well as causing a tendency to fly the aeroplane into the ground, resulting in a heavy touchdown (possibly nose-wheel first) and even a bounce.

THE AFTER-LANDING CHECK.

Once clear of the runway, stop the aeroplane, set idle rpm (1,000 to 1,200 rpm as recommended) and complete the After-Landing Check as specified in the Pilot's Operating Handbook. It will contain such items as:
- Flaps *RETRACT;*
- Carburettor heat check *COLD* (hot air may be unfiltered);
- Fuel pump *OFF* (if fitted);
- Throttle friction nut *LOOSEN*

AIRMANSHIP

Fly a neat circuit pattern, *on height* and *on speed.* Commence descent once on base leg to position the aeroplane for a turn that will have you lined up on final at or above 500ft AAL. Use flap as appropriate.

Fly a stabilised approach *on slope, on the extended centreline and on speed.* Maintain firm, positive and tight control of all three.

Although you will be very busy, still remain aware of other aircraft. Keep a good **Look Out.**

AIRWORK 13a —

AIM: To make an approach with power and land into-wind.

(21) Keep straight with rudder and wings level with aileron.

(17) Raise nose to reduce sink rate.

(22) STOP: using brakes as necessary.

(20) Gently lower the nose-wheel onto the runway.

(19) Touch down on main wheels and hold nose-wheel off, keeping straight with rudder.

(18) Progressively raise nose to hold-off just above the runway.

WINDSOCK

Pre-Landing checks commenced

DOWNWIND LEG *LOOK OUT*

—PATH— —OVER—

THE POWERED APPROACH AND NORMAL LANDING

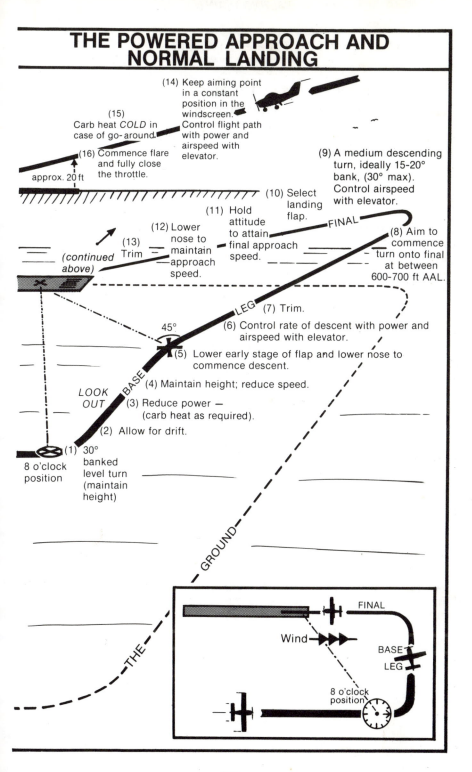

(14) Keep aiming point in a constant position in the windscreen. Control flight path with power and airspeed with elevator.

(15) Carb heat *COLD* in case of go-around.

(16) Commence flare and fully close the throttle.

approx. 20 ft

(9) A medium descending turn, ideally 15-20° bank, (30° max). Control airspeed with elevator.

(10) Select landing flap.

FINAL

(11) Hold attitude to attain final approach speed.

(8) Aim to commence turn onto final at between 600-700 ft AAL.

(12) Lower nose to maintain approach speed.

(13) Trim

(continued above)

LEG

(7) Trim.

(6) Control rate of descent with power and airspeed with elevator.

45°

(5) Lower early stage of flap and lower nose to commence descent.

BASE

(4) Maintain height; reduce speed.

LOOK OUT

(3) Reduce power — (carb heat as required).

(2) Allow for drift.

(1) 30° banked level turn (maintain height)

8 o'clock position

GROUND

THE

FINAL

Wind

BASE

LEG

8 o'clock position

229

FURTHER POINTS

SOME COMMON FAULTS IN THE LANDING.

Every Pilot learns how to land through experience. It is inevitable that many landings will be far from perfect, but progress will be made when you can recognise faults and correct them. Three very common faults are the 'balloon' (when the aeroplane moves away from the ground before touchdown), the 'bounced landing' (when it moves away from the ground after touchdown, perhaps after several touchdowns) and rounding-out too high.

THE 'BALLOON'.

A 'balloon' can be caused by either:
- too much back pressure on the control column; and/or
- too much power left on; and/or
- too high an airspeed; and/or
- a gust of wind.

To correct for a small 'balloon':
- relax some of the back pressure on the control column;
- allow the aeroplane to commence settling (sinking) again;
- when approaching the hold-off height, continue the backward movement of the control column; and
- complete the landing normally.

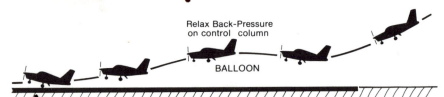

Fig.13a-15. Correcting for a Small 'Balloon'.

A Large Balloon may call for a go-around, certainly for inexperienced Pilots!

As experience is gained, it may be possible to reposition the aeroplane (possibly using power) for the flare and landing, but this uses up lots of runway. The decision to attempt a recovery from a large flare will therefore depend upon the extent of your experience and on the runway length remaining.

THE 'BOUNCED' LANDING.

A 'bounce' can occur due to:
- a failure to round-out sufficiently;
- touching down on the nose-wheel (possibly caused by looking over the nose);
- touching down too fast;
- excessive backward movement of the control column; or
- flaring too high.

An inexperienced Pilot should consider an immediate go-around following a bounce. With experience, however, a successful recovery from a bounce can be made (provided that the runway length is adequate) by relaxing the back pressure and adding power if necessary to re-position the aeroplane suitably to recommence the landing. Avoid pushing the nose down as a second bounced landing may result.

Avoid a second touchdown on the nose-wheel – a series of kangaroo hops down the runway is not a desirable way to land an aeroplane! Prior to touchdown, make sure that the aeroplane is in the correct nose-high attitude (even if it is the second touchdown).

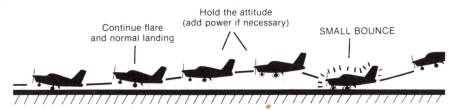

Continue flare and normal landing

Hold the attitude (add power if necessary)

SMALL BOUNCE

Fig.13a-16. Recovery from a Bounced Landing.

ROUNDING-OUT AND HOLDING-OFF TOO HIGH.

The hold-off is best completed within a foot or so of the ground. Any more than this and a landing somewhat heavier than usual will result.

If you recognise before 'impact' that you are too high, add power; this will break the descent rate somewhat and allow a less heavy touchdown. Immediately the wheels touch the ground, close the throttle, otherwise the aeroplane may not decelerate.

'Holding-off' too high usually results from either:
- not looking far enough into the distance, with the result that the ground rushing by is blurred and depth perception is poor; or
- a second attempt to land following a 'balloon' or 'bounce'.

NOTE: The more experienced you become, the less likely you are to find yourself bouncing, ballooning or rounding-out too high. It is part of the average Student Pilot's life to become somewhat of an expert at recovering from mis-judged landings, but this phase will not last too long.

THE GO-AROUND OR BAULKED APPROACH.

If at any stage during the approach or landing you feel uncomfortable about the situation, carry out a baulked approach (also known as a 'go-around', 'overshoot' or 'discontinued approach'). This manoeuvre is covered fully in the next chapter.

TOUCH AND GO LANDINGS.

The number of practice-circuits per hour can be greatly increased by doing 'touch and go' landings. This involves a normal approach and landing and then, when established in the landing run and after the nose-wheel has been gently lowered onto the ground (and with sufficient runway length remaining):
- move the flap to the take-off setting;
- apply full power and perform a normal take-off without having stopped.

In a touch-and-go take-off, the trim may not be set for take-off and so there will be a reasonable amount of forward pressure required on the control column to hold the nose in the climb attitude. Once established in the climb away from the ground, this pressure can be trimmed-off.

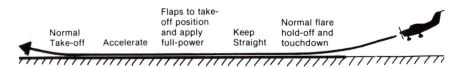

Fig.13a-17. The Touch and Go Landing.

If the landing is mis-judged and excessive runway is used, then bring the aeroplane to a stop as in a normal landing, rather than continue with a doubtful take-off on possibly insufficient runway with a degraded obstacle clearance in the climb-out.

TURBULENCE IN THE CIRCUIT AREA.

Friction affects the air flowing over the earth's surface, leading to the wind at ground level being different to that at circuit height and higher. Any change in wind speed and/or direction is called **windshear** and it can give rise to turbulence.

Uneven heating of the earth's surface will cause vertical convection currents also leading to turbulence. The Pilot experiences this as a bumpy ride with a fluctuating airspeed.

In turbulent conditions, it is advisable to carry a few extra knots on the approach to give you better controllability. A flapless approach should be considered, since it will make the aeroplane more responsive to a power increase (due to the lower drag).

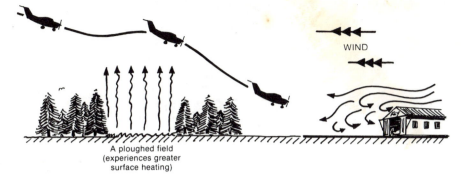

A ploughed field
(experiences greater
surface heating)

WIND

Fig.13a-18. Turbulence has Various Causes.

AVOID WAKE TURBULENCE FROM LARGE AIRCRAFT.

Significant wake turbulence can form behind the wingtips of large aeroplanes flying at high angles of attack (e.g. during take-off and landing). The vortices that cause the turbulence drift downwards and with the wind. **They are best avoided!** Never be afraid to delay a take-off or approach if you suspect wake turbulence from another aircraft could be a problem.

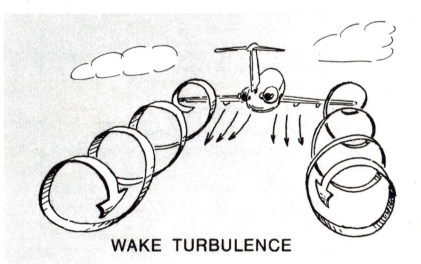

WAKE TURBULENCE

Fig.13a-19. Avoid Wake Turbulence.

13b

THE
GO-AROUND

AIM

To enter a climb from a flapped approach.

CONSIDERATIONS

GOING AROUND FROM AN APPROACH WITH FLAP EXTENDED.

It may be required to perform a go-around for various reasons:
- the runway is occupied by an aeroplane, a vehicle or animals;
- you are too close behind an aeroplane on final approach that will not have cleared the runway in time for you to land;
- the conditions are too severe for your experience (turbulence, windshear, heavy rain, excessive crosswind, etc.);
- your approach is unstable (in terms of airspeed or flight path);
- you are not aligned with the centreline or directional control is a problem;
- the airspeed is far too high or too low;
- you are too high at the runway threshold to touch down safely and stop comfortably within the confines of the runway;
- you are not mentally or physically at ease;
- following a 'balloon' or bounced landing.

FULL FLAP MAKES A CLIMB-AWAY DIFFICULT.

Full flap causes a significant increase in Drag. This has advantages in the approach to land – it allows a steeper descent path, the approach speed can be lower and the Pilot has a better forward view.

Full flap has no advantages in a climb – in fact establishing a reasonable Rate of Climb may not be possible with full flap extended. For this reason, when attempting to enter a climb from a flapped descent, consideration should be given to raising the flap. It should be raised in stages to allow a gradual increase in airspeed as the climb is established.

FLYING THE MANOEUVRE

ESTABLISH A DESCENT.

Follow the usual descent procedures and lower an appropriate stage of flap. Initially, it may be desirable to practise the go-around manoeuvre with only an early stage of flap extended (or perhaps none at all), as would be the case early in the approach to land.

A go-around with full flap requires more attention because of the aeroplane's poorer climb performance.

INITIATING A GO-AROUND.

A successful go-around requires that a positive decision be made and positive action taken. A sign of a good Pilot is a decision to go-around when the occasion demands it – the manoeuvre being executed in a firm, but smooth manner.

The procedure to use is similar to that already practised when entering a climb from a 'clean' descent; **'P-A-T'** – **Power** – **Attitude** – **Trim**. The additional consideration is flap, which will be raised when the descent is stopped and the climb (or level flight) is initiated.

To initiate a go-around, smoothly apply **Full Power** (counting "one-two-three" fairly quickly is about the correct timing to achieve full power) and move the Carburettor Heat to *COLD*.

Be prepared for a strong pitch-up and yawing tendency as the power is applied. These tendencies can be counteracted with forward pressure on the control column and rudder pressure. Hold the nose in the desired climb **attitude** for the flap that is set, and then **trim**. The initial pressure and trim required may be quite significant, especially with full flap.

Keep the aeroplane straight and the wings level.

Full flap creates a lot of drag and only a poor climb performance at a suitable airspeed may be possible. In this case level flight might be necessary whilst the flap setting is initially reduced. If only an early stage of flap is extended, a reasonable climb can be entered without delay.

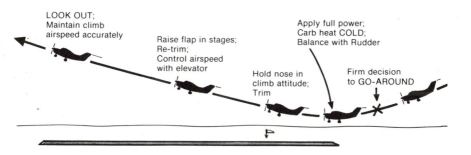

Fig.13b-1. The Go-around.

As the aeroplane accelerates to an appropriate speed, raise the flap in stages and adjust the pitch attitude to achieve the desired speeds and climb performance. Trim as required.

AIRMANSHIP

Make a positive decision to 'go-around', and then perform it decisively.

Exert firm, positive and smooth control over the aeroplane. Firm pressure must be held on the control column and rudder pedals when the power is applied. Correct trimming will assist you greatly.

Ensure that a safe airspeed is reached before each stage of flap is raised.

Once established comfortably in the climb-out, advise the Air Traffic Service Unit (and the other aeroplanes in the circuit) by radio that you are 'going-around'.

It is usual, once established in the go-around, to move slightly to one side of the runway so that you have a view of aeroplanes that may be operating off the runway and beneath you. The 'dead-side' away from the circuit direction is preferred.

Following the go-around, delay turning onto crosswind leg until at least at the upwind end of the runway to avoid conflict in the circuit.

AIRWORK 13b —
THE GO-AROUND

AIM: *To enter a climb from a flapped descent.*

With the aeroplane established in a flapped descent:

(1) Make firm decision to *"GO-AROUND"*;

(2) **P-A-T:**
- **Power** — throttle *OPEN FULLY* (carb heat *COLD*);
- **Attitude** — raise nose to appropriate pitch attitude;
- **Trim**

(3) Raise the flaps slowly, in stages.

(4) Adjust pitch attitude (higher as flaps are retracted) —
and maintain speed with elevator.

(5) Re-trim for the climb-out.

LOOK OUT
during the manoeuvre,
especially in a real
"Go-around" situation.

13c

DEPARTING
AND
JOINING THE CIRCUIT

The aim of this chapter is to become familiar with standard procedures and considerations when:

(1) Departing from the circuit after take-off on a flight to the training area or on a 'cross-country' flight; and

(2) When returning to the aerodrome from outside the circuit area with the intention of joining the circuit for an approach and landing.

CONSIDERATIONS

A lot of your early training will be carried out away from the airfield and this gives you a chance to develop good habits in departing from and rejoining the circuit. It should be noted that procedures for circuit departure and circuit joining vary between countries and, if flying overseas, you should ask to be briefed on them. The procedures here refer to the United Kingdom.

For flights away from the circuit area, you need to be confident of your:

• local area knowledge (landmarks and airspace restrictions);

• circuit departure and rejoining procedures for your particular aerodrome;

• altimetry procedures;

• radio procedures;

• en route or regular checks to ensure satisfactory operation of the aeroplane;

• ability to fly a particular heading using the Magnetic Compass.

DEPARTING THE CIRCUIT.

Follow any Air Traffic Control instructions given. If ATC is not active at your field, then you should plan a circuit departure that will not conflict with other aircraft in the circuit or joining it. Also, follow any special procedures applicable to your field.

An efficient means of departing an uncontrolled field is to extend the upwind leg as you climb out after take-off and then, when clear of other circuit traffic, manoeuvre to set heading for the Local Training Area, (or the first leg of your cross country flight).

Fig.13c-1. Departing the Circuit.

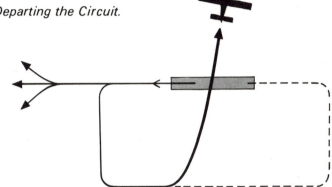

Once outbound to the Local Training Area, ensure that QNH is set in the subscale so that the Altimeter will read height Above Mean Sea Level. Heights of mountains, radio masts, etc., are shown as heights AMSL on charts.

JOINING THE CIRCUIT.

You should always have prior knowledge of the **elevation** of the aerodrome you intend to use.

Approaching the circuit, set the altimeter subscale to QNH or QFE (as advised by the ATS Unit) according to your normal procedure. With QNH set the altimeter will read height Above Mean Sea Level; with QFE set the altimeter will read height Above Aerodrome Level.

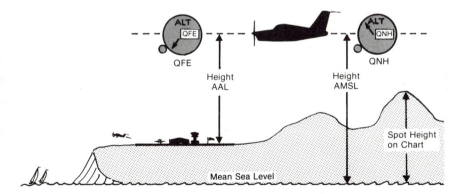

Fig.13c-2. The Altimeter Reads Height AMSL with QNH Set;
Height AAL with QFE Set.

When arriving at an aerodrome, follow any Air Traffic Control instructions given. If ATC is not active at your field, then you should plan an arrival that will not conflict with other aircraft in the circuit and follow any special procedures applicable to the field.

The usual methods of entering the circuit pattern are to either:
- join on downwind leg at circuit height, provided you know the circuit in use; or
- overfly at 2000 ft Above Aerodrome Level, determine the circuit direction (if not already known) from the windsock or signals area, descend to circuit height on the inactive ('dead') side and then join the circuit by crossing the upwind end of the runway.

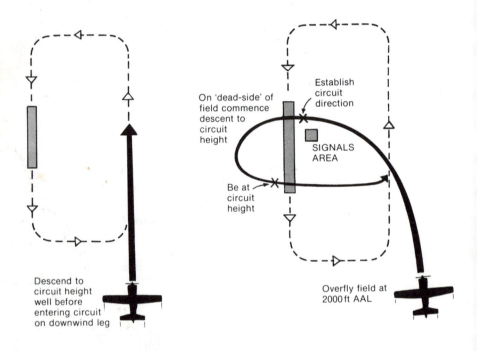

Fig.13c-3. Joining the Circuit.

FURTHER POINTS

FLYING MAGNETIC HEADINGS TO ASSIST IN ORIENTATION (i.e. Where You Are).

In poor visibility you may not be able to see the aerodrome from your local Training Area. You should become familiar with all the local landmarks (e.g. reservoirs, train lines, motorways, towns, villages, churches, other airfields, radio towers, etc.) that will lead you to your home field and you should also know the approximate magnetic heading to steer to return home.

The Magnetic Compass suffers **errors** when the aeroplane is **turning** or otherwise **accelerating** and gives accurate headings only when the aeroplane is in straight flight at a steady airspeed. Therefore, to maintain an accurate magnetic heading, fly straight at a constant speed, making use of external reference points on the horizon if you can.

If a turn is needed, select a new external reference point and turn onto it. Allow the compass to settle down and then check the heading. If you use the Direction Indicator, ensure that it is aligned with the Magnetic Compass during straight and steady flight. Being a gyroscopic instrument, the DI (once aligned correctly) is easier to use than the Compass.

QDM.

Some ATS Units are able to determine the position of an aircraft from its radio transmissions. This is a useful facility in the case of a Pilot being lost and requesting navigational assistance.

In such a situation, the ATS Unit will advise him of the Magnetic Track to the station, known as 'QDM'. The Pilot can then steer a suitable heading to allow for drift due to the wind to make good this track. The QDM may be revised by the ATS Unit, if necessary, as the return to the field progresses.

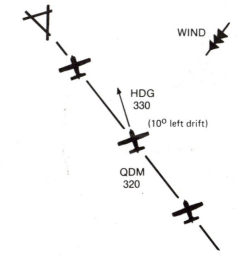

WIND

HDG
330

(10° left drift)

Fig.13c-4. An ATS Unit can provide a QDM (Magnetic Track) to the Aerodrome.

QDM
320

PERIODIC IN-FLIGHT CHECKS OF THE AEROPLANE.

Whilst flying the aeroplane for long periods, either en route, in the Local Training Area, or for prolonged periods in the circuit area, periodic checks (say every 15 minutes or so) should be made of the various systems that are vital to safe flight.

Your Flying Instructor will ensure that you perform the appropriate check, but it will contain items such as are included in this 'FREDA' check:

F – Fuel on and sufficient;
Fuel tank usage monitored;
Mixture Rich or Leaned as required;
Fuel Pump on (if fitted and if required) and fuel pressure checked.

R – Radio frequency correctly selected, volume and squelch satisfactory;
Make any necessary radio calls.

E – Engine: oil temperature and pressure; mixture set correctly; carburettor heat if required; check of other systems (ammeter for electrical system; suction gauge for air-driven gyroscopes if installed).

D – Direction Indicator aligned with Magnetic Compass (only realign the DI with the Magnetic Compass in steady straight and level flight).

A – Altitude checked and subscale setting correct (normally Regional QNH en route, and Aerodrome QNH or QFE if joining a circuit).

It is good airmanship to perform these checks at regular intervals on every flight and also just prior to entering the circuit area (where your workload generally increases).

IMPORTANT RADIO TRANSMISSIONS.

As well as the more usual traffic-type radio calls, you may occasionally hear Distress or Urgency Signals.

MAYDAY MAYDAY MAYDAY
GOLF ALFA BRAVO CHARLIE DELTA – CESSNA ONE SEVEN TWO
ENGINE FAILED
LOSING HEIGHT
INTEND TO LAND FIVE MILES SOUTH OF PONTELAND
PASSING TWO THOUSAND FEET
HEADING TWO EIGHT ZERO
STUDENT PILOT.

The use of the word 'MAYDAY' (an anglicised version of the French 'm'aidez' – 'help me') signifies a **Distress Signal** and it takes priority over all other calls. It informs ATC that the Pilot of the aeroplane registered G-ABCD has a serious problem.

Whilst ATC may offer helpful suggestions, the Pilot in distress must not be distracted from his main duty, which is to fly the aeroplane as safely as possible. Remember that an aeroplane does not need a radio to fly.

PAN PAN PAN
GOLF BRAVO CHARLIE DELTA ECHO – PIPER WARRIOR
UNSURE OF POSITION IN POOR VISIBILITY NORTH OF AIRDRIE
CRUISING TWO THOUSAND FEET
HEADING THREE FOUR ZERO
STUDENT PILOT

The use of the word 'PAN' signifies that this is an **'Urgency Signal'**. It informs ATC that the Pilot of G-BCDE is requesting assistance, but the use of 'PAN' indicates that the aeroplane is in no immediate danger. A 'PAN' call is also appropriate if you wish to report another aeroplane or ship in difficulties.

Hopefully, you will never have to make a Distress or Urgency Call of this nature but, if you do, remember to fly the aeroplane first and make radio calls second. If you hear another Pilot make such a call, then impose a temporary radio silence on yourself for a suitable period to avoid jamming these important transmissions and ATC responses.

13d

THE FLAPLESS APPROACH AND LANDING

AIM

To approach and land without the use of flaps.

CONSIDERATIONS

A flapless approach will be necessary if a failure of any part of the flap system occurs (a rare event) and is advisable in strong and gusty winds. Crosswind landings are often made in such conditions.

Compared to a normal approach and landing with flap, **the main features of a flapless approach and landing** are:
- a flatter flight path requiring an extended circuit;
- a higher approach speed (due to the higher stalling speed);
- a higher nose attitude and poorer forward vision;
- almost no round-out and a longer float (due to less drag) if the hold-off is prolonged before the aeroplane touches down;
- a risk of scraping the tail if the nose is raised too high on touchdown; and
- a longer landing run.

It is most important to control the flight path and airspeed fairly tightly on a flapless approach. As usual, airspeed is controlled with elevator and flight path with power. If too high, reduce power and lower the nose slightly – if the power is already at idle, consider a sideslip to increase the rate of descent and lose height.

A 'clean' wing has less drag than a flapped wing, which means that excess speed takes longer to 'wash-off', i.e. a flapless aeroplane is 'slippery'. This can lengthen the hold-off and float considerably. To avoid using too much runway and also to avoid the risk of scraping the tail, do not prolong the hold-off, particularly on a short runway.

Once the nose-wheel is on the ground, brakes can be used if required.

AIRWORK 13d —
THE FLAPLESS APPROACH & LANDING

AIM: To approach and land without the use of flaps.

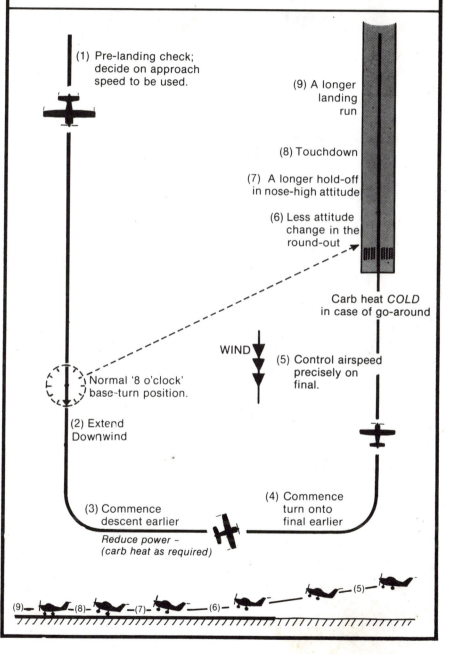

(1) Pre-landing check; decide on approach speed to be used.

(9) A longer landing run

(8) Touchdown

(7) A longer hold-off in nose-high attitude

(6) Less attitude change in the round-out

Carb heat *COLD* in case of go-around

Normal '8 o'clock' base-turn position.

(2) Extend Downwind

WIND

(5) Control airspeed precisely on final.

(3) Commence descent earlier
Reduce power – (carb heat as required)

(4) Commence turn onto final earlier

(9) (8) (7) (6) (5)

13e

THE GLIDE APPROACH AND LANDING

AIM

To carry out an approach and landing without using power.

CONSIDERATIONS

WHY NOT USE POWER IF IT IS AVAILABLE?

The glide approach and landing made without the assistance of power is very good for developing your judgement and is **good practice for emergency forced landings following an engine failure.** On a glide approach, the flight path angle to the runway is controlled mainly by the use of flaps to steepen it.

THE FLIGHT PATH ON A GLIDE APPROACH IS STEEP AND THE ROUND-OUT MORE PRONOUNCED.

On a normal, engine-assisted approach, power is used to control the rate of descent and the flight path to the aiming point on the runway. Without power, the descent rate is greater and the pitch attitude of the aeroplane must be lower to maintain the desired approach speed. The result is a steeper approach path to the runway on a glide approach and so the aeroplane must be positioned higher on final than normal. The lower nose position in the glide, especially with full flap, will mean that the change of pitch attitude required in the round-out will be greater.

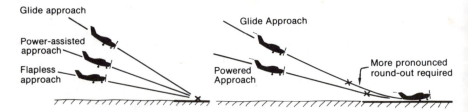

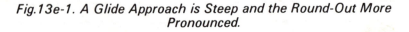

Fig.13e-1. A Glide Approach is Steep and the Round-Out More Pronounced.

FLYING THE MANOEUVRE

FLY A CLOSER BASE LEG FOR A GLIDE APPROACH, ESPECIALLY IN STRONG WINDS.

To achieve a steeper approach path to the aiming point on the runway, make the downwind leg shorter than normal, with base leg being flown closer to the field than in the normal power-assisted approach. In strong wind conditions, the base leg should be flown even closer to the field to ensure that you do not undershoot.

DELAY THE DESCENT FROM CIRCUIT HEIGHT ON A GLIDE APPROACH.

Descent point on base leg should be carefully chosen since the aim is, once power is removed, not to have to use it again. Use the amount of drift required on base to estimate the wind strength on final.

Ideally, if you have judged the closer base leg correctly, descent may be commenced when the runway is at 45° (as for a normal engine-assisted approach, except that the closer base leg means that you are closer to the runway). Initially, aim well down the runway (say 200 metres) so that the aeroplane is definitely higher than normal on approach. The approach can later be steepened with flap, whereas it cannot be flattened without the use of power.

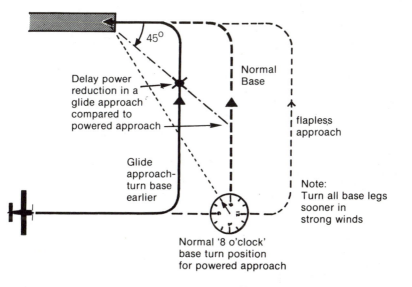

Fig.13e-2. Turn Base Earlier and Delay Descent for a Glide Approach.

USE FLAP TO CONTROL THE FLIGHT PATH, BACKED-UP BY TRACKING MODIFICATIONS.

Use of the flaps in stages will steepen the glide path and bring the aiming point nearer the threshold. It is preferable to be high on approach rather than too low.

If you are high on approach:
- extend some flap, lower the nose to achieve the correct airspeed, and re-trim; or
- widen out the base leg a little; or
- fly S-turns on final (but these can lead to an unstable approach and so are best avoided).

If you are low on approach:
- delay the selection of flap; and/or
- cut in on base leg to shorten final;

If hopelessly low, use power to re-position the aeroplane on the glide path or to go-around and start again.

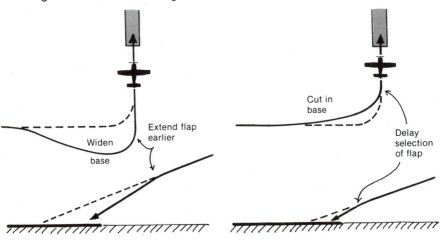

Fig.13e-3. Use Flap to Control Flight Path, Backed-Up by Tracking Modifications.

THE GLIDE PATH WILL STEEPEN IN A TURN.

Avoid steep gliding turns, since the descent rate will increase significantly and stalling speed will increase. Be prepared for an increased rate of descent and a steepening of the glide path in the medium turn onto final.

DO NOT TRY TO 'STRETCH' THE GLIDE.

Do not allow airspeed to get too low by trying to stretch the glide – it will not work! At very low airspeeds the flight path will steepen even though the nose position is high. Raising the flaps is not advisable, since it will initially cause the aeroplane to 'sink'. In a strong headwind, a slightly higher approach speed may give the aeroplane more 'penetration' even though the descent rate is increased. Apply power and go-around if the approach has been badly misjudged.

DELAY THE SELECTION OF LANDING FLAP UNTIL CERTAIN OF REACHING THE FIELD.

If the aiming point with partial flap is 200 metres down the runway, selection of more flap will give you a new aiming point nearer the threshold. Progressively lower the flap as required, but delay the selection of landing flap until you are absolutely certain that the runway will be reached comfortably. In a glide approach, a slight overshoot of the aiming point is preferable to an unrecoverable undershoot.

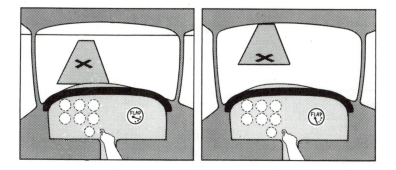

Fig.13e-4. Bringing the Aiming Point Closer by Lowering Additional Flap.

COMMENCE THE FLARE SLIGHTLY HIGHER THAN NORMAL.

With full flap and no power, the glide path will be steep and the nose attitude will be quite low to achieve the desired approach speed. The change of attitude in the round-out will be quite pronounced and a gentle flare should be commenced a little higher than normal. Make the appropriate type of landing applicable to the conditions (crosswind, short-field, soft-field, etc.).

AIRWORK 13e —
THE GLIDE APPROACH AND LANDING

AIM: *To carry out an approach and landing without the use of power.*

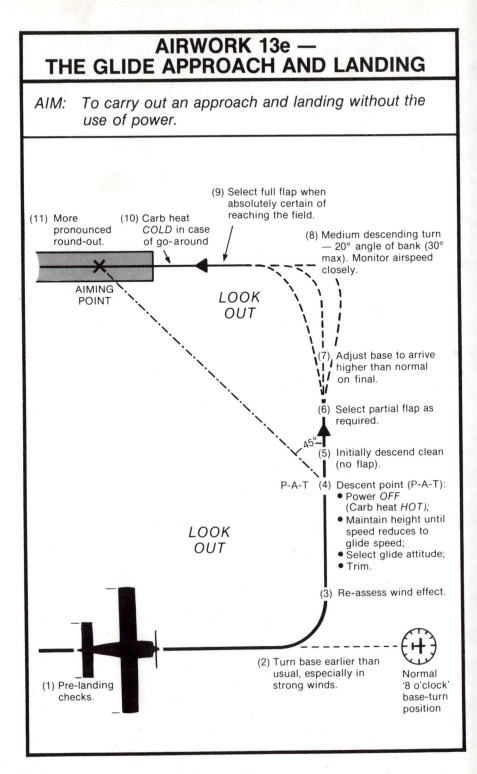

(9) Select full flap when absolutely certain of reaching the field.

(11) More pronounced round-out.

(10) Carb heat *COLD* in case of go-around

(8) Medium descending turn — 20° angle of bank (30° max). Monitor airspeed closely.

AIMING POINT

LOOK OUT

(7) Adjust base to arrive higher than normal on final.

(6) Select partial flap as required.

45°

(5) Initially descend clean (no flap).

P-A-T (4) Descent point (P-A-T):
- Power *OFF* (Carb heat *HOT);*
- Maintain height until speed reduces to glide speed;
- Select glide attitude;
- Trim.

LOOK OUT

(3) Re-assess wind effect.

(2) Turn base earlier than usual, especially in strong winds.

Normal '8 o'clock' base-turn position

(1) Pre-landing checks.

13f

CROSSWIND OPERATIONS

AIM

To take-off, fly a full circuit and land using a runway which is experiencing a significant crosswind component.

CONSIDERATIONS

Not all aerodromes have a runway which is facing into wind on a given day. For this reason, take-offs and landings on runways where there is a crosswind component are frequent events.

Each aeroplane type (from the smallest trainer up to the Airbus and Boeing 747) has a maximum crosswind component specified in the Flight Manual and Pilot's Operating Handbook. If the actual crosswind component on the runway exceeds the limit for the aeroplane and/or what you feel is your own personal limit, then use a different runway (which may even mean proceeding to a different aerodrome).

ESTIMATING THE STRENGTH OF THE CROSSWIND.

The crosswind component on a runway can be estimated from the wind strength and the angle that the wind direction makes with the runway. As a rough guide:

- a wind 30° off the runway heading has a crosswind component of $\frac{1}{2}$ the wind strength;
- a wind 45° off the runway heading has a crosswind component of $\frac{2}{3}$ the wind strength;
- a wind 60° off the runway heading has a crosswind component of $\frac{9}{10}$ the wind strength;
- a wind 90° off the runway heading is all crosswind.

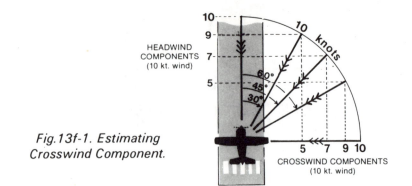

Fig.13f-1. Estimating Crosswind Component.

THE CROSSWIND CIRCUIT.

The crosswind circuit is a rectangular pattern over the ground and is based on the runway used. The standard names are given to the various legs of the crosswind circuit, even though the actual wind effect experienced on each of those legs may differ from what the name of the leg suggests.

Adjustments should be made to allow for the wind effect in the circuit, such as laying-off drift and modifying the turns. Since the wind at circuit height may differ in direction and strength to that at ground level, make use of ground features to assist in correct tracking around the circuit.

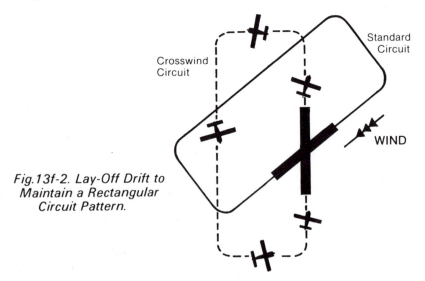

Fig.13f-2. Lay-Off Drift to Maintain a Rectangular Circuit Pattern.

When flying in a crosswind circuit, be aware that other aircraft may be operating in a standard into-wind circuit and that their traffic pattern may conflict with yours.

Aeroplanes in the standard circuit will generally have right-of-way, so the main responsibility for avoiding conflict is with the Pilot in the crosswind circuit. A crosswind circuit might sometimes be flown at a different level to avoid conflict with the standard circuit.

FLYING THE MANOEUVRE
The Crosswind Take-off

CROSSWIND CAUSES A WEATHERCOCKING TENDENCY.

In a crosswind, an aeroplane will tend to weathercock into-wind because of the large keel surfaces behind the main wheels.

Provided that the crosswind limit for your aeroplane is not exceeded, it will be possible **to keep straight with rudder on the ground** without too much difficulty. A crosswind from the right will require left rudder to counteract its effect – more rudder at slow speeds and less as the airflow over the rudder increases. Use whatever rudder is required to keep straight. Holding the nose-wheel firmly on the ground until lift-off will assist in directional control.

CROSSWIND TENDS TO LIFT THE INTO-WIND WING.

A crosswind blowing under the into-wind wing will tend to lift it. Counteract this effect and **keep the wings level with aileron,** i.e. move the control column into-wind. Whilst full deflection might be required early in the take-off run, this can be reduced as the faster airflow increases control effectiveness. You do not have to consciously think of aileron movement; just concentrate on keeping the wings level.

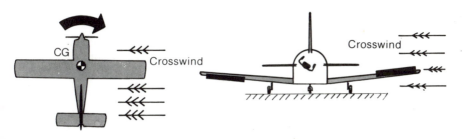

Fig.13f-3. Keep Straight with Rudder; and Wings Level with Ailerons.

THE CONTROLS ARE 'CROSSED' IN A CROSSWIND TAKE-OFF.

A right crosswind, for example, requires right control column and left rudder, i.e. 'crossed controls'. A glance at the windsock before you open the throttle for the take-off run will allow you to anticipate this and position the controls correctly.

As speed increases, the amount of aileron and rudder required will reduce until, at lift-off, there will probably be some rudder still applied, but little or no aileron. There is no need to consciously think about this; just:
- keep straight with rudder; and
- keep the wings level with the ailerons.

A CROSSWIND WILL CAUSE DRIFT AFTER TAKE-OFF, SO LIFT-OFF CLEANLY.

As the aeroplane enters the air mass after lift-off, it will tend to move sideways with it. Any tendency to sink back onto the ground should be resisted to avoid the strong sideways forces that would occur on the undercarriage.

For this reason it is usual, in a cross-wind take-off, to hold the aeroplane firmly on the ground during the ground run (with slight forward pressure on the control column) and then lift-off cleanly and positively with a backward movement of the control column. It may be advisable to delay lift-off until 5 kt or so past the normal rotation speed to achieve a clean lift-off.

Once well clear of the ground, turn into-wind sufficiently to counteract the drift and climb-out normally on the extended centreline of the runway. Any remaining 'crossed-control' should be removed once airborne by centralising the balance ball and keeping the wings level.

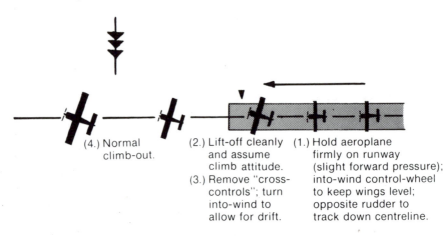

(4.) Normal climb-out.

(2.) Lift-off cleanly and assume climb attitude.

(3.) Remove "cross-controls"; turn into-wind to allow for drift.

(1.) Hold aeroplane firmly on runway (slight forward pressure); into-wind control-wheel to keep wings level; opposite rudder to track down centreline.

Fig.13f-4. The Crosswind Take-Off.

AIRMANSHIP

Maintain an exceptionally good **Look Out** and give way to aeroplanes using the into-wind runway and standard circuit, which may conflict with your circuit.

Exert firm, positive control during this manoeuvre and ensure a clean lift-off.

AIRWORK 13f —
THE CROSSWIND TAKE-OFF

AIM: *To take-off on a runway with a crosswind component (below limit for the aeroplane).*

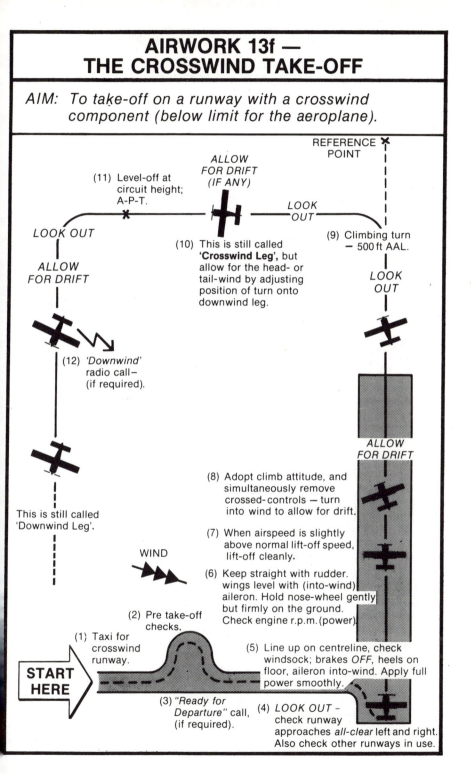

REFERENCE ✖
POINT

*ALLOW
FOR DRIFT
(IF ANY)*

(11) Level-off at circuit height; A-P-T.

*LOOK
OUT*

LOOK OUT

(9) Climbing turn — 500 ft AAL.

*ALLOW
FOR DRIFT*

(10) This is still called **'Crosswind Leg',** but allow for the head- or tail-wind by adjusting position of turn onto downwind leg.

*LOOK
OUT*

(12) *'Downwind'* radio call— (if required).

*ALLOW
FOR DRIFT*

This is still called 'Downwind Leg'.

(8) Adopt climb attitude, and simultaneously remove crossed-controls — turn into wind to allow for drift.

WIND

(7) When airspeed is slightly above normal lift-off speed, lift-off cleanly.

(6) Keep straight with rudder. wings level with (into-wind) aileron. Hold nose-wheel gently but firmly on the ground. Check engine r.p.m. (power).

(2) Pre take-off checks.

(1) Taxi for crosswind runway.

(5) Line up on centreline, check windsock; brakes *OFF*, heels on floor, aileron into-wind. Apply full power smoothly.

START HERE

(3) *"Ready for Departure"* call, (if required).

(4) *LOOK OUT* – check runway approaches *all-clear* left and right. Also check other runways in use.

FLYING THE MANOEUVRE –
The Crosswind Approach and Landing

Ensure that the crosswind component on the selected runway does not exceed the limit for the aeroplane (or your own personal limit).

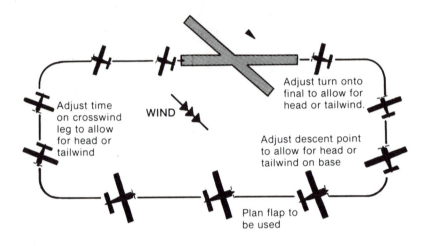

Fig.13f-5. Flying the Crosswind Circuit.

FLY THE CROSSWIND CIRCUIT ACCORDING TO THE WIND.

Planning for the crosswind approach and landing starts early in the circuit, even as you turn onto the 'crosswind' leg shortly after take-off. A following wind will tend to carry you wide, a headwind will hold you in too close. Adjust each leg of the circuit to position the aeroplane suitably with respect to the runway.

ANTICIPATE THE EFFECT OF A TAILWIND ON BASE LEG.

A tailwind on base leg will increase your speed over the ground and tend to carry you past the runway. For this reason, you should show some anticipation and:
- commence descent early;
- begin the turn onto final early; and
- continue the turn onto final beyond the runway heading to allow for drift.

NOTE: If you fly through final, avoid any tendency to overbank (30° bank angle is a reasonable maximum). Simply rejoin final from the other side.

FLYING INTO A HEADWIND ON BASE LEG, YOU CAN AFFORD TO DELAY.

A headwind on base leg will decrease your speed over the ground and so you can:

• delay descent until later than usual;

• delay the turn onto final until almost in line with the runway; and

• stop the turn short of runway heading to anticipate the expected drift.

If you turn too early then you may not reach final and a positive turn will have to be made into-wind to become established. **If you turn too late** and fly through final, fly the runway heading and the wind will most probably carry you back onto the extended centreline. Once in line with the runway, lay-off drift to track directly down final.

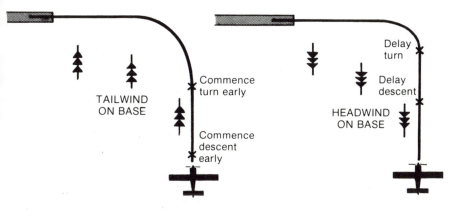

Fig.13f-6. Allow for Wind Effect when Turning Final.

POSITIVELY CONTROL TRACKING DOWN FINAL.

Because of the crab angle needed to maintain the extended centreline, the runway will appear to one side of the nose, but will still look symmetrical. On final for a crosswind landing, you should have a view directly down the runway centreline. If the aeroplane drifts downwind, then make a very definite turn into-wind and regain final without delay; (do not just aim the nose of the aeroplane at the runway!). Keep the aeroplane in balance.

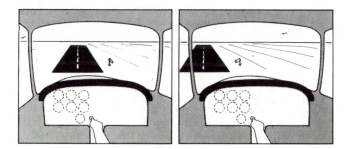

Fig.13f-7. An Into-Wind Approach; and A Crosswind Approach.

Wind strength often decreases near the ground, so continual adjustments to heading will have to be made to maintain your track down final. This is especially the case in strong and gusty conditions.

| *Left of* | *On* | *Right of* |
| *Extended Centreline* | *Extended Centreline* | *Extended Centreline* |

Fig.13f-8. Get Tracking Under Control Early on Final Approach.

Once tracking is under control, then achieving a stabilised descent path and a workmanlike landing becomes a simpler task. It is particularly true in the crosswind case that **a good landing requires a good approach.**

ON A CROSSWIND APPROACH, THE WHEELS WILL NOT BE ALIGNED WITH THE RUNWAY.

Whilst an aeroplane is airborne, the fact that its longitudinal axis is not aligned with the runway is not significant. It would be uncomfortable to touch down in this situation, however, since the wheels are not aligned with the path of the aeroplane down the runway in a crosswind. A strong sideways force on the undercarriage could do structural damage or, in an extreme case, tip the aeroplane over. On touchdown, the wheels should be aligned with the runway direction.

The 'trick' in a crosswind landing is to:
- align the axis of the aeroplane (i.e. the wheels) with the runway direction prior to touchdown; and to
- avoid any sideways drift across the runway before the wheels touch down.

To do this requires the co-ordinated use of the controls (ailerons, rudder, elevator and power). As your skills develop with practice, you will gain great satisfaction from consistently performing good crosswind landings.

There are three accepted crosswind landing techniques:

1. **The Crab Method;**
2. **The Wing-Down Method;**
3. **The Combination Method** (incorporating the best features of each of the above) – a crab approach and a wing-down landing.

Your Flying Instructor will teach you his or her preferred method.

SOME GENERAL CONSIDERATIONS IN CROSSWIND LANDINGS.

Strong crosswinds are often accompanied by gusts and turbulence and consideration should be given to using only partial or zero flap and a slightly higher approach speed than normal to give you better controllability.

The flare in a crosswind landing is normal, but the hold-off should not be prolonged (otherwise sideways drift could develop). The aeroplane should be placed on the ground, wheels aligned with the runway, while the flight controls are effective and with the aeroplane tracking along the runway centreline.

Once on the ground, directional control is more easily achieved if the nose-wheel is lowered onto the ground at an early stage in the landing run. Forward pressure on the control column may be required. The Pilot must retain firm control throughout the whole manoeuvre until the aeroplane is stopped or at least has slowed to taxying speed.

During the landing run:
- keep straight with rudder (the crosswind will cause an into-wind weathercocking tendency);
- lower the nose-wheel to the ground to assist in directional control;
- keep the wings level with progressive into-wind aileron as the airspeed decreases (the crosswind will tend to lift the into-wind wing). Full into-wind control column may be required by the end of the landing run.

AIRMANSHIP

Be firm and positive in your handling of the aeroplane. Be decisive!

Remember that your crosswind circuit may conflict with the standard circuit, so keep a good **Look Out.**

If at any stage you feel distinctly unhappy about the approach and landing, go-around and start again.

Method (i) — The Crab Method of Crosswind Landing

In the Crab Method, drift should be laid-off all the way down final and through the flare. This will keep the aeroplane tracking down the centreline, but the wheels will not be aligned with the landing direction.

Just prior to touchdown, yaw the aeroplane straight with smooth and firm rudder pressure to align its longitudinal axis (and the wheels) with the centreline of the runway. Keep the wings level with ailerons.

The hold-off period should not be prolonged and the main wheels of the aeroplane should be lowered onto the runway before any sideways drift has a chance to develop. Do not allow the nose-wheel to touch first as this could cause a bounce as well as overstress the structure, however the nose-wheel should be lowered to the ground early in the landing run to aid in directional control.

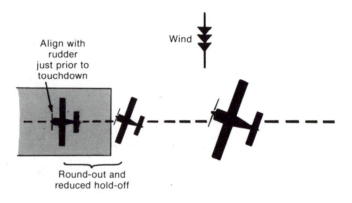

Fig.13f-9. In Crab Method, Align the Aeroplane Just Prior to Touchdown.

THE CRAB METHOD REQUIRES JUDGEMENT AND TIMING.

Judgement and timing are important when using the crab method. Failing to remove the crab angle prior to landing will result in the wheels touching-down sideways; removing it too early will allow a sideways drift to develop and, as well as landing downwind of the centreline, the wheels will still touch down with a sideways component. In both cases the landing will feel heavy and the undercarriage will be unnecessarily stressed. A reasonable touchdown can only be achieved with fine judgement in removing drift and contacting the ground.

If any sideways drift looks like developing before touchdown, it can be counteracted by:
• a small amount of wing-down into wind; and
• keeping straight with rudder.

This is really a lead-in to the next method of crosswind landing, the 'forward slip' or 'wing-down' method.

AIRWORK 13f, Method (i) —
CRAB METHOD OF CROSSWIND LANDING

AIM: To carry out a crosswind approach and landing by crabbing into wind until just prior to wheel contact on touchdown.

The Crab Method of Crosswind Landing

(1) On Final Approach:
- Track down extended centreline by heading aircraft into wind;
- Control airspeed with elevators, flight path with power and keep in-balance with rudder. The wings should be level except when adjusting crab angle.

(2) During the Flare:
- Reduce power and raise nose normally;
- Maintain track above centreline by crabbing into-wind.

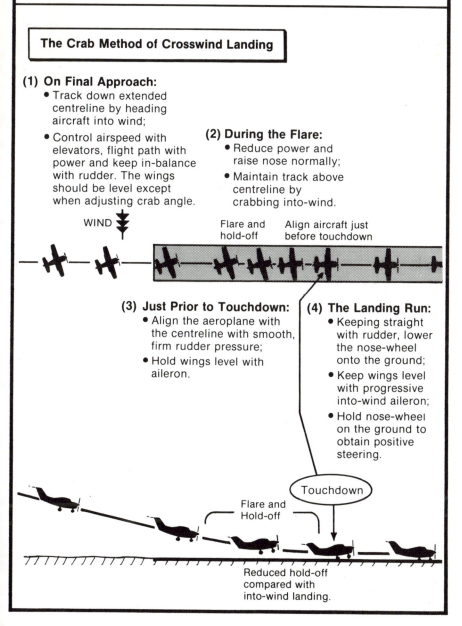

WIND

Flare and hold-off   Align aircraft just before touchdown

(3) Just Prior to Touchdown:
- Align the aeroplane with the centreline with smooth, firm rudder pressure;
- Hold wings level with aileron.

(4) The Landing Run:
- Keeping straight with rudder, lower the nose-wheel onto the ground;
- Keep wings level with progressive into-wind aileron;
- Hold nose-wheel on the ground to obtain positive steering.

Touchdown

Flare and Hold-off

Reduced hold-off compared with into-wind landing.

Method (ii) — The Wing-Down Method of Crosswind Landing

This method can be employed in the **latter stages of the approach.** In some places it is taught to be used all the way down final – in others, just for the last few feet. At this stage of your training we will discuss this method as applying to the last 300 ft or so.

The aeroplane is made to track down the extended centreline, not by crabbing, but by 'slipping'. Because the aeroplane tracks 'forward' towards the runway in a 'slip', this manoeuvre is called a 'forward-slip'.

To initiate a forward-slip:
- lower the into-wind wing a few degrees; and
- apply opposite rudder pressure to stop the aeroplane turning and to align its longitudinal axis with the runway centreline.

The aeroplane is out-of-balance and so the balance ball will not be centred. The stronger the crosswind, the more wing-down and opposite rudder required.

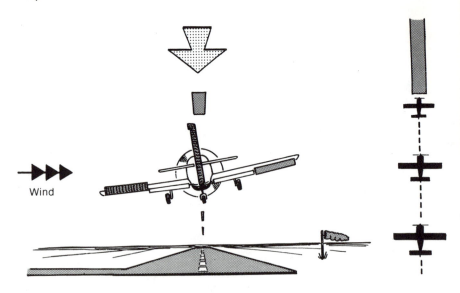

Wind

Fig.13f-10. The 'Wing-Down' or 'Forward-Slip' Crosswind Technique.

If the aeroplane starts to drift downwind across the runway, you have applied insufficient wing-down, so:
- lower the wing a few degrees further; and
- keep straight with rudder.

If the aeroplane starts to slip into-wind across the runway, you have applied too much wing-down, so:
- raise the wing a few degrees; and
- keep straight with rudder.

Stay aligned by varying the amount of wing-down and rudder pressure.
In gusty conditions especially, you will be continually varying the degree of wing-down and opposite rudder to remain aligned with the runway centreline.

TOUCHDOWN IS ON THE INTO-WIND MAIN WHEEL.

The wing-down and opposite rudder is held on through the flare and touchdown, which will occur on the into-wind main wheel. Throughout the manoeuvre the aeroplane will be tracking straight down the runway with its longitudinal axis aligned with the centreline. No sideways drift across the runway should be allowed to develop.

Fig.13f-11. The View from the Cockpit in a Left Crosswind.

When the wing-down main wheel touches first, there may be a tendency for the aeroplane to yaw into-wind, but the aeroplane can easily be kept straight with rudder. The other main wheel will touch down naturally, after which you should lower the nose-wheel onto the ground to allow more positive directional control.

In the landing run:
- keep straight with rudder, holding the nose-wheel on the ground; and
- keep wings level with into-wind aileron – full control wheel into-wind perhaps being required as the aeroplane slows down.

AN ADVANTAGE OF THE WING-DOWN METHOD.

Less judgement and timing is required in the actual touchdown using this method, since the aeroplane is aligned with the runway centreline throughout the flare and hold-off. There is no crab angle to remove and no sideways drift. It is of lesser importance if the aeroplane touches down a little earlier or a little later than expected, whereas with the crab method good judgement in aligning the aeroplane just before touchdown is required.

AIRWORK 13f, Method (ii) —
WING-DOWN CROSSWIND LANDING

AIM: *To land the aeroplane in a crosswind following a wing-down approach.*

The Wing-Down Crosswind Landing.

(1) On Final Approach, Aligned with Runway Centreline:
- Lower the into-wind wing and use rudder to remain aligned with runway centreline;
- Control airspeed with elevators, flight path with power and the track with wing-down (and opposite) rudder.

(2) During the Flare:
- Reduce power and raise nose normally;
- Maintain track along the centreline with wing down and opposite rudder.

(3) The Touchdown:
- The touchdown will be on the into-wind wheel because of that wing being down;
- The other main-wheel will follow naturally.

(4) The Landing Run:
- Keep straight with rudder;
- Lower the nose-wheel to the ground;
- Wings level with into-wind aileron.

Normal Circuit

WIND

Method (iii) — The Combination Method: A Crab Approach Followed By A Wing-Down Landing.

A distinct disadvantage of the wing-down technique being used all the way down final is that the controls are 'crossed' and the aeroplane out of balance (i.e. the ball is not centred). This is both inefficient and uncomfortable.

A more comfortable approach can be flown if drift is laid-off to maintain the extended runway centreline by 'crabbing' and the aeroplane is flown in balance (ball centred, pilot and passengers comfortable).

An easier crosswind landing can be made if, prior to touchdown, the wing-down method is employed by lowering the into-wind wing, simultaneously applying opposite rudder to align the aeroplane. This aligns the wheels with the track along the runway – the amount of 'wing-down' and opposite rudder required being determined by the strength of the crosswind.

At just what point you transfer from the crab to the wing-down depends upon your experience and the wind conditions. Initially, it may be better to introduce the wing-down at about 100 ft Above Ground Level but, as you become more experienced, this can be delayed until in the flare below 20 ft. **In strong and gusty crosswinds,** it is better to introduce the wing-down earlier than in steady conditions.

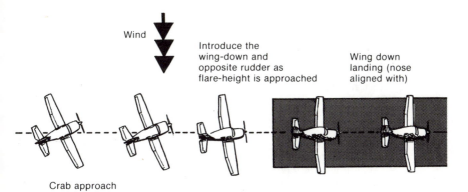

Wind

Introduce the wing-down and opposite rudder as flare-height is approached

Wing down landing (nose aligned with)

Crab approach

Fig.13f-12. The Combination Method of Crosswind Landing.

AIRWORK 13f, Method (iii) —
THE COMBINED CRAB APPROACH AND WING-DOWN CROSSWIND LANDING

AIM: *To land the aeroplane in a crosswind using a crab approach followed by a wing-down landing.*

The Combined Crab Approach and Wing-Down Crosswind Landing.

(1) On Final Approach:
- Adjust the heading to track (crab) down final along the extended runway centreline;
- Keep the wings level, and balance with rudder pressure.

(2) At or Approaching Flare Height (about 20 ft above the runway, or hangar height):
- Use smooth rudder pressure to align aeroplane with runway centreline – and stay aligned.
- Lower the into-wind wing to prevent sideways drift.

(3) During the Flare:
- Reduce power and raise the nose normally;
- Maintain centreline with wing-down and opposite rudder.

(4) The Touchdown:
- Touch down on the into-wind main-wheel and allow the other main-wheel to follow;
- Maintain directional control with rudder.

(5) The Landing Run:
- Keep straight with rudder;
- Lower nose-wheel to runway;
- Wings level with into-wind aileron (full control wheel movement may be required).

Crab approach

WIND

Introduce wing-down and opposite rudder as flare height approached.

Wing-down landing

13g

SHORT-FIELD OPERATIONS

AIM

To operate safely and efficiently out of and into a short-field.

CONSIDERATIONS

WHAT IS A SHORT-FIELD?

A short-field is one at which the runway length available and/or the obstacle-clearance gradients are only just sufficient to satisfy take-off and landing requirements.

REFER TO THE PERFORMANCE CHARTS.

The Take-Off and Landing Performance charts for your aeroplane should be consulted to ensure that a short field in a confined area is indeed adequate for the planned operations under the existing conditions. **An inspection** on foot of the proposed take-off and landing surface and the surrounding area may be necessary. During the inspection remember that the take-off is not complete until all obstacles are cleared in the climb-out, so not only the take-off surface, but also the surrounding area, need to be considered.

CONDITIONS:
Flaps 10°
Full Throttle Prior to Brake Release
Paved, Level, Dry Runway
Zero Wind

TAKEOFF DISTANCE

SHORT FIELD

NOTES:
1. Short field technique as specified in Section 4.
2. Prior to takeoff from fields above 3000 feet elevation, the mixture should be leaned to give maximum RPM in a full throttle, static runup.
3. Decrease distances 10% for each 9 knots headwind. For operation with tailwinds up to 10 knots, increase distances by 10% for each 2 knots.
4. For operation on a dry, grass runway, increase distances by 15% of the "ground roll" figure.

WEIGHT LBS	TAKEOFF SPEED KIAS		PRESS ALT FT	0°C		10°C		20°C		30°C		40°C	
	LIFT OFF	AT 50 FT		GRND ROLL	TOTAL TO CLEAR 50 FT OBS	GRND ROLL	TOTAL TO CLEAR 50 FT OBS	GRND ROLL	TOTAL TO CLEAR 50 FT OBS	GRND ROLL	TOTAL TO CLEAR 50 FT OBS	GRND ROLL	TOTAL TO CLEAR 50 FT OBS
1670	50	54	S.L.	640	1190	695	1290	755	1390	810	1495	875	1605
			1000	705	1310	765	1420	825	1530	890	1645	960	1770
			2000	775	1445	840	1565	910	1690	980	1820	1055	1960
			3000	855	1600	925	1730	1000	1870	1080	2020	1165	2185
			4000	940	1775	1020	1920	1100	2080	1190	2250	1285	2440

Fig.13g-1. Consult the Performance Charts.

FLYING THE MANOEUVRE

THE SHORT-FIELD TAKE-OFF.

There are generally two considerations in the short-field take-off:
1. Use of only a short ground run.
2. Avoidance of obstacles in the take-off and climb-out flight path.

A Short-Field Take-off is a normal take-off, except that you should pay special attention to the following points to achieve the shortest ground run and steepest climb-out:

- take-off as much into-wind as possible;
- use the best flap setting for take-off;
- ensure that the take-off run is commenced from as close to the end of the field as possible;
- apply power with toe-brakes on, holding the control column back to avoid damage to the propeller, releasing the brakes as full power is reached (although, if loose stones could damage the propeller, a rolling start is preferred);
- lift-off at the minimum recommended flying speed with elevator;
- assume the nose attitude for the best-angle climb to avoid obstacles (a higher pitch attitude than in a normal climb);
- at a safe height, when clear of obstacles, enter a normal climb.

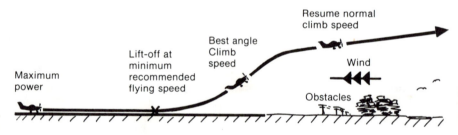

Fig.13g-2. The Short-Field Take-Off.

THE SHORT-FIELD LANDING.

The short-field landing is useful when the chosen landing area:
- is of marginal length (obviously); or
- has a surface of which the Pilot is unsure.

Land as much into-wind as possible, since this will allow a steeper approach and a shorter landing run. Position the aeroplane as for a normal approach – the preferred technique being a power-assisted approach at a low speed, with an aiming point as close to the threshold as practicable. The aeroplane should touch down without much float as soon as the throttle is closed.

Fly as slow an approach speed as is safe. Full flap is preferred if wind conditions are suitable (i.e. no significant gustiness), since this allows a lower approach speed and there will be less float prior to touchdown due to the extra drag. A shorter landing distance will result. **The recommended approach speed** for a short-field landing may be less than for the normal approach (check your Pilot's Operating Handbook), however it should never be less than 1.3 times the actual stall speed to give you a 30% safety buffer over the stall when on approach.

Use power to control the flight path and elevator to maintain airspeed. If you are on 'the Back Side of the Power Curve' (also known as 'the Back Side of the Drag Curve'), then frequent and positive adjustments to power and attitude will be required to maintain the desired flight path and airspeed.

Fly the approach so as to clear all obstacles. Obstacles in the approach path may require that an aiming point further into the short-field be chosen. Having cleared the obstacles, do not reduce power unduly, otherwise a high sink rate and a heavy touchdown may result (since at a low speed the aeroplane has less-effective controls and a reduced flaring capability). Given a choice, a Pilot should select an approach path that does not have obstacles.

If there are no obstacles in the approach path, then a slightly undershooting approach may be considered, with power being used to ensure that you clear the nearside fence safely.

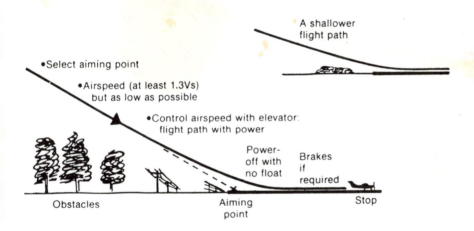

Fig.13g-3. Clear All Obstacles in the Approach Path.

Do not prolong the hold-off and touchdown; then use brakes as required. Aim to cross the airfield boundary at the selected speed and at the minimum height consistent with adequate obstacle clearance and with power on.

Since the nose will be higher than in a normal landing due to the lower speed and higher power, not as great a flare will be required and the round-out should be commenced closer to the ground than normal. Some power should be left on at the commencement of flare if the speed is low; touchdown will follow immediately the throttle is closed.

If a high sink rate develops add power to prevent a heavy landing. Power may be required all the way to the ground – if so, close the throttle as soon as the wheels touch.

If an especially short landing run is required, brakes may be used once all the wheels are firmly on the ground. Early in the landing run, the wings will still be producing some lift and so all of the weight will not be on the wheels. Excessive braking at this time may cause skidding.

13h

SOFT-FIELD OPERATIONS

AIM

To operate safely and efficiently from a 'soft' field.

CONSIDERATIONS

WHAT IS A SOFT-FIELD?

A soft field could be an area which has a soft surface such as sand or snow, a wet grassy surface or a rough surface. A soft-field may be quite long and with no obstacle-clearance problems in the climb-out or approach path. It may also be short, which means the short-field consideration of obstacle-clearance also becomes important. For this exercise, we assume a long take-off surface and no obstacle-clearance problems.

Soft surfaces create extra frictional drag and stress on the wheels and therefore **degrade the acceleration** in the take-off run. The wheels may have a dangerous tendency to 'dig-in'. Only use a soft-field if you are totally satisfied that a safe take-off and/or landing can be made.

FLYING THE MANOEUVRE

THE SOFT-FIELD TAKE-OFF.

The main concern in a soft field take-off is to shift the weight from the wheels to the wings as soon as possible and achieve a short ground run. Consequently **optimum flap** and **maximum power** should be used.

During the take-off run, **keep the weight off the nose-wheel** with the control column held well back. Lift the aeroplane off the ground as soon as possible (at a lower speed than in a normal take-off) and accelerate to climb speed close to the ground. The aeroplane can fly in 'ground effect' at a lower speed than when it is well away from the ground. For this reason, do not climb more than about 10 ft above the ground until a safe flying speed is attained, at which time a normal climb-out can proceed.

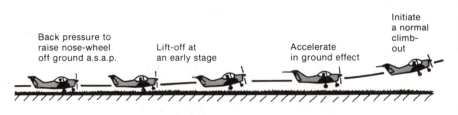

Fig.13h-1. The Soft-Field Take-Off.

THE SOFT-FIELD LANDING.

Since the tendency on a soft-field is for the nose-wheel (and, to a lesser extent, the main wheels) to dig in, the aim should be to:
• land as slowly as possible; and
• hold the nose up as long as possible during the landing roll.

Use Full Flap if Conditions Permit. Full flap reduces the stalling speed and so touchdown can be made at a very low speed. If field length is not a problem, a normal approach can be flown, with a slightly modified round-out. Some power can be left-on in the flare as the nose is raised higher than normal in a prolonged hold-off. The higher the nose attitude and the lower the speed on touchdown the better.

Fig.13h-2. The Soft-Field Landing.

14

FIRST SOLO

Intentionally Blank

14

FIRST SOLO

To fly solo and be the Pilot-in-Command of an aeroplane for the first time.

FLYING THE MANOEUVRE

First solo is a great experience! When your Instructor steps out of the aeroplane and leaves you to your first solo flight you are being paid a big compliment. You may feel a little apprehensive, but remember that he is trained to judge the right moment to send you solo. He will have a better appreciation of your flying ability than anybody (including you).

Fly your first solo circuit in the same manner as you flew those circuits before he stepped out. The usual standards apply to your take-off, circuit and landing. Maintain a good look out, fly a neat circuit, establish a stabilised approach and carry out your normal landing. Be prepared for a better performance of the aeroplane without the weight of your instructor on board. If at any stage you feel uncomfortable, go-around.

If an emergency, such as engine failure, occurs – (and this is an extremely unlikely event) – carry out the appropriate emergency procedure that you have been well trained in. Your Flying Instructor, when he sends you solo, not only considers you competent to fly a circuit with a normal take-off and landing, he also considers you competent to handle an emergency.

One take-off, circuit and landing will admit you to the 'Fraternity of Pilots'.

CONSOLIDATION FLYING.

Further refinement and consolidation of the basic skills that you now possess will follow, with Solo periods being interspersed with Dual periods. The Dual flights allow your Flying Instructor to refine your skills and develop them further. In the solo periods you will develop the skills of a Captain, making your own decisions and acting upon them.

Your initial solo flights will be in the circuit area, practising take-offs and landings, but, quite soon, you will be proceeding solo to the Local Training Area to practise other manoeuvres.

Intentionally Blank

15

ADVANCED TURNING (STEEP TURNS)

15a

THE
STEEP LEVEL TURN

AIM

To perform a steep level turn, maintaining constant height and airspeed.

CONSIDERATIONS

A steep turn is a turn in which the bank angle exceeds 45°. It is a high performance manoeuvre which requires good co-ordination and positive control.

A STEEP LEVEL TURN REQUIRES INCREASED LIFT.

In straight and level flight, the Lift produced by the wings balances the Weight of the aeroplane. In turns, the Lift force is tilted and consequently the Lift generated by the wings must be increased to provide not only a vertical component to balance the Weight but also a horizontal component (known as the centripetal force) to pull the aeroplane into the turn. In a 60° banked turn, for example, the Lift produced must be double the Weight if height is to be maintained.

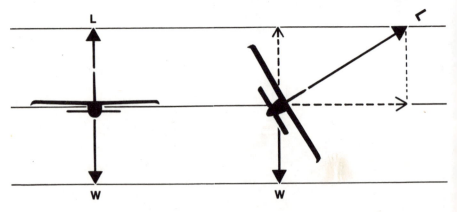

Fig.15a-1. A Steep Level Turn Requires Increased Lift.

The increased Lift in a turn is generated by back pressure on the control column which increases the angle of attack. The back pressure required to maintain height is quite significant in a steep turn.

THE LOAD FACTOR AND STALLING SPEED INCREASE SIGNIFICANTLY IN A STEEP TURN.

When the Pilot feels an increased g-loading in a turn then he is simply experiencing an increased Load Factor (which is the ratio 'Lift/Weight'). The normal load factor is one (1) when the aeroplane is either stationary on the ground or in steady straight and level flight. The Pilot experiences this as '1g', i.e. his normal weight. In a 60° banked turn the Load factor is 2 and the Pilot will feel twice his normal weight because the Lift generated by the wings is now double the aeroplane's Weight. The human body soon becomes accustomed to these 'g-forces'.

The steeper the turn, the greater the angle of attack required to generate sufficient Lift, and consequently the stalling angle of attack will be reached at a higher airspeed than when the wings are level. In a 60° banked turn, for example, the stalling speed is some 40% greater (e.g. an aeroplane which stalls at 50 kt straight and level will stall at 70 kt when pulling 2g).

The greater the load factor, the higher the stalling speed. Feeling a g-force is a signal that the aeroplane structure is under additional stress and that stalling speed has increased. **At any hint of stalling in a steep turn,** some of the back pressure on the control column should be released. This will reduce the angle of attack and move the wings away from the stalling angle. Reducing the bank angle or adding power (if there is any in reserve) will also assist in avoiding a stall in this situation.

DRAG INCREASES SIGNIFICANTLY IN STEEP TURNS.

The greater angle of attack used to generate the increased Lift required in a steep turn also creates additional Induced Drag. This must be balanced by increased Thrust if the aeroplane is not to slow down. Whereas it was acceptable to lose a few knots in medium turns, it is very important to maintain airspeed in steep turns because of the higher stalling speed.

As well as co-ordinating the use of aileron, rudder and elevator (as in medium turns) power now becomes an added ingredient as the **maximum achievable bank angle in a steady steep turn** is determined by the amount of power available.

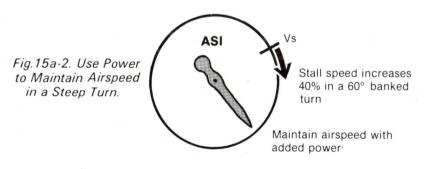

Fig.15a-2. Use Power to Maintain Airspeed in a Steep Turn.

ASI

Vs

Stall speed increases 40% in a 60° banked turn

Maintain airspeed with added power·

FLYING THE MANOEUVRE

The g-forces in a 45° steep turn are nowhere near as great as in a 60° banked turn. For this reason, you may find it easier to practise steep turns at a 45° bank angle initially, progressing to 60° bank angle turns later on in your training.

Prior to practising steep turns, your Training Organisation may require you to carry out the pre-aerobatic **'HASELL'** check (as described in Chapter 10a).

ROLLING INTO A STEEP LEVEL TURN.

Trim the aeroplane for straight and level flight at the desired airspeed and height. **Look Out** for other aeroplanes and select a reference point on the horizon for the roll-out.

Roll into the turn just as you would into a normal medium turn except that as the bank angle increases through 30°:
- smoothly add power;
- progressively increase the back pressure on the control column;
- adjust the bank angle and back pressure to place the nose in the correct position relative to the horizon; and
- balance with rudder.

Do not apply too much back pressure entering the turn or the aeroplane will climb – just gradually increase it as you steepen the bank. The back pressure required in a steep turn will probably be much greater than you had anticipated. Do not trim as the turn is only a transient manoeuvre.

MAINTAINING A STEEP LEVEL TURN.

The 'secret' of flying an accurate steep level turn is to hold the nose in the correct position relative to the horizon (even if it takes a lot of back pressure), ensuring the airspeed is maintained by adding sufficient power.

Keep a very good **Look Out** during the steep turn to monitor the nose position and the approach of your roll-out reference point, as well as to look for other aircraft, especially in the direction of your turn.

An occasional glance at the instruments will confirm that the turn is proceeding satisfactorily, but do not sacrifice your outside reference by concentrating on the instruments. In just a second or two you can quickly check:
- **Height** on the Altimeter and Vertical Speed Indicator;
- **Airspeed** on the Air Speed Indicator;
- **Bank Angle** on the Attitude Indicator;
- **Balance** on the Balance Indicator (ball in the centre).

Adjusting the bank angle and nose position is a continuing requirement throughout the steep turn and keeps the Pilot quite busy. That is why it is such a good training manoeuvre! The sooner the corrections are made, the smaller they can be and the better the steep turn.

If height is being gained in the steep turn, it means that the vertical component of the Lift force is too great and so either:
- steepen the bank angle; and/or
- relax some of the back pressure.

If height is being lost then the vertical component of the Lift force is insufficient. To regain height:
- reduce the bank angle slightly;
- raise the nose with back pressure; and
- once back on height, reapply the desired bank angle and back pressure.

If the nose drops below the horizon during a steep turn, trying to raise the nose with back pressure will only tighten the turn rather than raise the nose. Should the height loss rapidly increase, roll out to straight and level, climb back to your desired height and start again.

STALL BUFFET.

If the aeroplane turns through more than 360°, you may in fact strike your own slipstream and feel some turbulence. This is not the stall buffet, but the sign of a well-executed steep turn. If, however, the stall buffet is felt, **then release some of the back pressure** to reduce the angle of attack before the stall actually occurs. To avoid losing height, you will have to decrease the bank angle slightly as back pressure is released.

When practising steep turns aim to achieve an accuracy of ±200 ft and ±10 kt initially and then, as your training progresses, accept no variations at all.

Fig.15a-3. Typical Nose Attitudes while Flying the Manoeuvre.

ROLLING-OUT OF A STEEP TURN.

This is the same as rolling-out of a medium turn, except that:
- greater anticipation is required to roll-out on your reference point;
- there is a great deal more back pressure to be released, otherwise height will be gained; and
- power must be reduced to cruise power.

Remember to keep the aeroplane in balance with rudder.

Concentration is required in the roll-out, especially to avoid gaining height since you may be a little reluctant to relax all of the back pressure. Rolling-out of a 45° banked turn, relaxing back pressure is usually sufficient. Rolling-out of a 60° banked turn the release of back pressure is so great that it may feel as though you have to push the control column forward.

Do not forget to reduce the power as you roll-out otherwise airspeed will rapidly increase.

After some practice at steep turns to the left and right, your Flying Instructor may suggest that you roll from a steep turn one way immediately into a steep turn the other way.

AIRMANSHIP

Practise steep turns in an appropriate area and keep a very good **Look Out** for other aircraft.

Note various landmarks that will assist in orientation during and after the turn. It is easy for an inexperienced Pilot to become disoriented in steep turns which involve large changes of heading.

Handle the power smoothly and monitor the gauges to ensure engine limitations are not exceeded.

Exert smooth, but firm, control over the aeroplane.

AIRWORK 15a —
STEEP LEVEL TURNS

AIM: To perform a steep level turn, maintaining constant height and airspeed.

(1) Entry:
- Complete the *'HASELL'* check;
- *LOOK OUT;*
- Select a reference point on the horizon;
- Roll-on bank with aileron;
- Balance with rudder;
- Apply sufficient back-pressure on control column to maintain height;
- Add power progressively to maintain airspeed.

(2) Maintaining the Steep Turn:
- *LOOK OUT;*
- Maintain bank with ailerons;
- Maintain balance with rudder;
- Maintain height with elevator;
- Maintain airspeed with power;
- Notice increased downwards view.

- If Height is Gained:
- Reduce Back Pressure and consider steepening the angle of bank temporarily (do not over-bank).

- If Height is Lost:
- Reduce angle of bank;
- Raise nose with increased back pressure; and then
- Re-apply bank.

(3) Roll-out:
- *LOOK OUT;*
- Locate roll-out reference point (anticipate by 30°).
- Roll-off bank with ailerons;
- Balance with rudder;
- Release elevator back pressure to maintain height;
- Progressively reduce power to maintain airspeed.

FURTHER POINTS

MAXIMUM PERFORMANCE TURNS.

A maximum performance steep level turn at a particular airspeed is flown like a normal steep turn except that power is progressively applied as the bank angle is increased, until maximum power is reached.

The ability to maintain height and airspeed in this manoeuvre depends upon the amount of power available. For most training aeroplanes, the performance limit is reached at about 65° of bank.

Turning performance is measured in terms of:
- the rate of turn (the greater, the better); and
- the radius of turn (the smaller, the better).

At a constant airspeed, turning performance increases with bank angle. **At a constant bank angle,** turning performance is better at low airspeeds. Therefore, the best turning performance can be achieved at a relatively low airspeed and a high bank angle (providing the aeroplane is not stalled or the airframe overstressed).

DO NOT OVERSTRESS THE AIRFRAME IN A STEEP TURN.

The Lift which can be generated by the wings with full rearward movement of the control column is far greater at high airspeeds than at low airspeeds and results in greater load factors occurring. For example, pulling the control column fully back at 150 kt will increase the g-loading considerably more than at 50 kt. **At high airspeeds,** therefore, there is a danger of overstressing the airframe by exceeding the maximum allowable load factor (+3.8g for most training aeroplanes).

MANOEUVRING SPEED (V_A).

Large elevator deflection at high airspeed can cause the wings to generate so much lift that the aeroplane's limit-load-factor is exceeded without the wings reaching their stalling angle of attack. **At low airspeeds** the aeroplane will stall before the limit-load-factor is reached, i.e. the airframe is 'protected' aerodynamically.

The airspeed at which maximum elevator deflection causes the stall to occur right at the limit-load-factor is called the Manoeuvring Speed (V_A). **The best aerodynamic turning performance** can be achieved at this speed provided sufficient power is available.

For most training aeroplanes the engine performance is the limiting factor in maximum performance steep turns.

V_A for maximum weight is specified in the Flight Manual. **At airspeeds less than the Manoeuvring Speed** (V_A), full elevator deflection will not overstress the airframe – **above V_A it will.** At lesser weights, when stalling speed is lower, the actual V_A will be a few knots less than that published.

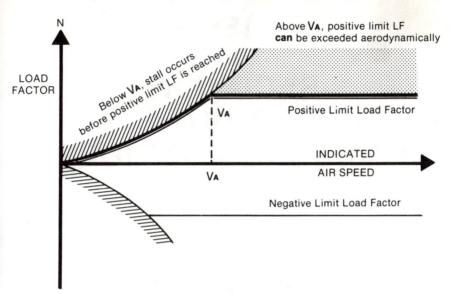

Fig.15a-4. Airspeed (V) versus Allowable Load Factor (n).

15b

RECOVERY FROM UNUSUAL ATTITUDES

AIM

To recognise and recover from an unusual aeroplane attitude which has developed.

CONSIDERATIONS

Whilst a steep turn should be a straightforward manoeuvre, it is possible that early in your steep turn training some unusual attitudes may develop. It would be appropriate for you to re-read Sections 10 and 11 at this stage.

WHAT IS AN 'UNUSUAL ATTITUDE'?

The two fundamental unusual attitudes are:
- nose-high with a decreasing airspeed; or
- nose-low with an increasing airspeed.

Unusual attitudes generally result from some form of mis-handling by the Pilot. For example, the relatively low power available in most training aeroplanes will not allow a steady climb to be maintained in a steep turn. A 'nose-high/low speed' unusual attitude can result if the nose is raised in an attempt to achieve a steep climbing turn.

FLYING THE MANOEUVRE

NOSE-HIGH AND A STEEP BANK — BEWARE OF A STALL OR A SPIN.

If the nose is well above the horizon and the speed is low and/or decreasing, a stall is a possibility.

To recover from a 'nose-high/low airspeed' unusual attitude **following a stall:**
- ease the control column forward;
- apply sufficient rudder to prevent further yaw;
- apply maximum power; and
- when the airspeed increases as the wings become unstalled, level the wings with co-ordinated use of rudder and ailerons, ease out of the descent and resume the desired flight path.

If a full spin develops from a mishandled steep turn, probably as a result of the nose being raised too high and the speed allowed to drop too low, then recover using the recommended **spin recovery**. The technique is:
- throttle closed, flaps up and ailerons neutral;
- verify the spin direction on the Turn Co-ordinator;
- apply full opposite rudder;
- **pause;**
- progressively ease the control column forward (to unstall the wings) until the rotation stops;
- centralise the rudder once the rotation has stopped;
- level the wings and gently ease out of the ensuing dive; and
- as the nose rises through the horizon, add power and climb away.

NOSE-LOW AND A HIGH AIRSPEED — BEWARE OF AN OVERSPEED OR A SPIRAL DIVE.

If the nose is low, especially if power is applied, exceeding the **maximum allowable airspeed** (VNE – shown on the ASI as a red line) is a danger as this could overstress the aeroplane. A steep bank angle and a low nose attitude may develop into a spiral dive.

To recover from a 'nose low/high airspeed' unusual attitude:
- reduce power (close the throttle);
- roll the wings level with aileron and rudder;
- ease out of the ensuing dive; and
- as the nose passes through the horizon, re-apply power and climb away.

A 'nose low/increasing speed' attitude, if not corrected, can develop into a spiral dive, which can be recognised by:
- a high g-loading;
- a rapidly increasing airspeed (that distinguishes it from a spin); and
- a rapid loss of height, probably with the rate of descent increasing.

The recovery from the spiral dive is the same as above, but avoid excessive elevator deflection in easing out of the dive, otherwise the limit load factor for the aeroplane could be exceeded, overstressing the airframe. It is permissible to use the ailerons as firmly as needed to roll the wings level.

AIRWORK 15b —
RECOVERY FROM UNUSUAL ATTITUDES

AIM: *To recognise and recover from an unusual aeroplane attitude which has developed.*

(1) 'Nose High/Low Airspeed'
— Recognised primarily from ASI.

Recovery:
- Simultaneously ease control column forward and roll wings level;
- Add power.

(If close to stall, do not use aileron until certain the wings are un-stalled).

(2) 'Nose Low/High Airspeed'
— Recognised primarily from Air Speed and Vertical Speed Indicators.

Recovery:
- Reduce power;
- Roll wings level with aileron and balance with rudder;

- Ease out of dive;
- Add power as nose passes through the horizon.

15c

THE STEEP DESCENDING TURN

AIM

To perform a steep turn whilst descending.

CONSIDERATIONS

A steep descending turn can be made in:
- a glide; or
- a powered descent.

FLY FASTER IN A STEEP DESCENDING TURN BECAUSE OF THE INCREASED STALLING SPEED.

It is usual to increase the flying speed as a steep descending turn is commenced to retain an adequate safety margin above the stalling speed (which increases during a turn). Typical speed increases are:
- 10 kt for a 45° steep descending turn; and
- 20 kt for a 60° steep descending turn.

In a steep gliding turn, the rate of descent will increase markedly. It can be controlled by reducing the bank angle or by adding power.

FLYING THE MANOEUVRE

A steep descending turn is flown like a steep level turn except that the **increased airspeed is maintained with the elevator.**

The nose will tend to drop in a descending turn and so, even though the nose position is lower to achieve a higher airspeed, some back pressure on the control column will be needed to stop it dropping too far.

If airspeed becomes excessive:
- ease-off the bank angle with ailerons;
- raise the nose with elevator; and
- re-establish the desired steep turn.

The lack of slipstream in a glide will mean that more rudder is required when rolling in one direction than when rolling in the other.

Simply exerting increased back pressure on the control column in a steep descending turn may tighten the turn and increase the g-loading beyond acceptable limits. A spiral dive may also result if attitude and airspeed are not monitored.

AIRMANSHIP

Be aware of your proximity to the ground since the rate of descent will be quite high in a gliding steep turn.

Allow the airspeed to increase and **maintain** a safe margin above the stall, but do not let a spiral dive develop.

Keep a very good **Look Out,** especially below.

AIRWORK 15c —
STEEP DESCENDING TURNS

AIM: To perform a steep turn whilst descending.

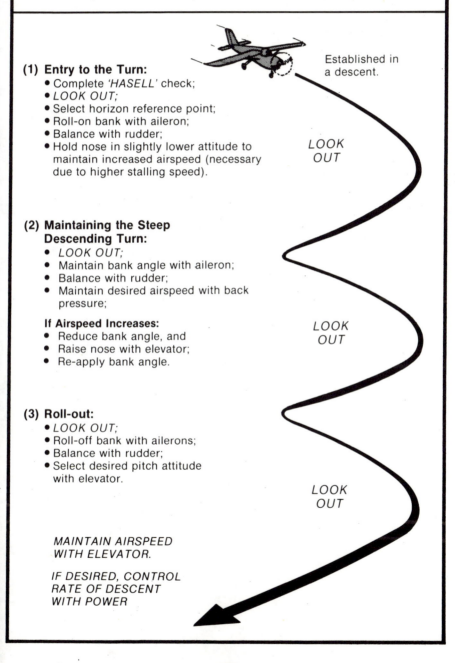

(1) Entry to the Turn:
- Complete *'HASELL'* check;
- *LOOK OUT;*
- Select horizon reference point;
- Roll-on bank with aileron;
- Balance with rudder;
- Hold nose in slightly lower attitude to maintain increased airspeed (necessary due to higher stalling speed).

Established in a descent.

LOOK OUT

(2) Maintaining the Steep Descending Turn:
- *LOOK OUT;*
- Maintain bank angle with aileron;
- Balance with rudder;
- Maintain desired airspeed with back pressure;

If Airspeed Increases:
- Reduce bank angle, and
- Raise nose with elevator;
- Re-apply bank angle.

LOOK OUT

(3) Roll-out:
- *LOOK OUT;*
- Roll-off bank with ailerons;
- Balance with rudder;
- Select desired pitch attitude with elevator.

LOOK OUT

MAINTAIN AIRSPEED WITH ELEVATOR.

IF DESIRED, CONTROL RATE OF DESCENT WITH POWER

Intentionally Blank

16

LOW LEVEL FLYING

16

LOW LEVEL
FLYING

AIM

1. To fly the aeroplane safely at a low level.

2. To observe the misleading visual effects caused by a strong wind at low levels.

CONSIDERATIONS

WHY FLY AT A LOW LEVEL?

A low level is generally considered to be 500 ft Above Ground Level or lower. Low level flying may be necessary:
- **in poor weather conditions** such as low cloud and/or poor visibility;
- **to inspect a field** in preparation for a forced landing with power available;
- in the **VFR Entry/Exit Lanes** which provide access to certain aerodromes beneath airspace reserved for Instrument Flight Rules (IFR) operations.

PILOT RESPONSIBILITY IN LOW LEVEL FLYING.

Do not fly within 500 ft of any person, building, animal, etc., except when taking-off or landing. There are other restrictions regarding flight over built-up areas (1500 ft) and large open-air gatherings (3000 ft), which are covered in Aviation Law – Volume 2.

Low cloud or some other unforeseen situation may force you below the minimum legal levels. As a visual Pilot, you are not qualified to enter cloud and this should be avoided at all costs. If low cloud is encountered, it is better to fly slowly beneath it closer to the ground and turn back as soon as possible, rather than to enter it. This is because, in cloud, all visual contact with the ground and the horizon will be lost and the consequences for an untrained Pilot are usually fatal!

Be aware that **radio communication,** which depends on 'line-of-sight' transmission, may be poor at low levels.

Around the country there are some areas which have been set aside for local training. Other aircraft may be operating there at the same time as you, so maintain a good **Look Out** for them (and for obstructions such as TV masts and transmission wires). Do not forget that balloons, helicopters, sailplanes, hang-gliders and micro-light aircraft may also be operating at low levels.

OBSTACLE-CLEARANCE WHEN LOW FLYING.

A close study of maps of the area is advisable prior to flight – special attention being given to the height of the ground above sea level, the nature of the terrain and the position of obstacles.

Flying at a low level the Pilot has a limited field of vision and surface features move rapidly through it. The Pilot needs to **anticipate any features and recognise them quickly.** Obstacles such as overhead cables, radio masts, chimneys and rising ground deserve particular attention. These can be noted prior to commencing low level flight.

Aeronautical charts generally show only obstacles higher than 300 ft Above Ground Level (AGL). If you fly 500 ft higher than the highest spot height shown on the chart for the area, your obstacle-clearance may in fact be only 200 ft. Flying at 300 ft you may have no obstacle-clearance at all, especially if altimeter errors have crept in. Charts specify terrain and obstacles in terms of height Above Mean Sea Level. If you are using a map to determine vertical clearance from obstacles, then QNH should be set in the subscale so that the Altimeter reads height AMSL.

Some commonsense rules for obstacle-clearance are:
- anticipate rising ground and climb early to remain at the desired height above it;
- ensure that the aeroplane can actually out-climb the rising ground, especially if a wind is blowing down its slopes;
- avoid areas of rising ground associated with a lowering cloud base;
- always be prepared to turn back.

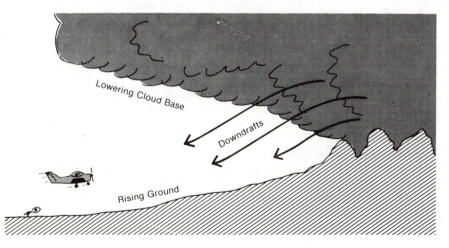

Fig.16-1. Avoid a Lowering Cloud Base and Rising Ground.

SELECT GROUND FEATURES SUITABLE FOR LOW LEVEL FLYING.

Features with vertical characteristics are good landmarks for low level navigation. Hills, peaks, high monuments, factory chimneys and radio or television masts fall into this category.

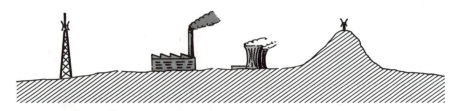

Fig.16-2. Choose Landmarks Suitable for Low Level Flight.

STRONG WINDS AT LOW LEVELS MAY CAUSE MISLEADING VISUAL EFFECTS.

When flying at high levels, the Pilot is less aware of his passage over the ground, which may seem to be in slow-motion. In low level flight, however, both **speed and drift are very obvious.**

The aeroplane flies in the air mass – its Indicated Air Speed having much more significance than its ground speed, and balanced flight being achieved when the ball is centred (even if it appears to be slipping or skidding over the ground because of a crosswind).

A tailwind causes a false impression of high speed. An aeroplane flying with an airspeed of 70kt in a 25kt tailwind will have a ground speed of 95 kt. The nearness of the ground will give an impression of speed much greater than 70kt, but the Pilot must resist any temptation to slow down. Reducing the groundspeed to what feels like 70 kt would require an airspeed of 45 kt, which may be below the stalling speed. **Check the airspeed on the ASI regularly.**

In a headwind the reverse is the case. The groundspeed is lower than the airspeed, giving an impression of low (rather than high) speed. Since there is no temptation to slow down, this situation is not as dangerous as the former one.

Sideways drift over the ground due to a crosswind causes false impressions of balance. In strong crosswinds, especially if the airspeed is low, the aeroplane will experience a large drift angle over the ground even though it is in-balance.

The false impression of slip or skid, especially when turning, can tempt an inexperienced Pilot to use rudder to counteract it. This would place the aeroplane out-of-balance and degrade its performance. **Confirm balance with the Balance Ball.** Since airspeed tends to fall in a turn, it is also good airmanship when flying low to have your hand on the throttle to adjust the airspeed if necessary.

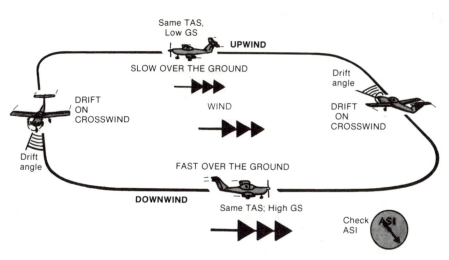

Fig.16-3. Wind Effect is Very Noticeable in Low Level Flight.

OBSTACLES.

Remain downwind of obstacles, especially when turning, to avoid the wind carrying the aeroplane into them.

INCREASED TURBULENCE AND WINDSHEAR AT LOW LEVEL.

The air is often more turbulent near the ground than at higher levels for various reasons – the main ones being:
• surface friction slowing down strong winds;
• changes in wind speed and/or direction (i.e. windshear); and
• uneven heating of the earth's surface creating convection currents.

The possibility of turbulence at low level is another reason why it is good airmanship to **keep your hand on the throttle** most of the time to enable an immediate response to airspeed variations if they occur.

CONSIDER THE 'PRECAUTIONARY' CONFIGURATION FOR LOW FLYING.

In good visibility and over open country, the normal cruise configuration of 'clean' wings may be suitable for low level flying. In poor visibility or in confined areas where good manoeuvrability is required, however, the precautionary configuration with an early stage of flap lowered may be preferable.

Using the precautionary configuration allows:
• better vision because of the lower nose attitude with flap extended;
• a lower cruise speed because of the reduced stalling speed;
• better manoeuvrability and smaller radius turns because of the lower airspeed;
• better response to elevator and rudder, due to the extra power required causing a greater slipstream effect.

A disadvantage of having flap extended for long periods, however, is the increased fuel consumption and the reduced range capability.

FLYING THE MANOEUVRE

BE WELL PREPARED BEFORE DESCENDING TO A LOW LEVEL.

As it is important that the Pilot maintains a very good **Look Out** when flying at a low level, a 'Low Flying Check' of items in the cockpit should be completed prior to descending. The 'FREDA' check, outlined previously, may be adequate:

F – Fuel on and sufficient;
Fuel tank usage monitored;
Mixture Rich;
Fuel Pump on (if fitted) and fuel pressure checked.

R – Radio frequency correctly selected, volume and squelch satisfactory, and make any necessary radio calls (reception will decrease at low levels).

E – Engine: oil temperature and pressure; carburettor heat if required; check other systems (ammeter for electrical system, suction gauge for air-driven gyroscopes if installed).

D – Direction Indicator aligned with Magnetic Compass, and your position on the map checked.

A – Altitude checked and subscale setting correct (normally Regional QNH; possibly QFE if joining a bad weather circuit).

Additional check items prior to low level flight should include:
- the security of the aeroplane (doors and harnesses) and take steps to make the aeroplane more visible (landing lights, rotating beacon and strobe lights on if appropriate);
- check the surface wind direction;
- assume the desired configuration ('clean' or an early stage of flap in the 'precautionary' configuration);
- trim.

A good **Look Out** is essential! View the ground even before you commence the descent to a low level to ensure that an adequate height above obstacles can be maintained and also look out for other aircraft. Beware of rising ground, especially if a wind is blowing down its slopes.

Vital points when flying low are:
- monitor the airspeed (resisting any temptation to slow down in a tailwind);
- keep in balance;
- stay well clear of obstacles and turn downwind of them.

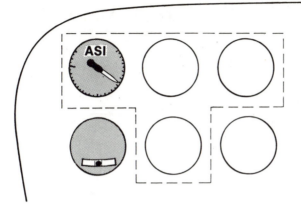

Fig.16-4. Monitor Airspeed and Balance when Flying at Low Level.

ALLOW FOR AEROPLANE INERTIA.

The aeroplane will take time to respond to any control movements due to inertia (which is a 'resistance to change'). Commence climbs and turns early to avoid obstacles. Avoid harsh manoeuvres (such as steep turns or high-g pull-ups) which may lead to an accelerated (or 'high speed') stall.

KEEP IN-TRIM WHEN LOW FLYING.

An aeroplane that is correctly trimmed is easier to fly and more likely to maintain height. Since your attention is directed out of the cockpit for most of the time in low level flying, **a well-trimmed aeroplane is essential**. A very slight nose-up trim will help ensure that an unintentional descent does not occur.

AIRMANSHIP

Maintain a very high visual awareness. Avoid 'congested areas' and maintain a suitable height.

Beware of false impressions caused by the wind effect, best counteracted by reference to the Air Speed Indicator and Balance Ball.

AIRWORK 16 —

AIMS: (a) To fly the aeroplane safely at a low level.

(b) To observe the misleading visual effects caused by a strong wind at low levels.

(1) Prior to Descending to Low Level:
- Complete *"FREDA"* check (refer to full version earlier in text):
  - F — Fuel system checks;
  - R — Radio correctly set;
  - E — Engine and systems for normal operation;
  - D — Direction Indicator aligned correctly and position on map checked;
  - A — Altitude and altimeter sub-scale checked, (QNH or perhaps QFE set).

- Additional considerations:
  - Security of the aeroplane (doors and harnesses, etc.) and its visibility (landing lights, beacon, strobes *ON*).
  - Note surface wind direction;
  - Aeroplane configuration (clean or early stage of flap);
  - Trim;
  - Decide on suitable IAS for the operation.

- Awareness of Low Flying Regulations.

LOOK OUT
for obstacles and
other aircraft – including
balloons, microlights, gliders, parachutists,
airships, towers, masts, hang-gliders,
large birds and flocks
of birds.

LOW LEVEL FLYING

(2) Descent to Low Level:
- Commence descent, hand on throttle, keeping a good *LOOK OUT;*
- Fly no lower than 500 ft AGL*;
- Estimate height visually, with back-up from the altimeter and known height AMSL of the ground.

  *or as advised by your flying instructor.

*LOOK
OUT*

(3) Establish Cruise Flight at the Desired Level:
- Set-up desired airspeed and height;
- Trim;
- Consider increasing power in the medium turns to maintain airspeed.

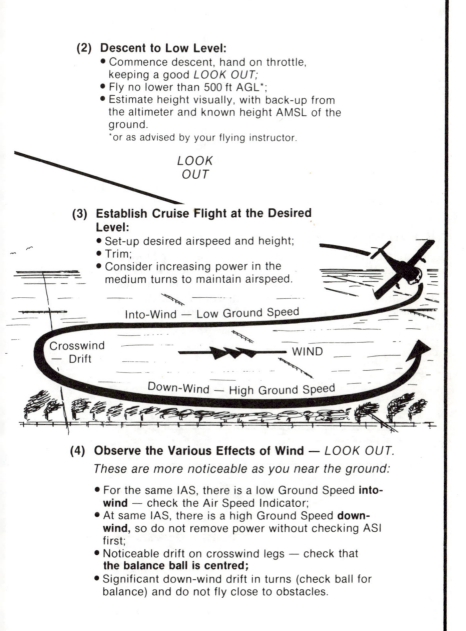

Into-Wind — Low Ground Speed

Crosswind — Drift

WIND

Down-Wind — High Ground Speed

(4) Observe the Various Effects of Wind — *LOOK OUT.*

These are more noticeable as you near the ground:

- For the same IAS, there is a low Ground Speed **into-wind** — check the Air Speed Indicator;
- At same IAS, there is a high Ground Speed **down-wind,** so do not remove power without checking ASI first;
- Noticeable drift on crosswind legs — check that **the balance ball is centred;**
- Significant down-wind drift in turns (check ball for balance) and do not fly close to obstacles.

FURTHER POINTS

LOW FLYING IN BAD WEATHER.

Poor visibility, a descending cloud base or rising ground may require some unplanned low flying. If you are 'caught-out' in really marginal conditions, maintain as much separation from the ground as possible, but **avoid entering cloud** – an estimated 100 ft beneath it is adequate.

Use any aircraft systems that can assist you in coping with bad weather, such as carburettor heat (if required), pitot heaters, window demisters, etc. Make your aeroplane more visible by switching the Rotating Beacon and Strobe on.

If the legal requirements of minimum visibility and distance from cloud cannot be satisfied, then consideration should be given to either:
- diverting to an area where better weather exists;
- landing at a nearby aerodrome, or requesting radar guidance if navigation is a problem;
- making a 'precautionary landing' in a field, (this procedure is discussed in Chapter 17b).

THE BAD WEATHER CIRCUIT.

A circuit in bad weather (i.e. poor visibility and/or a low cloud base) should be organised so that visual contact with the field is not lost. This may require a tight circuit flown at low level in the 'precautionary' configuration. Aim for a circuit height of at least 500 ft Above Ground Level if possible, **but do not enter cloud!** Maintain a clearance of at least 300 ft vertically from obstacles.

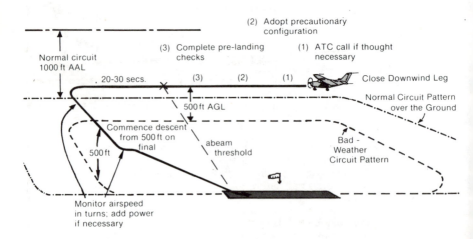

Fig. 16-5. The Bad-Weather Circuit.

17

FORCED LANDING

17a

THE FORCED LANDING WITHOUT POWER

AIM

To carry out a safe approach and landing following engine failure.

CONSIDERATIONS

WHY WOULD AN ENGINE FAIL?

A forced landing due to a mechanical malfunction or a structural problem is a rare event with modern aeroplanes. However, occasionally it happens, so a Pilot should be prepared.

*Fig.17a-1. Safe Forced Landings
Can Be Made in Small Fields.*

Fuel starvation is often the cause of an engine stopping in-flight. Fuel gauges can be inaccurate and fuel agents have on rare occasions loaded incorrect or contaminated fuel. A visual inspection of the fuel tanks and of the fuel itself during your pre-flight inspection should prevent insufficient or incorrect fuel causing a forced landing.

Forgetting to switch from a near-empty fuel tank in-flight to an alternative tank, incorrect use of the Mixture Control and failure to use Carburettor Heat can all lead to an engine stoppage through fuel starvation.

Performance data published in Flight Manuals is obtained from test results obtained by experienced Test Pilots flying new aeroplanes under ideal conditions. Similar results will be difficult for an average Pilot in a well-used aeroplane to achieve. The published fuel consumption and range capability assumes **correct leaning** of the mixture. If this is not done by the Pilot when cruising at 75% Maximum Continuous Power or less, the manufacturer's range figures will not be attained.

As the Captain of an aeroplane, you must show good airmanship and **always be aware of the real fuel situation.** Never allow fuel starvation to force you into an unwanted landing.

Other possible causes of engine stoppage include faults in the magneto system, the Pilot inadvertently switching the magnetos *OFF,* mechanical failure (possibly due to insufficient oil) or an engine fire. Bad luck sometimes plays a role – a bird strike damaging a propeller for instance.

FORCED LANDINGS WITHOUT POWER CAN BE MADE QUITE SAFELY.

All Pilots must be able to cope with an emergency landing without the use of engine power, possibly on an unprepared surface. This can be done quite successfully. The low landing speed of a modern training aircraft and its robust construction allow it to be landed safely in quite small fields, provided the Pilot positions the aeroplane accurately.

No new flying aspects are introduced with this exercise; it is simply a matter of putting together what you already know – making sound decisions fairly quickly and acting on them.

An aeroplane that glides at 700 ft/min rate of descent will allow a Pilot only 3 minutes from a height of 2000 ft AGL. Always be aware that:
- flying the aeroplane is number one priority – maintain a satisfactory airspeed and keep it in trim;
- planning and executing the approach comes next, with an attempt (if you think it advisable) to restart the engine.

Partial power from an engine that has not completely failed may give you extra time and the possibility of gaining some extra distance, but do not rely upon it. The engine may fail completely at a most inopportune moment, so plan your approach and landing as if no power is available.

A FORCED LANDING FOLLOWING COMPLETE ENGINE FAILURE AT ALTITUDE.

Height means time to a Pilot and the amount of time that you have available determines what options you have. If the engine fails, convert any excess speed into height by a gentle climb or into useful distance by maintaining height until the airspeed decays to gliding speed, and then establish a glide with the aeroplane in-trim.

When the aeroplane is comfortably under control, perform some simple emergency actions and attempt an engine restart – provided that you think restarting the engine is a good idea. It is possible that a restart is not advisable, say following an engine fire or mechanical damage. This is a command decision that only the Pilot in Command can make.

IF YOU DECIDE TO ATTEMPT AN ENGINE RESTART.

An experienced Pilot may decide very quickly to attempt an immediate restart and will perform the required actions while he is allowing the aeroplane to slow down to gliding speed.

A less-experienced Pilot may be advised to concentrate just on flying the aeroplane – first establishing it in the glide and trimming it before performing any restart actions. Your Flying Instructor will advise you on this point.

Some obvious items to be considered in an attempted restart of the engine are:

- **a fuel problem:**
    - change fuel tanks;
    - fuel pump on (if fitted);
    - mixture *RICH;*
    - primer locked;
- **an ignition problem:**
    - check magneto switches individually *(BOTH – LEFT – RIGHT)*. If the engine operates on one magneto as a result of a fault in the other magneto system, then leave it there, otherwise return to *BOTH;*
- **an icing problem:**
    - carburettor heat *FULL HOT.*

NOTE: Following a **mechanical failure** or **fire,** the engine should be stopped immediately. If the failure is **partial,** resulting in reduced or intermittent running, then use the engine at your discretion.

There is a likelihood that it may fail at a critical stage, so it may be best not to rely on it and simply assume a total failure. Following a failure due to **faulty operation by the Pilot,** restart the engine in the glide.

FLYING THE MANOEUVRE (i)
An **Actual** Forced Landing Without Power

MANY FORCED LANDING SCENARIOS ARE POSSIBLE.

Many scenarios are possible and your actions will depend upon the situation at the time, the height above ground at which the failure occurs, the surface wind, and the availability of good fields (possibly even an airfield).

We will consider a very general situation which is capable of modification to suit your precise set of conditions.

If the engine fails at a reasonable height (say 3000 ft or more Above Ground Level), a basic pattern that may be followed is:
• convert excess speed to height or to useful distance;
• set up a safe glide;
• attempt a restart;
• select a suitable field and plan an approach to it;
• make a Distress (MAYDAY) radio call;
• attempt to resolve the emergency (whilst maintaining a safe glide);
• carry out a safe approach and landing (in the case of training, a go-around rather than a landing will usually be performed).

KNOW THE GROUND WIND AT ALL TIMES.

Whilst flying along, it is good airmanship (commonsense) to keep an eye on the surface wind. A forced landing into-wind is generally safer because of the lower ground speed on touchdown and the shorter landing run. **Indicators of surface wind** include:
• smoke;
• a windsock;
• cloud shadows on the ground (especially if the clouds are low);
• the drift angle of the aeroplane over the ground;
• wind lanes on water.

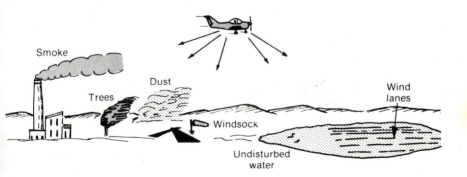

Fig.17a-2. Always Be Aware of the Surface Wind Direction.

ESTIMATE THE GLIDING RANGE.

A typical training aircraft has a Lift/Drag ratio of approximately 9:1, which means that, when flown at the correct gliding speed, 9000 ft (or 1.5 nm) can be gained horizontally for each 1000 ft lost in height.

Losing 1000 ft vertically in 9000 ft horizontally is an angle of depression (down from the horizontal) of about 7° (easy to work out using the 1 in 60 rule, following your Navigation studies).

To estimate gliding range in still air conservatively, lower your arm about 10° from the horizontal. You should be pointing at a position on the ground to which a glide in still air is possible.

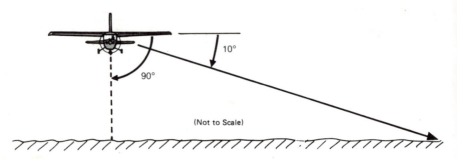

Fig.17a-3. An Approximate Estimate of Gliding Range in Nil Wind.

A headwind will reduce the gliding range; a tailwind will increase it. A windmilling or stopped propeller will also decrease it. In your training so far, you have become familiar with the glide path achievable with the engine idling and the propeller turning over.

If the engine has failed, the propeller (either stopped or windmilling) will cause a significant increase in drag. The nose of the aeroplane will have to be lowered to maintain airspeed and the Rate of Descent will increase. The increased drag will mean a steeper glide path and a reduced gliding range.

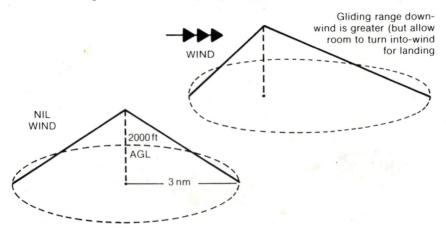

Fig.17a-4. Wind Affects Gliding Range Over The Ground.

SELECT A SUITABLE FIELD.

Following an engine failure, convert excess speed above gliding speed to height or useful distance, then adopt the gliding attitude and speed and trim the aeroplane. Change fuel tanks.

An **experienced Pilot** might attempt a restart at this stage but, at all times, it is most important to fly the aeroplane first.

When **settled into the glide,** select a suitable field for a forced landing. It is safest to **select a field well within your gliding range** and to fly a pattern around it, rather than to try a long straight glide to a distant field. This makes correct judgement of the glide easier and gives you more flexibility and room to correct if your original estimates are not perfect.

Keep turns towards the field and do not turn your back on it – it is possible to lose sight of the field and waste time re-identifying it.

The easiest place to look for a field is out of the left window. Ideally, select a field downwind of your present position, since that is where the gliding range of the aeroplane will be greatest.

The forced landing field should:
- be well within gliding range;
- be large and preferably surrounded by other suitable fields;
- have no obstacles on the approach and overshoot areas;
- be level or slightly uphill;
- have a suitable surface (ideally an aerodrome, but pasture or stubble may be satisfactory; wetness, often indicated by dark green areas, may be a disadvantage; crops and beaches in general should be avoided – the preferred order being pasture, stubble, ploughed fields, beaches, standing crops. Avoid roads if possible);
- be close to civilisation, (communication and assistance may be valuable).

Apply the **five S's:**
- – Size;
- – Shape;
- – Surface;
- – Slope;
- – Surroundings.

PLANNING THE APPROACH.

The basic plan that you formulate depends mainly upon the height above the ground. Various patterns and key points around a field can assist you in flying a suitable glide descent.

Each Flying Training Organisation and each Flying Instructor will have a preferred technique, but the aim is the same in every case – consistently good positioning for a glide approach and landing. We discuss various planning techniques. Your Flying Instructor will give you sound advice on which to use.

METHOD (A): THE '1000 ft AGL CLOSE BASE LEG' TECHNIQUE.

The basic aim using this technique is to arrive at 1000 ft AGL on a close base leg, from which a comfortable glide well into the field can be made. If the engine is stopped, the drag from the propeller will steepen the glide path compared to the glide angle when the engine is idling (as in the practice manoeuvre), so allow for this possibility.

A wide base leg allows little room for error, but a close base leg gives flexibility in the case of over- or under-shooting the field, allowing adjustments to be made quite easily. According to your position when the engine fails, choose either a left or right 1000 ft base point, with a long base leg and a short final. Left turns provide a better view of the field for the Pilot. Noting a ground reference point near the 1000 ft position will assist in re-identifying the turning-base point if you are distracted.

A suitable distance for the downwind leg is approximately ⅓ nm from the selected landing path. In flying a square pattern around the selected field, approximately 1000 ft per leg will be lost and this must be considered in your planning.

Stay close to the field and make all turns towards it.

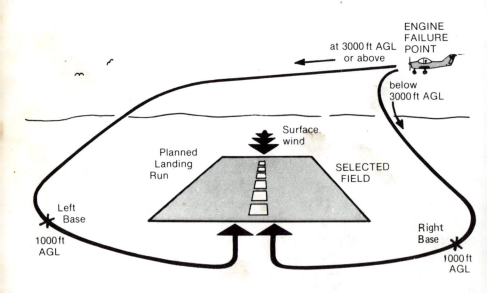

Fig.17a-5. A Very Basic Circuit Plan For A Forced Landing.

METHOD (B): THE 'HIGH KEY' AND 'LOW KEY' TECHNIQUE.

The advantage of using the 'high key' and the 'low key' is that they are closely related to the selected landing strip and therefore are easily re-identified:

- the **'Low Key'** – 1500 ft AGL about ⅓ nm abeam the landing threshold (a similar position to where the aeroplane would be using Method A);
- the **'High Key'** – 2500 ft AGL in line with and about ¾ to 1 nm upwind of the far end of the selected landing strip.

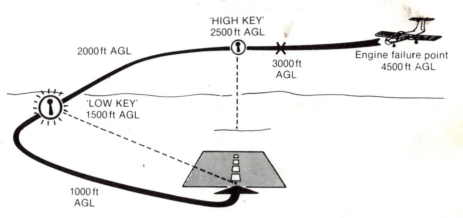

Fig.17a-6. The 'High Key' And The 'Low Key'.

The first aim in the descent is to glide to 'high key' keeping the field in sight. The purpose of the 'high key' is simply to assist your judgement in reaching the 'low key', which is of course the more important key point. After some practice glide descents, you may find that you can glide direct to the 'low key' without any definite consideration of the 'high key'. Engine failure at a low height (say 2000 ft AGL) will also mean flight direct to the low key.

Monitor Descent To The Key Points And Plan On A Long Base And A Short Final. If too high, widen out; if too low, cut in.

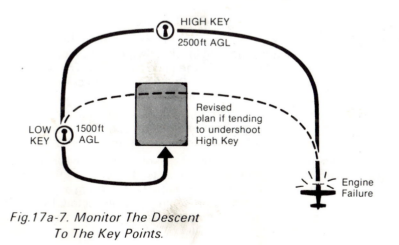

Fig.17a-7. Monitor The Descent To The Key Points.

Estimates of familiar heights (such as 1000 ft AGL circuit height) will generally be reasonably accurate. You should develop the same skill with other heights.

Assess the wind during the descent to assist in choosing a suitable base point. A reasonably long base leg allows:
- more time to judge wind strength (using the drift angle on base);
- better judgement of height (since it is easier to judge height out to one side of the aeroplane than straight ahead);
- flexibility in adjusting the descent path:
  - cutting in if too low;
  - widening out, lengthening the base leg or extending flap if too high.

A short final allows for a glide path steeper than expected.

ATTEMPT TO RECTIFY THE ENGINE PROBLEM.

When established in the glide, there may be time to look for the cause of the failure and to remedy it. The Pilot's Operating Handbook will contain a list of the appropriate items to check. It will include:
- fuel;
- mixture;
- carburettor heat;
- throttle linkage;
- fuel pump on (if fitted);
- primer (locked);
- magneto switches.

If the propeller is rotating, then fuel and ignition *ON* should be enough to restart the engine, otherwise the starter may be required. Whilst attempting to rectify the problem, the continuing descent towards the key points should be monitored and the suitability of the field confirmed. If you decide that your chosen field is unsuitable, then select another as early as possible.

ADVISE OTHERS OF YOUR PLANNED FORCED LANDING.

Make a 'MAYDAY' Distress Call (in a real forced landing, but not when practising). VHF radio signals may not be effective from very low levels, so the sooner a MAYDAY call is made in the glide the better. The 'MAYDAY' call should be made on 121·5 MHz as this frequency secures best ATC assistance.

Keep radio conversations brief and do not be distracted from your main duty, which is to **fly the aeroplane.** Squawk Transponder Code 7700, as this helps ATC radar to identify an aeroplane experiencing an emergency.

Advise your passengers of your intentions. Request them to remain calm, to remove sharp objects from their pockets, to remove glasses and dentures and ensure they are buckled in. Use of soft clothing or pillows will protect them if a sudden deceleration or impact is expected. Harnesses should remain fastened until the aeroplane stops. Be firm and brook no interference. Request silence.

APPROACHING THE 'LOW KEY' POINT — 1500 ft AGL.

As normal circuit height is approached, all of your attention needs to be focussed on positioning for the approach and landing. Further attempts to re-start would only distract you from this. **Secure the aeroplane,** placing it in a safer condition for a landing on an unprepared field by carrying out the required **'Security Check'** (also known as the 'Crash or Impact Check'):
- fuel *OFF;*
- ignition *OFF;*
- radio *OFF;*
- master switch *OFF* (unless flaps are electrically operated);
- cabin heater *OFF;*
- brakes *OFF;*
- harnesses very secure;
- doors unlatched (if appropriate to your aeroplane type);
- all loose items secured and the position of safety items noted (e.g. fire extinguisher, first aid kit).

WHERE TO TURN ONTO BASE LEG.

From the 'Low Key' abeam the touchdown point, extend downwind according to the wind. The stronger the wind, the shorter the extension of the downwind leg, bearing in mind that it is preferable to be a little high on final approach than to be too low. If the surface wind is:
- greater than 20 kt, commence base turn at the 'Low Key' point abeam the aiming point for landing, i.e. at about 1500 ft AGL;
- between 10–20 kt, commence base turn when the aiming point for landing appears about one-half chord length behind the trailing edge (for a low wing aeroplane), which will occur at about 1300 ft AGL;
- less than 10 kt, commence base turn when the aiming point for landing appears about one chord length behind the trailing edge (for a low wing aeroplane), which will occur at about 1100 ft AGL.

WHEN TO USE FLAPS.

A typical technique is to lower:
- the first stage of flap at the Low Key on downwind leg;
- the second stage when turning base leg;
- full flap on final and when assured of 'getting in'.

If the aeroplane appears to be **high on base leg,** then:
- lengthen the base leg; or
- widen the base leg; or
- extend some flap; or
- sideslip (if permitted – refer to the Pilot's Operating Handbook); or
- carry out some S-turns (but try and avoid this).

If the aeroplane appears to be **low on base leg,** then you can:
- shorten the base leg;
- cut in towards the field for a shorter final; or
- delay the use of flap.

A long base leg and a short final give you the greatest flexibility.

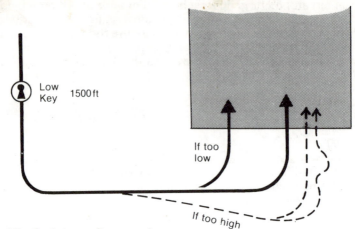

*Fig.17a-8. A Long Base and
A Short Final Gives You Some Flexibility.*

MONITOR AIRSPEED AND BANK ANGLE CLOSELY IN THE GLIDING TURN ONTO FINAL.

It is most important that you maintain the correct gliding speed, especially when turning. A **gliding turn near the ground should not be steep** because:

• stalling speed increases with increasing bank angle and wing loading; and

• rate of descent in a glide increases with bank angle.

Be very conscious of your airspeed during the turn onto final and limit the angle of bank to 15–20° (30° maximum). Do not stall or even allow the aeroplane to approach the stall!

Turn onto final so that the aiming point is well into your chosen field, say ½ to ⅓ into the field, to ensure that you make it. It is better to land too far in than to undershoot the field and hit a fence or some other obstacle. It is best, of course, to land comfortably over the field boundary and have sufficient distance to stop well before the far boundary without any drama.

FINAL APPROACH.

Once certain that you can glide well into the field, continue extending flap in stages to steepen your approach and bring the aiming point closer to you.

Keep the aiming point comfortably past the near boundary so that, even if an undershoot occurs, a safe landing in the field can still be made. It is safer to hit an obstacle at the far end at slow speed than to hit the fence before landing. It is safest, of course, to judge your aiming point so that neither occurs and so that you land comfortably into the field. Ensure that the Master Switch is *OFF* once electrically-operated flaps have been placed in the landing position.

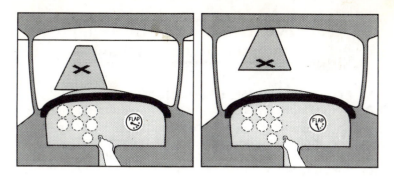

Fig.17a-9. Use of More Flap Brings the Aiming Point Closer.

If you are **too high** on final approach:
● extend flap;
● make shallow S-turns (but avoid this if possible);
● dive-off excess height (but avoid this also if possible).

If you are **too low** on final approach, delay extending flap. Do not fall into the trap of trying to stretch the glide by raising the nose. Airspeed will fall and the flight path will in fact be steeper. In an extreme case you may have to land in a nearer field.

LANDING.

A Forced Landing with **full flap** is generally safest because:
● the touchdown speed is low (due to the lower stalling speed);
● the landing run is shorter; and
● the stress on the airframe will be less if the field is rough.

Touch down on the main wheels, holding the (less-robust) nose-wheel off to avoid unnecessary stress. Once all three wheels are on the ground, brakes can be used to shorten the ground run.

Unseen obstacles and ditches could be a problem. If collision with an obstacle is imminent (say the far fence), apply rudder, braking on one side only to initiate a controlled ground loop if possible.

HAVING BROUGHT THE AEROPLANE TO A HALT.

A forced landing is not complete until the aeroplane is stopped, the passengers evacuated, the aeroplane made secure and assistance obtained. So as soon as the aeroplane stops:
● set the brakes to *PARK;*
● secure the aeroplane (check all switches *OFF,* fuel *OFF,* control locks *IN);*
● evacuate;
● chock the aeroplane;
● remove any items thought necessary;
● protect the aeroplane, e.g. keep animals away;
● seek assistance and telephone the Chief Flying Instructor and the appropriate authorities. If possible, leave someone in charge of the aeroplane.

Do not attempt to take-off!

FLYING THE MANOEUVRE (ii)
Simulated Forced Landing

ENSURE CORRECT ENGINE OPERATION
(AND A FEW OTHER THINGS).

So far we have covered the genuine engine-failure situation. In practice, however, we only **simulate an engine-failure** and, once having demonstrated that we could have made a safe landing, go-around off the approach from a safe height (say 500 ft AGL in the Low Flying Training Area). To ensure that the engine will respond at the time of go-around:

- ensure that the mixture is *RICH* and move the carburettor heat control to *HOT* to avoid carburettor icing (prior to reducing power in the simulated engine-failure). If a fuel pump is fitted, switch it *ON;*
- clear the engine and keep it warm by increasing rpm for a few seconds every 500 or 1000 ft on descent;
- when applying power for the go-around, check mixture *RICH* and carburettor heat full *COLD* (most engine manufacturers recommend apply power first, then move carburettor heat to *COLD).*

Simulate the Trouble Check, MAYDAY call and Security Check that you would carry out in a real forced landing, i.e. call them out at the appropriate time in your glide descent, but **do not action them.** For example, call "fuel *OFF,* magneto switches *OFF",* etc., but do not action them.

Keep a good **Look Out.** Other aircraft may be practising glide approaches to the same field in the Training Area, possibly from the other direction in calm wind conditions. Ensure that the climb-out area following the go-around is clear of obstacles. Check this well before you descend to a point where the go-around could become marginal.

Practising forced landings requires steady concentration. It is practising for an emergency and has its own peculiar risks. You are calling out items associated with a real forced landing, yet operating the aeroplane so that it will function normally when you carry out a go-around from a safe height. Be quite clear that, in practice, you should not do anything that would endanger the aeroplane (e.g. actually stop the engine).

Practising forced landings without the use of engine power (i.e. with the engine idling) is good training in developing the skills of command. One of these skills is to manage your resources effectively and efficiently in an 'emergency' situation.

AIRMANSHIP

When **Practising Forced Landings** without the use of engine power:
- **Look Out,** especially in the latter stages of the glide approach – other aircraft may be practising forced landings into the same or a nearby field;
- clear the engine by increasing rpm at least every 1000 ft on descent;
- do not descend below the authorised 'break-off height';
- know your checks thoroughly and execute them in the correct sequence;
- do not turn your back on the field – keep it in sight at all times;
- do not make any unnecessary changes in which field you select;
- make command decisions in a calm but firm manner.

When carrying out an **Actual Forced Landing** without the use of engine power:
- most of the points above related to 'practising' also apply in the real forced landing situation;
- do not rely on a partially-failed engine;
- ensure that the 'Trouble Check', MAYDAY call and 'Security Check' are actioned and not just called out, as in practice;
- ensure the safety of your aeroplane and passengers;
- notify the authorities as soon as possible.

AIRWORK 17a —

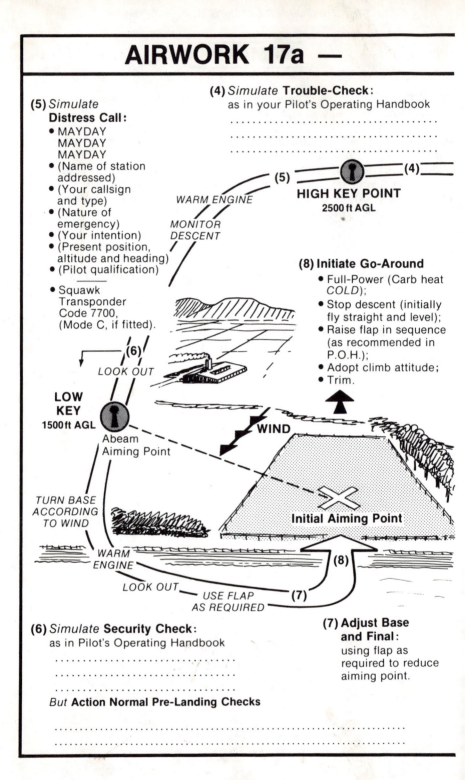

(4) *Simulate* **Trouble-Check:**
as in your Pilot's Operating Handbook

....
....
....

(5) *Simulate*
Distress Call:
- MAYDAY
  MAYDAY
  MAYDAY
- (Name of station
  addressed)
- (Your callsign
  and type)
- (Nature of
  emergency)
- (Your intention)
- (Present position,
  altitude and heading)
- (Pilot qualification)

- Squawk
  Transponder
  Code 7700,
  (Mode C, if fitted).

(5) ═══ **(4)** ═══

HIGH KEY POINT
2500 ft AGL

WARM ENGINE

MONITOR
DESCENT

(8) Initiate Go-Around
- Full-Power (Carb heat
  COLD);
- Stop descent (initially
  fly straight and level);
- Raise flap in sequence
  (as recommended in
  P.O.H.);
- Adopt climb attitude;
- Trim.

(6)
LOOK OUT

LOW
KEY
1500 ft AGL
Abeam
Aiming Point

WIND

TURN BASE
ACCORDING
TO WIND

Initial Aiming Point

WARM
ENGINE

LOOK OUT *USE FLAP*
AS REQUIRED

(8)

(7)

(6) *Simulate* **Security Check:**
as in Pilot's Operating Handbook

....
....
....

But **Action Normal Pre-Landing Checks**

....
....

(7) Adjust Base
and Final:
using flap as
required to reduce
aiming point.

PRACTISING THE FORCED LANDING

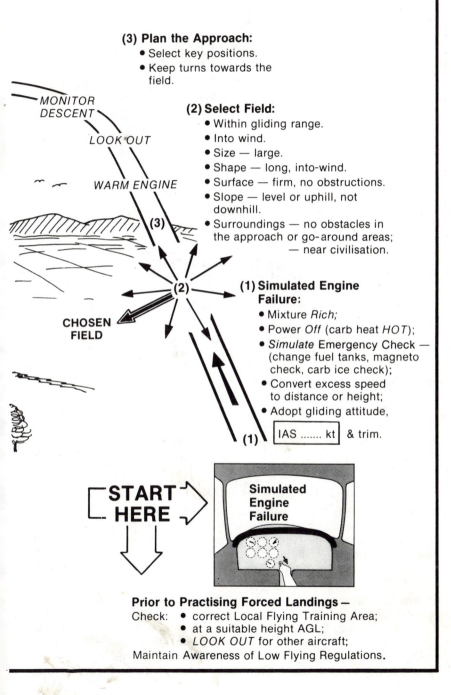

(3) Plan the Approach:
- Select key positions.
- Keep turns towards the field.

MONITOR DESCENT

LOOK OUT

WARM ENGINE

(3)

(2) Select Field:
- Within gliding range.
- Into wind.
- Size — large.
- Shape — long, into-wind.
- Surface — firm, no obstructions.
- Slope — level or uphill, not downhill.
- Surroundings — no obstacles in the approach or go-around areas; — near civilisation.

(2)

CHOSEN FIELD

(1) Simulated Engine Failure:
- Mixture *Rich*;
- Power *Off* (carb heat *HOT*);
- *Simulate* Emergency Check — (change fuel tanks, magneto check, carb ice check);
- Convert excess speed to distance or height;
- Adopt gliding attitude,

| IAS .... kt | & trim.

(1)

```
┌ START ┐
└ HERE ┘
```

Simulated
Engine
Failure

Prior to Practising Forced Landings —
Check: • correct Local Flying Training Area;
- at a suitable height AGL;
- *LOOK OUT* for other aircraft;

Maintain Awareness of Low Flying Regulations.

17b

THE PRECAUTIONARY SEARCH AND LANDING

AIM

To carry out a safe powered-approach and landing at an unfamiliar field.

CONSIDERATIONS

WHY LAND AT AN UNFAMILIAR FIELD OR ON AN UNPREPARED SURFACE?

A Pilot may be faced with the decision to land away from an aerodrome for a number of reasons. These include suspected engine or airframe problems; a sudden deterioration in weather, with low cloud and decreasing visibility making further flight unsafe; or as a result of deficient flight planning or navigation. Being totally lost, having insufficient fuel or insufficient daylight remaining are good enough reasons to consider making a precautionary landing in a field.

Impending incapacitation of the Pilot, say due to food poisoning, is best coped with on the ground.

DECIDE TO LAND EARLIER RATHER THAN LATER.

If any doubt exists as to the advisability of continuing the flight, the Pilot should make the decision to land whilst there is still time to do so with the aeroplane under full control and before conditions deteriorate to a dangerous level. It is better to land before you run out of either fuel, daylight or visibility, even if the landing is in a field rather than at an aerodrome.

Estimate what time you do have available. Slowing the aeroplane down, possibly lowering some flap, may assist the Pilot greatly. Slow flight gives a Pilot more time to observe the ground and to plan, as well as making the aeroplane more manoeuvrable. Turning performance is better at slow speeds and forward vision from the cockpit is improved. Slow flight may reduce the problems facing the Pilot and may even eliminate them.

FLYING THE MANOEUVRE

SEARCH FOR A SUITABLE LANDING AREA.

Once the decision to land has been taken, immediately search for a suitable landing area. Ideally, choose an active aerodrome; otherwise select the most suitable landing field as outlined in *'Forced Landings Without Power'*. Consider advising Air Traffic Control of your intentions by radio on the normal frequency and, if not satisfactory, on the emergency frequency 121·5 MHz.

Items to consider when selecting a field include:
- its alignment with respect to the surface wind;
- size (larger is better than smaller);
- no obstacles in the approach or go-around areas;
- level or slightly uphill – (a downslope is bad news);
- a firm surface with no obstructions;
- near civilization.

If no suitable field is obvious then searching downwind will allow you to have a higher ground speed and so cover more area.

USE AN APPROPRIATE AIRCRAFT CONFIGURATION.

If low cloud, poor visibility or a restricted manoeuvring area are involved, then adopt the 'bad weather (or precautionary) configuration'. Use the optimum stage of flap, which may be just the first stage. Extending some flap allows:
- slower speeds (due to reduced stalling speed);
- a smaller turn radius and a higher rate of turn (due to the reduced speed);
- better visibility from the cockpit (due to lower nose position); and
- improved elevator and rudder response due to higher power and greater slipstream effect over the tail (possibly).

Staying in the one configuration allows the Pilot to fly the whole sequence (descents, straight and level, and climbs) at a constant airspeed, thereby removing one variable. Fly the attitude for the desired speed, and control descent, level flight and climb-out with the use of power.

INSPECT THE SELECTED LANDING AREA.

Several inspection runs should be made in the precautionary configuration and a circuit pattern and circuit height established. With no restrictions, a normal circuit pattern should be suitable.

In bad weather, a low and tight circuit (e.g. 500 ft AGL) may be advisable. The heights at which the circuits are flown and the number of inspection runs carried out depend upon the situation. Command decisions must be made by the Pilot.

The Low Flying Check should be completed before descent to a low level. It is good airmanship to keep your workload to a minimum in low level flight. Flying low to inspect a surface means accurate flying and a good **Look Out.** Keep the aeroplane in trim or, if anything, trim slightly nose-up so that the aeroplane will have no tendency to descend whilst your attention is directed outside.

AIRMANSHIP

Fly the aeroplane into a position for a normal engine-assisted approach. Consider making a 'short-field landing' to minimise stress on the aeroplane during the touchdown and landing run if the field is rough. Complete the appropriate pre-landing checks. If time is not a consideration, be prepared to go-around if not totally satisfied with the approach.

Be aware of the usual illusions of low flying resulting from the wind effect. Keep your turns accurate and balanced in spite of the deceptive appearance of the ground if there is a strong wind. Add power to maintain airspeed in the turn if necessary and monitor the Air Speed Indicator.

Even though three preliminary circuits are used in the Airwork example (which follows), adapt the procedure according to your requirements. Learn to **make command decisions quickly and efficiently.**

Adapt your plan to suit the conditions (e.g. low cloud, imminent darkness, low fuel). Possibly a 500 ft AGL, close-in circuit with only one inspection run might be called for, with no delay in making a landing.

When practising the Precautionary Search and Landing:
- ensure that you are in the correct Local Flying Area and keep a good **Look Out** for other aircraft;
- consider any regulations or local rules (such as no descents below 500 ft AGL, do not frighten animals, etc.), and obey them;
- align the Direction Indicator with the landing direction (either on 360 or 180) to help with orientation.

Your Flying Instructor will give you plenty of practice at this procedure in many different situations. Adapt to each situation as you see fit.

FURTHER POINTS

IF THERE ARE NO TIME, FUEL OR WEATHER RESTRICTIONS.

If three inspection circuits are thought necessary, a suitable plan might be:

Circuit 1. At 1000 ft AGL to establish circuit and note landmarks and magnetic headings. Some Flying Instructors may consider this preliminary circuit superfluous. Complete low flying checks before descent.

Circuit 2. To select and make a preliminary evaluation of the actual landing path. Descend on final and make a 500 ft AGL run (or 300 ft AGL run – refer to your Flying Instructor) slightly right of the landing path to give you a good view of the approach path and the landing surface out of your left cockpit window. Search for large obstacles and obstructions, ditches, animals, wires, fences, etc. Return to circuit height as you near the end of the field.

Circuit 3. Descend on final and make a run to the right of and along the landing path at a lower, but still safe, level (say 100 ft or 50 ft AGL) for a closer inspection of the landing surface itself. Return to circuit height.

Circuit 4. A normal circuit followed by a short-field landing.

Make each inspection run alongside the selected landing path at a constant height and not as a slow descent that necessitates a frantic climb at the far boundary to avoid obstacles.

AIRWORK 17b —

AIM: To carry out a safe approach and landing at an unfamiliar field with engine power available.

For the purpose of this exercise, the scenario is a cloud base of 600 ft AGL, poor visibility and 20 mins flight time available before night sets in.

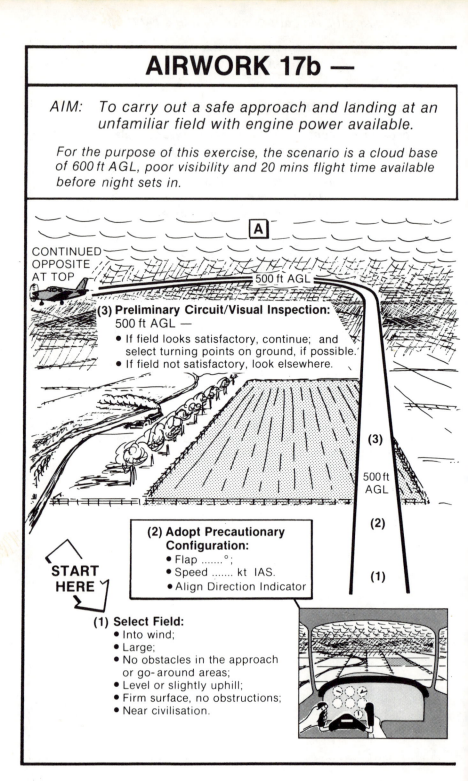

A

CONTINUED OPPOSITE AT TOP

500 ft AGL

(3) Preliminary Circuit/Visual Inspection:
500 ft AGL —
- If field looks satisfactory, continue; and select turning points on ground, if possible.
- If field not satisfactory, look elsewhere.

(3)

500 ft AGL

(2) Adopt Precautionary Configuration:
- Flap ....°;
- Speed .... kt IAS.
- Align Direction Indicator

(2)

(1)

START HERE

(1) Select Field:
- Into wind;
- Large;
- No obstacles in the approach or go-around areas;
- Level or slightly uphill;
- Firm surface, no obstructions;
- Near civilisation.

THE PRECAUTIONARY SEARCH AND LANDING

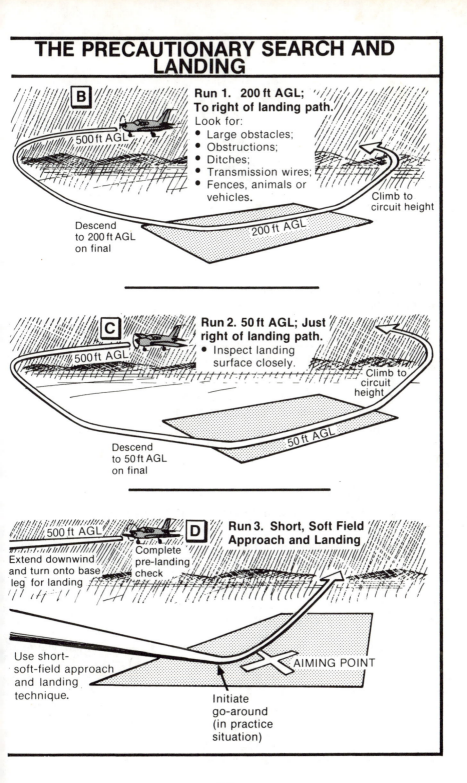

B

500 ft AGL

**Run 1. 200 ft AGL;
To right of landing path.**
Look for:
- Large obstacles;
- Obstructions;
- Ditches;
- Transmission wires;
- Fences, animals or vehicles.

Climb to circuit height

Descend to 200 ft AGL on final

200 ft AGL

C

500 ft AGL

Run 2. 50 ft AGL; Just right of landing path.
- Inspect landing surface closely.

Climb to circuit height

Descend to 50 ft AGL on final

50 ft AGL

---

500 ft AGL

D

Complete pre-landing check

Run 3. Short, Soft Field Approach and Landing

Extend downwind and turn onto base leg for landing

Use short-soft-field approach and landing technique.

AIMING POINT

Initiate go-around (in practice situation)

17c

DITCHING IN WATER

AIM

To alight on water as successfully as possible, if ditching is the best available option.

CONSIDERATIONS

Being forced to ditch in the ocean is a remote possibility, however it is worthwhile having a suitable procedure in the back of your mind.

Try to land near a ship or in a shipping lane if possible and make a *MAYDAY* radio call before too much height is lost to ensure the best chance of reception by ground stations.

LANDING DIRECTION.

If the water is smooth, or smooth with a very long swell, then land into-wind.

If there is a large swell or a rough sea, then land along the swell, even if you have to accept a crosswind. This avoids the danger of nosing into a big wave. **Waves** generally move downwind except near a shoreline or in fast moving estuaries, however **swells** may not bear any relationship at all to surface wind direction.

Clues to wind direction include:
- wave direction;
- wind lanes (the streaked effect being more apparent when viewed downwind);
- gust ripples on the water surface;
- aeroplane drift.

FLYING THE MANOEUVRE

IF YOUR ENGINE IS RUNNING, USE A POWERED APPROACH FOR DITCHING.

From altitude, water generally appears to be calmer than what it is. Fly low and study the water surface before ditching.

Generally ditch with an early stage of flap set, using a low speed, a high nose attitude (tail-down) and a low rate of descent controlled by power (if available). Power gives you a lot more control over the touchdown point, so avoid running out of fuel prior to ditching.

Touch down with as low a flying speed as possible, but do not stall in.

ALERT THE PASSENGERS.

Warn the passengers. Buckle up and don life-jackets, if available, but do not inflate them until in the water, as they may restrict the evacuation. Remove headsets and anything else that may get in the way during the evacuation.

Be prepared for a double impact – the first when the tail strikes the water, the second (and greater) when the nose hits the water. The aircraft may also slew to one side.

Evacuation (if possible) should be carried out as calmly as possible, life-jackets being inflated outside the cabin. The Pilot in Command should supervise.

Intentionally Blank

18

PILOT
NAVIGATION

18

PILOT NAVIGATION

AIM

To fly cross-country, navigating with visual reference to the ground.

CONSIDERATIONS

Cross-country flying is another step forward in your training which, so far, has been restricted to the local training area and has concentrated on:
- **basic flying skills** (climbing, turning, landing, etc.); and
- **basic procedures** (circuits, forced landings, low level flying, etc.).

Flying to another aerodrome, perhaps quite distant, requires the additional skills and knowledge encompassed in **Flight Planning and Navigation.** This chapter acts as a summary of Volume 3 of this series, which is devoted to these subjects.

FLIGHT MANAGEMENT.

As the Pilot-in-Command of a cross-country flight you have certain duties to perform, both on the ground and in-flight. The prime tasks are:
- **to fly the aeroplane;** and
- **to navigate it to the destination,** which involves:
    - flight planning; and
    - en route navigation.

You have limited resources in the cockpit and they need to be managed efficiently. For example, it is difficult to measure tracks and distances on a chart in flight whilst trying to fly in rough air. Better management would have seen the chart work done on the ground prior to flight.

The better the flight planning, the easier the en route navigation!

PERSONAL NAVIGATION EQUIPMENT.

The two most vital instruments in visual navigation are the Magnetic Compass and the Clock, **so always carry a serviceable watch.** Provided that the aeroplane's position has been fixed within the previous twenty minutes or so, and its speed is known (at least approximately), its position during flight can be deduced from the direction it has travelled and the time taken from the fix.

A **flight case** or satchel that fits comfortably within reach in the cockpit should be used to hold your navigational equipment. A typical flight case should contain:
- relevant charts covering at least 50 nm either side of your planned track;
- a navigation computer (the *Airtour CRP-1* is excellent);
- a scale rule and protractor (or a plotter);
- pens and pencils;
- appropriate flight information publications, e.g. *Pooley's Flight Guide;*
- spare flight log forms;
- sun glasses.

THE FLIGHT LOG.

The flight log is designed to keep the necessary data and calculations orderly. There are various presentations and the one illustrated below is quite typical.

FROM /TO	SAFETY ALT	ALT		RAS	TAS	W/V	TR °T	DRIFT	HDG °T	VAR	HDG °M	G/S	DIST	TIME	ETA	HDG °C
		TEMP														

Fig.18-1. Layout of a Typical Flight Log Form.

FLIGHT PLANNING

WEATHER CONSIDERATIONS.

For your planned areas and aerodromes of operation, check the **meteorological information** obtainable:
- in aerodrome Briefing Offices; (where, at certain aerodromes, print-outs of Area Forecasts and Aerodrome Forecasts are available – as advised in UK AIP MET 1-1); or
- by telephone; (Area Forecasts from the *AIRMET* telephone recording service, as advised in UK AIP MET 2-7/8; Aerodrome Forecasts from the appropriate Forecast Office as listed in UK AIP MET 1-6).

Note: For flights outside the area of coverage of UK area forecasts, a Special Forecast may be obtained from a Weather Office, but four hours notice is required for flights exceeding 500 nm, and two hours notice for flights less than 500 nm. (See Chapter C11 in Vol. 2.)

Establish from the forecasts that the planned flight can be completed in visual conditions. Note the Altimeter Setting Regions (ASRs) you will pass through en route.

OPERATIONAL CONSIDERATIONS.

Check the official documentation for considerations that may affect your operation:
- NOTAMs for urgent and short notice items;
- Aeronautical Information Circulars (AICs) and the Aeronautical Information Publication (AIP) for 'permanent' items of long standing.

ROUTE SELECTION, MAP PREPARATION AND COMPILING A FLIGHT LOG.

Select the route over which you want to fly. Note the nature of the terrain and of the airspace along this route and to either side of it:
- **terrain:** check the height of any obstacles within (say) 10 nm of track;
- **airspace:** check the route for:
  - Controlled Airspace;
  - Special Rules Zones or Special Rules Areas;
  - Prohibited Areas, Restricted Areas or Danger Areas;
  - Military Air Traffic Zones (MATZs);
  - Air Traffic Zones (ATZs);
  - Radar Advisory Service Areas;
  - other aerodromes.

The break-up of airspace is shown on the aeronautical charts (at all levels on the 1:500 000 series, but only below 3000 ft AMSL on the 1:250 000 series).

Airspace information is overprinted on both series, except for details about Danger Areas for which you need to refer to the **Chart of Airspace Restrictions and Danger Areas** or the **Aeronautical Information Publication.**

It may be best to avoid particularly high or rugged terrain and areas of dense air traffic.

Choose turning points and check points which will be easily identified in-flight and which cannot be confused with other nearby ground features. Mark the route on your chosen aeronautical map (1:500 000 or 1:250 000 series, the former usually being preferable).

Use a Chinagraph pencil if possible, since it will write on plastic-coated surfaces (e.g. charts) and can be erased easily.

Enter the check points on the flight log.

Note any suitable **alternate aerodromes** available on, or adjacent to, the route in case of an unscheduled landing becoming necessary. Also note the en route radio frequencies and any other relevant information.

SAFETY ALTITUDES AND CRUISING ALTITUDES.

For each leg of the flight, calculate a **'safety altitude'** that is 1000 ft higher than any obstacle within the distance either side of track (15, 10 or 5nm) as specified by your Flying Training Organisation, and enter it on the flight log. This provides a reasonable minimum altitude to fly at if, for instance, cloud forces you down. Also check the meteorological information to confirm that the forecast cloud is above this minimum safety altitude.

Select a suitable cruising altitude for each leg and enter it in the flight log. Considerations should include:
- terrain;
- overlying airspace restrictions; and
- the cloud base.

TRACKS AND DISTANCES.

For each leg of the flight, mentally estimate the track in °T and the distance in nautical miles before measuring it accurately (ensuring that you are using the correct scale). **Mentally estimating track and distance prior to actual measurement will avoid gross errors.** Insert these measured figures on the flight log.

FROM/TO	SAFETY ALT	ALT / TEMP	RAS	TAS	W/V	TR °T	DRIFT	HDG °T	VAR	HDG °M	G/S	DIST	TIME	ETA	HDG °C
ELSTREE															
	1920	2400				069						60			
IPSWICH															
	1772	2400				286						40			
CAMBRIDGE															
	1920	2400				208						38			
ELSTREE															
												138			

Fig.18-2. The Flight Log at this Stage.

DISTANCE MARKERS OR TIME MARKERS.

To assist you in flight, it is suggested that each leg be subdivided and small marks placed at intervals on the track lines drawn on the chart. The usual means of subdividing (your Flying Instructor will advise you of his preferred method) is to use one of the following:
- distance markers each 10 nm; or
- distance markers at the ¼, ½ and ¾ points; or
- time markers each 10 min; or
- time markers at the ¼, ½ and ¾ points.

NOTE: the time markers will of course have to wait until you have calculated Ground Speeds and time intervals. Once in-flight, these may vary from the flight planned values, unlike the distance markers.

TRACK GUIDES.

To allow easier in-flight estimation of any deviation from the desired track, it is useful to draw in 5° and 10° guides either side of track emanating from each turning point. This avoids having to use a protractor or plotter in-flight.

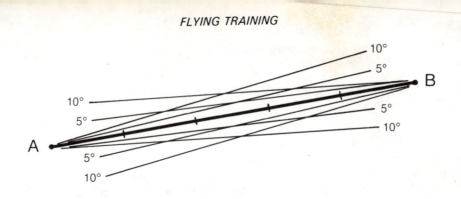

Fig.18-3. Track Guides and Distance Markers.

CALCULATE THE REQUIRED HEADINGS, EXPECTED GROUND SPEEDS AND TIME INTERVALS.

Insert the forecast winds for each leg, the selected cruising altitude and the TAS onto the flight log.

Remember that for a given Indicated Air Speed, the True Air Speed will be greater at higher altitudes and temperatures because of the decreased air density. Converting IAS to TAS is easily done on the calculator-side of the computer.

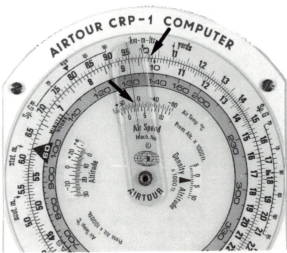

Fig.18-4. If Necessary,
Convert IAS to TAS
(using Pressure Altitude
and Temperature).

On the **wind-side of the computer,** use the forecast wind to set up the 'triangle of velocities' and calculate Drift, **Heading** and **Ground Speed**.

NOTE: It is most important when using the wind-side of the computer that you work either completely in °TRUE or completely in °MAGNETIC. Do not mix them! Either method is satisfactory – it being most common for Private Pilots in the UK to **work in** °T. Use of the computer is covered in detail in the Navigation volume (3) of this series.

Having obtained the values for GS and HDG(T), insert them on the flight log. Magnetic Variation, found on the chart, is then used to convert the True Heading into Magnetic Heading – required when using the Magnetic Compass and the Direction Indicator during the flight.

Having measured the distance of each leg and calculated the expected Ground Speed, determine the Estimated Time Interval and insert it on the Flight Log.

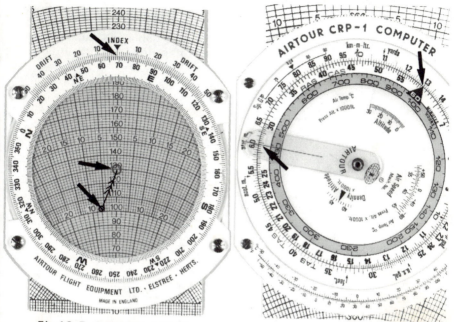

Fig.18-5. Calculate Heading   Fig.18-6. Calculate the Estimated
and Ground Speed.   Time Intervals.

Add all of the individual time intervals together and obtain the **total time interval** for the whole flight.

It is good airmanship at this point to compare this with the total distance for the flight and verify that it is a reasonable result, considering the average GS expected to be achieved. Also, confirm that you will arrive with adequate daylight remaining.

FROM/TO	SAFETY ALT	ALT / TEMP	RAS	TAS	W/V	TR °T	DRIFT	HDG °T	VAR	HDG °M	G/S	DIST	TIME	ETA	HDG °C
ELSTREE	1920	2400 / +10	98	102	270/30	069	−6	063	5W	068	130	60	28		
IPSWICH															
CAMBRIDGE	1772	2400 / +10	98	102	270/30	286	−5	281	5W	286	73	40	33		
ELSTREE	1920	2400 / +10	98	102	270/30	208	+15	223	5W	228	84	38	27		
										ToT.		138	88		

Fig.18-7. The Flight Log at this Stage.

FUEL CALCULATIONS.

The fuel consumption for various power settings is published in the Flight Manual and Pilot's Operating Handbook. These figures assume **correct leaning of the fuel/air mixture** at higher levels (usually above 5000 ft) when cruising at less than 75% Maximum Continuous Power. Leaning the mixture can decrease fuel consumption by up to 20%.

From the Estimated Time Interval for the whole flight and the published fuel consumption rate, **calculate the expected Flight Fuel. Reserve Fuel** should also be carried to allow for in-flight contingencies including diversions, fuel consumption poorer than that published, unexpected headwinds en route, etc. **At least 45 minutes reserve fuel is recommended.**

Insert the fuel calculations onto the flight log.

CONSUMPTION RATE 7 USG/hr		
Stage	mins	US Gal
Route	88	10·3
Reserve	45	5·3
Fuel Required	133	15·6 = 16
Margin	180	21
Total Carried	313	37

Fig.18-8. Fuel Calculations.

WEIGHT AND BALANCE.

At this stage in your flight planning, knowing the fuel required and the passenger and baggage load, it is appropriate to consider Weight and Balance. **For a flight to be legal,** the aeroplane must not exceed any weight limitation and must be loaded so that the Centre of Gravity lies within the approved range throughout the flight. Complete a Load Sheet (if necessary) to verify that the requirements are met.

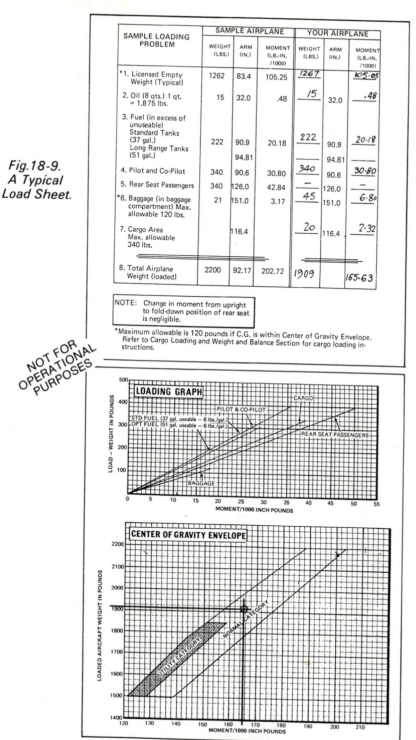

Fig.18-9.
A Typical
Load Sheet.

NOT FOR
OPERATIONAL
PURPOSES

SAMPLE LOADING PROBLEM	SAMPLE AIRPLANE			YOUR AIRPLANE		
	WEIGHT (LBS.)	ARM (IN.)	MOMENT (LB.-IN. /1000)	WEIGHT (LBS.)	ARM (IN.)	MOMENT (LB.-IN. /1000)
*1. Licensed Empty Weight (Typical)	1262	83.4	105.25	1267		105.05
2. Oil (8 qts.) 1 qt. = 1.875 lbs.	15	32.0	.48	15	32.0	.48
3. Fuel (in excess of unuseable) Standard Tanks (37 gal.) Long Range Tanks (51 gal.)	222	90.9 94.81	20.18	222	90.9 94.81	20.18
4. Pilot and Co-Pilot	340	90.6	30.80	340	90.6	30.80
5. Rear Seat Passengers	340	126.0	42.84	—	126.0	—
*6. Baggage (in baggage compartment) Max. allowable 120 lbs.	21	151.0	3.17	45	151.0	6.80
7. Cargo Area Max. allowable 340 lbs.		116.4		20	116.4	2.32
8. Total Airplane Weight (loaded)	2200	92.17	202.72	1909		165.63

NOTE: Change in moment from upright to fold-down position of rear seat is negligible.

*Maximum allowable is 120 pounds if C.G. is within Center of Gravity Envelope. Refer to Cargo Loading and Weight and Balance Section for cargo loading instructions.

LOADING GRAPH

LOAD – WEIGHT IN POUNDS

PILOT & CO-PILOT
CARGO
STD FUEL (37 gal, useable – 6 lbs./gal.)
OPT FUEL (51 gal, useable – 6 lbs./gal.)
REAR SEAT PASSENGERS
BAGGAGE

MOMENT/1000 INCH POUNDS

CENTER OF GRAVITY ENVELOPE

LOADED AIRCRAFT WEIGHT IN POUNDS

NORMAL CATEGORY
UTILITY CATEGORY

MOMENT/1000 INCH POUNDS

TAKE-OFF AND LANDING PERFORMANCE.

Having considered Weight and Balance, you will know the expected Take-Off Weight and Landing Weight of the aeroplane. If any doubt exists regarding the suitability of the departure, destination and alternate aerodromes, then reference should be made to the Take-Off and Landing **Performance Charts** in the Flight Manual. The official source of **aerodrome data** is the AGA section of the Aeronautical Information Publication (AIP). **Meteorological data** affecting the performance (i.e. wind and temperature) can be obtained from the forecast.

TAKE-OFF DISTANCE

ASSOCIATED CONDITIONS:

Power — Maximum
Flaps — Up
Runway — Hard surface (level & dry)
Fuel Mixture — Full throttle climb, mixture leaned above 5000 feet to smooth engine operation

NOTES:
1. Decrease distance 4% for each 5 knots headwind. For operation with tailwinds up to 10 knots increase distance by 10% for each 2.5 knots.
2. Where distance value is shaded, climb performance after lift-off, based on the engine operating at takeoff power at takeoff speed, is less than 150 feet per minute.
3. If takeoff power is set without brakes applied, then distances apply from point where full power is attained.

NOT FOR OPERATIONAL PURPOSES

WEIGHT LBS	TAKEOFF SPEED KIAS (MPH) LIFT OFF	CLEAR 50 FT.	PRESS. ALT. FT.	0°C (32°F) GROUND ROLL	0°C (32°F) CLEAR 50 FT.	10°C (50°F) GROUND ROLL	10°C (50°F) CLEAR 50 FT.	20°C (68°F) GROUND ROLL	20°C (68°F) CLEAR 50 FT.	30°C (86°F) GROUND ROLL	30°C (86°F) CLEAR 50 FT.	40°C (104°F) GROUND ROLL	40°C (104°F) CLEAR 50 FT.
2200	56 (64)	63 (73)	S.L.	754	1374	836	1522	925	1681	1020	1850	1120	2029
			2000	897	1625	996	180						
			4000	1071	1927	1189	213						
			6000	1282	2290	1423	253						
			8000	1538	2730	1707	302!						
2000	53 (61)	60 (69)	S.L.	600	1102	665	122						
			2000	714	1304	792	144						
			4000	852	1546	946	171						
			6000	1020	1838	1132	203						
			8000	1223	2190	1358	242						
1800	50 (58)	57 (66)	S.L.	466	864	517	95						
			2000	554	1022	615	113						
			4000	662	1212	724	134						
			6000	792	1441	879	159						
			8000	950	1717	1054	190						

LANDING DISTANCE

ASSOCIATED CONDITIONS:

Power — Off
Flaps — Down
Runway — Hard surface (level & dry)
Braking — Maximum

NOTES:
1. Decrease distance 4% for each 5 knots headwind.
2. For operations with tailwinds up to 10 knots, increase distance by 9% for each 2.5 knots.

Fig. 18-10. Consider if Performance Charts Need to be Consulted.

WEIGHT LBS	SPEED AT 50 FT. KIAS	MPH	PRESS. ALT. FT.	0°C (32°F) GROUND ROLL	0°C (32°F) CLEAR 50 FT.	10°C (50°F) GROUND ROLL	10°C (50°F) CLEAR 50 FT.	20°C (68°F) GROUND ROLL	20°C (68°F) CLEAR 50 FT.	30°C (86°F) GROUND ROLL	30°C (86°F) CLEAR 50 FT.	40°C (104°F) GROUND ROLL	40°C (104°F) CLEAR 50 FT.
2200	61	70	S.L.	366	1057	375	1086	385	1114	394	1144	404	1173
			2000	385	1116	396	1148	406	1180	417	1212	428	1245
			4000	432	1183	419	1218	431	1253	443	1289	455	1325
			6000	432	1257	445	1296	458	1335	471	1375	485	1415
			8000	460	1342	474	1384	489	1428	504	1472	518	1516
2000	60	69	S.L.	342	986	351	1011	359	1037	368	1063	377	1090
			2000	360	1038	369	1067	379	1095	388	1125	398	1154
			4000	379	1098	390	1130	400	1162	411	1194	422	1227
			6000	402	1165	413	1200	425	1236	437	1272	449	1308
			8000	427	1241	440	1280	453	1319	466	1359	480	1399
1800	58	67	S.L.	381	912	325	934	333	957	341	980	348	1004
			2000	333	959	342	984	350	1009	359	1035	367	1062
			4000	351	1012	360	1040	369	1068	379	1097	389	1126
			6000	371	1072	381	1103	391	1134	402	1166	413	1199
			8000	393	1139	405	1174	416	1209	428	1244	440	1280

FLIGHT NOTIFICATION.

Prior to flight the Pilot should contact the relevant Air Traffic Service (ATS) Unit and either:

• Book Out; or
• File a Flight Plan.

A Flight Plan may be filed with ATC for any flight and is advisable when planning to fly more than 10 nm from the coast or over sparsely populated or mountainous areas, especially if the aeroplane is not equipped with radio.

For most visual flights, however, it is sufficient to 'Book Out' with the ATS Unit. This may be done by radio prior to taxying, by telephone, or in person if necessary. 'Booking Out' details should include the aircraft registration, the destination, flight time, endurance and the number of persons on board.

AEROPLANE DOCUMENTATION AND PREPARATION FOR FLIGHT.

Check that the Certificate of Airworthiness is valid and that the Maintenance Document confirms that the aeroplane is **airworthy.**

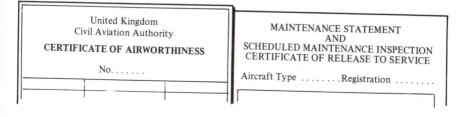

Fig.18-11. Check the CofA and the Maintenance Document.

Ensure that there is **adequate fuel on board** and complete your normal pre-flight duties, i.e. the external ('walk-around') inspection and internal inspection. Never hurry this aspect of the flight. It is most important that the pre-flight preparation is thorough and, even if you are running behind schedule because of flight planning taking longer than expected (a common reason), **do not rush your normal pre-flight duties.**

Settle into the cockpit and place your navigation equipment and charts where they are readily accessible. Ensure that the charts are folded so that at least 20 nm either side of track is visible. Ensure that no metallic or magnetic objects are placed near the Magnetic Compass. Check on the comfort of your passengers (at this stage, your Flying Instructor).

These final checks are worthwhile since, once the engine starts, the noise level will be higher, communication will be slightly more difficult and you will be busier with the normal workload of manipulating the aeroplane.

THE FLIGHT

START-UP, TAXI (and 'Book Out' if not already done).

Following normal procedures, start the engine, switch on the radio, 'Book Out' with the ATS Unit (if this has not already been done) and taxi to the take-off position. If in any doubt about the exact time, confirm it with an ATS Unit and ensure that your clock is set correctly. Complete all of the normal pre-flight checks.

Ensure that your navigation equipment is accessible, but will not restrict the controls in any way.

TAKE-OFF AND SET HEADING.

When aligned on the runway, but not accelerating, check that the Magnetic Compass is reading correctly and that the Direction Indicator is aligned with it.

Following take-off, the easiest method of **setting heading** is from directly overhead the airfield, at which time you would mentally note your 'Set Heading' time (or Actual Time of Departure).

NOTE: for various reasons, it is not always possible to set heading over the top (for example, at aerodromes with a low level Entry/Exit lane or if there is overlying controlled airspace) and you must fly to intercept the planned track some short distance en route. Once on track, you should estimate what the actual time of departure from overhead would have been.

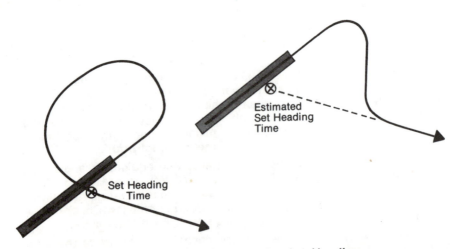

Estimated
Set Heading
Time

Set Heading
Time

Fig.18-12. Two Methods of Setting Heading.

To use the Magnetic Compass precisely, you should refer to the Compass Deviation Card in the cockpit so that the Magnetic Heading can be modified if necessary to the slightly more accurate Compass Heading. (Deviation is usually less than 3° and so is not operationally significant.)

Once well clear of the circuit area, enter the 'set heading' time on the Flight Log and estimate the arrival time at the destination and at selected points en route. Regional QNH (obtainable by radio from an ATS Unit) should be set in the altimeter subscale so that 'height Above Mean Sea Level' is indicated, i.e. altitude. Look well ahead to ensure that visual flight and the required separation from cloud can be maintained and, if not, consider a diversion.

When established outbound from the aerodrome:
- arrange the chart so that your planned track runs up the page, making it easier for you to read 'map to ground';
- confirm that the Direction Indicator is aligned with the Magnetic Compass; and
- positively check a definite ground feature or group of features within the first 10 nm to ensure that you are indeed on track and that no gross error has been made – misreading the Compass or misaligning the Direction Indicator is always a possibility.

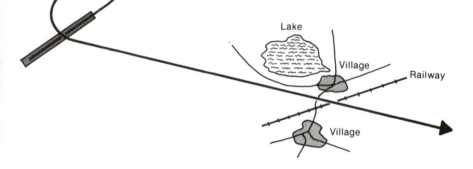

Fig.18-13. Check that Tracking is Correct Soon After Setting Heading.

EN ROUTE NAVIGATION.

It is important to maintain **steady headings for known times** when flying cross-country.

There is no need to refer to the chart all the time, but be sure to keep it handy (and usually on your lap). It is best to select certain ground features that will occur at intervals of 10 minutes or so (which at a Ground Speed of 120 kt puts them about 20 nm apart) to verify that you are on or near track. Selecting check-points this far apart allows time for your other duties, which include flying the aeroplane, making radio calls and carrying out periodic checks of the aeroplane systems ('FREDA').

At the appropriate time, look ahead for the next check point which should be coming into view – in other words, look at the chart, note the features that should shortly come into view and then look outside with the expectation of seeing them. **Read from Map to Ground** – then use features to either side of track and well ahead to confirm your position.

MAKE REGULAR CHECKS OF THE GROUND SPEED AND REVISE YOUR ETAs.

The actual Ground Speed is easily calculated from 'distance/time', using the time and distance between two fixes or crossing two position lines. For example, if you cover 5 nm in 3 minutes, then the GS is 100 kt (3 minutes = 1/20th of an hour, therefore GS = 20 x 5 = 100 kt). These calculations can be done mentally or on the computer. Mentally is better if you can manage it.

Once you know the GS, you can revise your ETA for the next check-point (and others further on). Again, this can be done mentally or by computer. For example, if it is 40 nm to the next check point, then at 100 kt this should take 40/100ths (i.e. 4/10ths) of 1 hour = 4 x 6 minutes = 24 minutes. If the time now is 1343 UTC, ETA at the check point is 1407 UTC.

Checking the actual time at the ¼, ½ or ¾ points along the way makes the mental calculation of the next ETA very easy. Also, it is good airmanship to log the times at fixes (or mark them on the map), so that you have some record of what positions the aeroplane passed over and when.

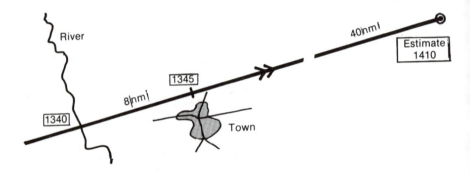

Fig.18-14. Calculate Ground Speed and Revise ETAs.

OFF-TRACK CORRECTIONS.

It is usual to find that the actual Track Made Good over the ground differs from the desired track plotted on the map, possibly because the wind is different to that forecast.

Whatever the cause, it is quite a simple calculation to revise the heading to re-intercept track. There are various means of doing this and your Flying Instructor will show you his preferred method. It can be done by computer or it can be done mentally (which leaves your hands free for other duties and avoids having your 'head in the cockpit' for too long). It is good airmanship to log the heading changes and the time at which they were made.

In each of the three methods in the next figure, the same result (turn 12° to the right) is obtained. Having regained track, turn 4° left to maintain it.

(1) 1:60 rule

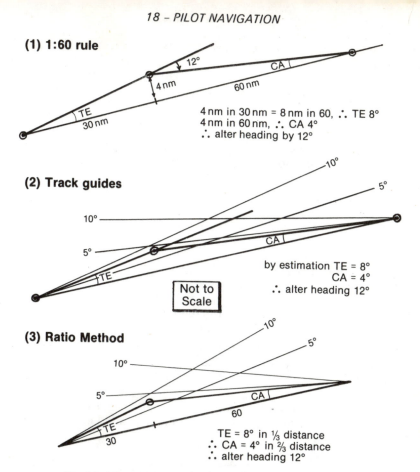

4 nm in 30 nm = 8 nm in 60, ∴ TE 8°
4 nm in 60 nm, ∴ CA 4°
∴ alter heading by 12°

(2) Track guides

Not to Scale

by estimation TE = 8°
CA = 4°
∴ alter heading 12°

(3) Ratio Method

TE = 8° in ⅓ distance
∴ CA = 4° in ⅔ distance
∴ alter heading 12°

Fig.18-15. Various Methods of Revising Heading.

REGULAR CHECKS.

The correct operation of the aeroplane and its systems should be checked on a regular basis (about every 15 minutes, or just prior to arrival overhead a check-point). A very suitable periodic check is 'FREDA', as described in Chapter 13c of this manual.

TURNING POINTS.

Just prior to reaching a turning point, check that the DI is indeed aligned with the Magnetic Compass (part of the 'FREDA' check). Take up the new heading over the turning point, log the time and calculate the ETA for the next check-point. Then, within 10 nm of passing the turning point, confirm from ground features that you are on the desired track and that no gross error has been made.

USE OF THE RADIO.

The radio is a very useful aid to a Pilot. En route and ouside controlled airspace, you will normally select the FIR frequency (shown on the charts) to enable immediate contact with the Air Traffic Service if desired. If passing close to other airfields, Military Air Traffic Zones, Special Rules Areas, controlled airspace, etc., make contact on the appropriate frequency prior to penetrating the airspace. Advise each frequency change before making it.

Do not be afraid to request the Radar Advisory Service if it is available in your area.

A typical position report will contain your:
- aircraft identification (i.e. callsign);
- position;
- time;
- level;
- next position and ETA.

ARRIVAL AT THE DESTINATION.

If appropriate, make radio contact with the ATS Unit at the aerodrome some 10 minutes prior to your ETA. This will allow time for you to obtain the aerodrome information (e.g the wind, the runway in use, and the QFE or QNH) so you can plan your arrival.

Normal procedures are either to join on downwind leg at circuit height or to overfly at 2000 ft Above Aerodrome Level and let-down to circuit height on the 'dead' side of the traffic pattern. The latter method is preferred at non-radio fields.

Having landed and taxied in, secure the aeroplane and 'Book In'. Refuelling may be a consideration, as well as payment of any landing fees.

FURTHER POINTS

DIVERSIONS.

A successful cross-country flight does not necessarily mean arriving at the destination. Sometimes conditions are such that continuing to the destination would expose your flight to unnecessary risk.

Weather Forecasters are not infallible. If the **actual** weather conditions ahead deteriorate to such a degree that onward visual flight would be unsafe (or less safe than you wish it to be), then to divert is good airmanship.

Never be afraid to divert if you feel it is the appropriate thing to do. There will always be pressures to press on from, for example, passengers wanting to get home; a sense of failure if you do not make it to the planned destination; the inconvenience of having to overnight away from home unexpectedly, etc.

When faced with an operational decision of 'what to do?', forget all of these secondary problems! They are irrelevant to your decision of whether to divert or not, which should be made purely on **flight safety** and nothing else.

Having decided to divert, (perhaps in difficult conditions such as turbulence), there is a **basic diversion procedure** that you should follow:
- make your decision to divert earlier rather than later;
- if possible, plan to divert from a prominent ground feature ahead, so that the diversion is commenced from a known point (e.g. a town);
- mark the diversion track on the map (free-hand if necessary) and estimate track and distance – estimate the track in °T with reference to the latitude-longitude grid and estimate the distance in nm;
- at the prominent feature, take up the estimated diversion **heading,** which you have calculated from the estimated track, allowing for magnetic variation and wind drift. **Your heading is extremely important** at this stage – even more important than distance (within reason);
- log the time at the diversion point and your new heading;
- refer to the chart and look for a positive ground feature soon after altering heading to ensure that no gross error has been made;
- when time permits, measure the track and distance accurately (ideally this would be done prior to the actual diversion);
- estimate the Ground Speed and the ETA at the diversion aerodrome or next turning point;
- inform the nearest Air Traffic Service Unit by radio of your actions;
- continue with normal navigation until you reach the diversion aerodrome (i.e. adjust heading and ETAs as required, contact the ATS Unit at the diversion field when about 10 nm away, obtain QNH or QFE, landing direction and other information);
- join the circuit normally, land, 'Book In' (and consider if the original destination aerodrome should be advised), and then advise your home base of the situation.

LOW LEVEL NAVIGATION.

If a diversion is due to a lowering cloud base you may find yourself involved in low level navigation. Low level flying itself has been covered in Chapter 16, but navigational aspects worth noting are:

if possible, perform any required checks before descent to a low level;

the possible advantages of using the 'precautionary' configuration (which allows slower flight, a better forward view, better manoeuvrability, but poorer fuel consumption);

your small field of vision at low level and the greater speed at which features pass through it;

check features need to be close to track to fall within this field of vision and must be prominent in profile (i.e. when seen from the side);

you must anticipate reaching the ground features, because they may not be in your field of vision for long; and

keep your eyes 'out of the cockpit' as much as possible.

UNCERTAIN OF POSITION.

Being 'temporarily uncertain of your position' is **not** being lost. A DR ('dead reckoning') position can be calculated which, hopefully, can shortly be backed-up with a positive fix over or abeam a ground feature.

If, at any time, you feel uncertain of your position:

1. Log your heading (Compass and Direction Indicator) and the time.
2. If the DI is incorrectly set, then you have the information needed to make a reasonable estimate of your actual position. Re-set the DI and calculate a HDG and time interval to regain the desired track.
3. If the DI is aligned correctly with the compass, then the non-appearance of a landmark, whilst it will perhaps cause you some concern, need not indicate that you are grossly off-track. You may not have seen the landmark for some perfectly legitimate reason (bright sunlight, poor visibility, a change in features not shown on the chart, cloud, etc.).
4. Make an **Urgency Call** (PAN, PAN, PAN, etc.) on 121·5 MHz. This should immediately enable ATC to fix your position by 'auto-triangulation', allowing you to resume normal navigation.
5. If still unable to fix your position, follow the procedure below.

PROCEDURE WHEN LOST.

Becoming lost is usually the result of some human error. Careful pre-flight planning followed by in-flight attention to the simple navigational tasks will ensure that you never become lost. You may become 'temporarily uncertain of your exact position', but this is not 'being lost' because you can calculate an approximate DR position.

If you ever become lost, then **formulate a plan of action** and do not just fly around aimlessly. Make use of the **Radar Advisory Service,** if available; see point 4 above.

When lost:

1. It is important that you initially maintain the HDG (if terrain, visibility and what you know of the proximity of controlled airspace permit) and carry **out a sequence of positive actions.**
2. If a vital check point is not in view at your ETA, then continue to fly for 10% of the time since your last positive fix.
3. Start from the chart position of your last known fix, **check the headings flown since that last fix,** and ensure that:
   - the magnetic compass is not being affected by outside influences such as a camera, portable radio, or other magnetic material placed near it;
   - the gyroscopic Directional Indicator (DI) is aligned with the magnetic compass correctly;
   - magnetic variation and drift have been correctly applied to obtain your HDGs flown;
   - an estimate of the track direction on the chart against that shown on the flight plan is correct.
4. **When Lost, read from Ground to Chart,** i.e. look for significant **ground** features or combinations of features and try to determine their position on the chart.
5. Establish a **'Most Probable Area'** in which you think you are. There are several ways in which this can be done, and we recommend you consult your Flying Instructor for his preferred method.

Two Suggested Methods of establishing a 'Most Probable Area':

Method (1). Estimate the distance flown since the last fix and apply this distance, plus or minus 10%, to an arc 30 degrees either side of what you estimate the probable Track Made Good (TMG) to be.

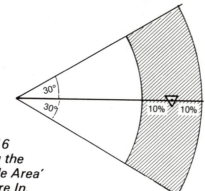

MOST PROBABLE
POSITION

*Fig. 18-16
Estimating the
'Most Probable Area'
That You Are In.*

Method (2). Estimate your 'most probable position' and around it draw a circle of radius equal to 10% of the distance flown since the last fix.

- **Establish a safety altitude** to ensure adequate clearance of all obstacles in what you consider the general area to be – being especially careful in conditions of poor visibility or low cloud.
- **Check large features** within this area of the chart with what can be seen on the ground. Try and relate features seen on the ground with those shown on the chart, i.e. **read from ground to chart.** Confirm the identification of any feature by closely observing secondary details around the feature.

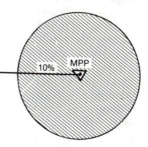

*Fig. 18-17. Another Means of Estimating
the Most Probable Position.*

At all times continue to fly the aircraft safely, maintaining an awareness of time, especially with respect to Last Light and your Fuel State.

When you do positively establish a fix, re-check your DI and recommence normal navigational activity. Calculate the HDG, GS and ETI for the next check feature and set course for it.

If you are Still Unable to Fix Your Position, you should consider taking one of the following actions :

(a) Increase your 'most probable area' by 10%, 15% or 20% of the distance flown since the last fix.

(b) Climb to a higher altitude to increase your range of vision.

(c) Turn towards a prominent 'line-feature' known to be in the area, e.g. a coastline, large river, railway line or road, and then follow along it to the next town, where you should be able to obtain a fix.

(d) Steer a reciprocal heading and attempt to return to your last fix.

Note the following important points:

- If you want to cover as much ground as possible with the fuel available, you should fly the aeroplane for best **Range.**
- Keep a **Navigation Log** going.
- Remain positively Aware of Time. Keep your eye on the fuel and on the amount of time remaining until last light. If last light is approaching, remember that it will be darker at ground level than at altitude and, if you are flying in the tropics, that it will become dark very quickly following sunset.
- If you decide to carry out a precautionary search and landing, allow sufficient time and fuel to do this, because two or three inspections might have to be made before finding a suitable landing area.

Why Did You Become Lost?

If at any stage you became lost, try to determine the reason systematically (either in-flight or post-flight) so that you can learn from the experience.

Common reasons for becoming lost include:

- incorrectly calculated HDGs, GSs, and ETIs (hence the need to make mental estimates of approximate answers to these items);
- an incorrectly synchronised Directional Indicator (DI), i.e. the gyroscopic DI not aligned correctly with the magnetic compass – the DI should be checked every 10 or 15 minutes against the compass;
- a faulty compass reading (due to transistor radios, cameras and other metal objects placed near the compass);
- incorrectly applied Variation (Variation West, Magnetic Best, etc);
- incorrectly applied Drift (compared to Track, Heading should be into-wind);
- an actual wind velocity significantly different to that forecast, and not allowed for in flight by the pilot;
- a deterioration in weather, a reduced visibility, or an increased cockpit workload;
- an incorrect fix, i.e. mis-identification of a check feature;
- a poorly planned diversion from the original desired track;
- not paying attention to carrying out normal navigational tasks en route.

With regular checks of the DI alignment with the compass, reasonably accurate flying of Heading, and with position fixes every 10 or 15 minutes, none of the above errors should put a Pilot far off-track. It is only when he is slack and lets things go a bit too far that he becomes lost.

19

USING THE
FLIGHT
INSTRUMENTS

19

USING THE FLIGHT INSTRUMENTS

AIM

To fly accurately using the flight instruments and no external visual clues.

CONSIDERATIONS

THE FLYING TECHNIQUE IS THE SAME VISUALLY AND ON INSTRUMENTS.

The Pilot controls the **performance** of the aeroplane by:
- selecting the **attitude** with the control column; and;
- selecting the **power** with the throttle.

This is called **attitude flying.** The Visual Pilot uses the natural horizon as attitude reference; the Instrument Pilot uses the Attitude Indicator (AI) on the instrument panel and thinks of the AI and the Tachometer as the **control instruments.**

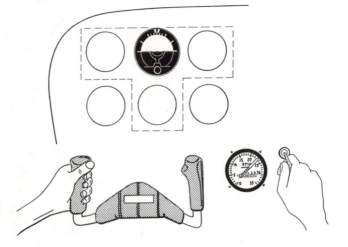

Fig.19-1. Power + Attitude = Performance.

350

WHY FLY ON INSTRUMENTS?

Flight in conditions of low visibility requires reference to instruments, both to achieve the desired aeroplane performance and to navigate. The appropriate pilot qualification for this fully-fledged instrument flying is the Instrument Rating (IR).

Flight in visual conditions does not require constant reference to instruments but, if they are used properly, the level of precision and safety is improved. This introduction to flying on instruments is designed for this purpose and not to achieve an Instrument Rating. Your Instrument Flight (I.F.) training will be practised with a Flying Instructor on board to act as a safety pilot and to maintain a watch outside whilst your vision is restricted to inside the cockpit.

THE FLIGHT INSTRUMENT PANEL.

The main flight instruments are usually installed on the panel in a 'Basic-T' configuration, which has proved very satisfactory over many years. The 'Basic-T' can be found in the smallest training aeroplanes as well as in the latest passenger jets (with slight modifications).

The **master instrument** (the Attitude Indicator) has the top central position with subsidiary instruments to either side and below it.

Fig.19-2. The 'Basic-T' is Found in Almost All Aeroplanes.

THE ATTITUDE INSTRUMENT IS THE MASTER INSTRUMENT.

The Pilot can visualise the aeroplane's **attitude** by reference to the AI (which may be thought of as a small 'porthole' through which the Pilot can see the horizon directly ahead). The AI provides information on **pitch attitude** and **bank angle,** but does **not** indicate whether the aeroplane is climbing, descending or flying level.

Fig.19-3. The Attitude Indicator is the Master Instrument.

The position of the index aeroplane (especially the small central dot) relative to the horizon bar gives a direct picture of the aeroplane's pitch attitude (within the limitations of the instrument). Roll is also indicated by the angle the wings on the index aeroplane make with the horizon, and by the 'sky pointer' at the top of the instrument.

The index (or model) aeroplane on some Attitude Indicators can be adjusted in relation to the horizon bar, but this should only be done when the aeroplane is on level ground or in straight and level flight.

Many Attitude Indicators will topple and give false indications if the aeroplane is placed in extreme attitudes (usually at least 60° nose-up or down). In normal flight this should not occur. Attitude Indicators driven by 'suction' usually have a caging knob so that the gyroscope that provides the horizon reference in the AI can be caged during aerobatics and when the aeroplane is parked.

THE 'CONTROL' INSTRUMENTS.

Aeroplane performance is controlled by the Pilot selecting the **power** and the **attitude**. These are indicated on the **Tachometer** and the **Attitude Indicator,** which can be referred to as the 'control instruments'.

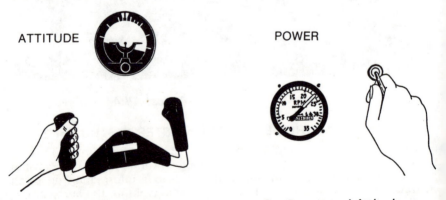

ATTITUDE   POWER

Fig.19-4. The Control Instruments to Set Power and Attitude.

VERTICAL PERFORMANCE.

Having set the power and the attitude, the Pilot can monitor the vertical performance of the aeroplane using the Air Speed Indicator, the Altimeter and the Vertical Speed Indicator (all of which are pressure instruments).

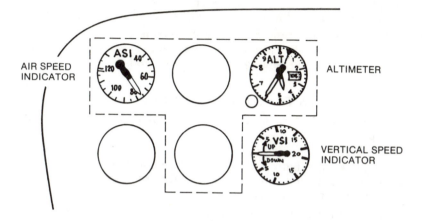

Fig.19-5. The Vertical Performance Instruments.

(a) **The Airspeed Indicator,** if showing the desired airspeed, indicates that the nose position is correct for the power being used. In this sense, the ASI is a back up instrument to the Attitude Indicator and verifies that you have selected the correct pitch attitude. If the airspeed is too high or is increasing, then the nose position is too low for the power selected (and vice versa). Allow some time for the airspeed to settle down following any change of attitude. **Do not chase the airspeed.** When cross-referenced with the Altimeter, the Air Speed Indicator will verify that the correct nose position has been selected for level flight at the power being used.

(b) **The Altimeter** is used to indicate height, but it can also be used as a back-up indicator of correct pitch attitude. For example, if straight and level flight is desired but the altimeter indicates an increasing altitude, then the pitch attitude is too high. If indicating a climb (and a climb is desired), then it acts as a check that the attitude and power may be reasonably correct.

(c) **The Vertical Speed Indicator** will indicate zero (or fluctuate about zero) during level flight and will indicate steady rates of climb or descent once the aeroplane is established in a steady climb or descent. It provides useful confirmation of the indications of the other instruments (e.g. the Altimeter and the Air Speed Indicator) and provides a convenient check on desired rates of climb or descent. The VSI responds more quickly than the Altimeter but will tend to fluctuate in turbulence.

Each of the above three instruments is pressure-operated and will experience some lag, i.e. any change of indication will take a little time to register.

BANK ATTITUDE IS SHOWN BY THE ATTITUDE INDICATOR.

A direct picture of the aeroplane's attitude in bank or roll (within the limitations of the AI, which is usually at least 90°) is given by:
- the position of the index aeroplane and central dot relative to the horizon bar;
- the position of the pointer on the angle of bank scale (the 'sky pointer') and also the angle that the model wings make with the horizon bar.

NOTE: Remember that selecting the desired bank angle with the ailerons requires the co-ordinated use of rudder pressure to keep the aeroplane in balance, verified by the balance ball being centred.

THE INSTRUMENTS THAT INDICATE TURNING PERFORMANCE.

The turning performance achieved by the aeroplane is determined by:
- the airspeed; and
- the bank angle selected by the Pilot.

Having selected the bank angle on the Attitude Indicator, the **turning performance** will be indicated by the Turn Co-ordinator and the Direction Indicator (both gyroscopic instruments), or by the Magnetic Compass.

The Standard Turn used in Instrument Flying is one in which the heading changes by 3°/sec, i.e. it would take 2 minutes for a complete turn of 360°, 1 minute for a turn of 180°, etc. This is called a **Rate One** turn. The higher the airspeed, the greater the angle of bank that is required to achieve a Rate 1 turn; a simple means of estimating the required angle of bank in degrees is to take $\frac{1}{10}$ of the airspeed and add 7.

- At 60 kt a Rate 1 turn will be achieved at (6 + 7 =) 13° bank angle.
- At 100 kt a Rate 1 turn will be achieved at (10 + 7 =) 17° bank angle.
- At 150 kt a Rate 1 turn will be achieved at (15 + 7 =) 22° bank angle.
- At 200 kt a Rate 1 turn will be achieved at (20 + 7 =) 27° bank angle.

For aeroplanes with ASIs calibrated in statute miles per hour (the familiar 'mph'), the formula for Rate 1 turn angle of bank is $\frac{1}{10}$ airspeed in mph+5.

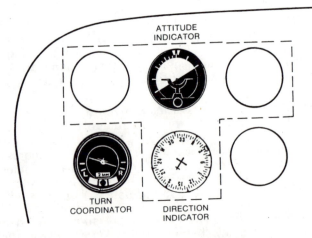

ATTITUDE
INDICATOR

TURN
COORDINATOR

DIRECTION
INDICATOR

Fig.19-6. Turning Performance.

The Rate of Turn Indicator shows the rate and direction of turn. It may take the form of a **Turn Co-ordinator** or a **Turn Indicator**. It is a gyroscopic instrument, electrically-operated in most modern aeroplanes, and can generally be relied upon not to topple.

Fig.19-7. The Turn Co-ordinator and The Turn Indicator.

Both instruments incorporate a Balance Ball that should normally be kept centred with appropriate rudder pressure. It is possible to fly straight with the wings banked and the ball out of centre (i.e. with 'crossed-controls'), but for accurate, efficient and comfortable flight, the ball must be centred. In **balanced flight,** any indication of turning on the Turn Co-ordinator means that the aeroplane is banked, and a constant zero reading means that the wings are level.

NOTE: The Turn Co-ordinator does **not** indicate pitch attitude or angle of bank, but only rate and direction of turn.

The Direction Indicator (DI) indicates magnetic heading, provided it has been aligned with the Magnetic Compass when the aeroplane is neither accelerating nor turning (which cause the Magnetic Compass to experience significant errors). Be aware that the DI may not give accurate indications if the aeroplane is allowed to exceed 55° or thereabouts in pitch or roll.

THE INSTRUMENT SCAN (or cross-referencing the instruments).

Instrument flight is not all that different from normal visual flight. Your eyes are still the main source of information, except the information is gathered from the instruments rather than from the outside world.

Scan all of the flight instruments and do not concentrate on any one. The information portrayed should be seen as a whole, i.e. pitch and bank attitude, airspeed, heading, rate of turn, climb or descent. Not every instrument need be referred to, but only those relevant to a particular phase of flight.

If your scan is good, then the aeroplane will never be allowed to stray far from the desired attitude and flight path, and only small control movements to correct minor variations will be required. Smooth Pilots are continually making subtle and almost imperceptible changes in control pressures – much more comfortable and effective than occasional large control movements.

Concentrate on the major flight instrument (the Attitude Indicator) and glance at the other instruments one at a time as required – your eyes then returning to the Attitude Indicator. For example, in a climb, the pitch attitude shown on the AI is of prime importance, with back-up information from the Altimeter and VSI.

Your eyes should only dwell on a particular instrument long enough to register its indications and then move on to the next one in your scan – one or two seconds being more than enough for any one instrument. With experience, you will even receive information through your peripheral vision, i.e. without even looking directly at the particular instrument.

Do not let outside influences (such as talking passengers and radio chatter) distract you from your main task of a fast and efficient scan. There will be a tendency for inexperienced Pilots to increase their dwell time when distracted; the experienced Pilot can handle other tasks and distractions whilst still maintaining a good scan.

In steady flight, it is adequate to scan only the instruments in the 'Basic-T', with occasional glances at the Turn Co-ordinator, the Vertical Speed Indicator and the Engine Instruments (rpm, temperatures and pressures).

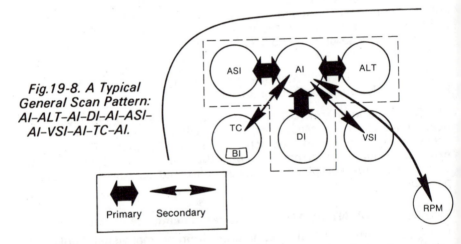

Fig.19-8. A Typical General Scan Pattern: AI–ALT–AI–DI–AI–ASI– AI–VSI–AI–TC–AI.

A comfortable scan pattern for each manoeuvre will develop quite early in your instrument training (with guidance from your Flying Instructor). Just which flight instruments are scanned (in between referencing the Attitude Indicator) when altering the flight performance of the aeroplane will depend upon whether you are monitoring:
- performance in the vertical plane; or
- turning performance.

SENSORY ILLUSIONS — ONLY THE EYES CAN BE TRUSTED.

The balance mechanism within the human ear can be seriously disturbed by the accelerations that may occur in instrument flight, so do not trust your sense of balance. Rely only upon your eyes and the indications that they receive from the flight instruments.

FLYING THE MANOEUVRE

FLIGHT PRINCIPLES AND CONTROL TECHNIQUE.

To become a competent Instrument Pilot you must have a knowledge of the forces involved in flight. It is appropriate at this early stage in your instrument training to review the basic manoeuvres of straight and level, climbing, descending and turning.

Inertia (resistance to change) will cause a delay in the response of the aeroplane to any control change. It will take time for the flight path and/or airspeed to settle. The Pilot must allow for this when using the pressure instruments (Air Speed Indicator, Altimeter and Vertical Speed Indicator), e.g. any change in pitch attitude will not be reflected immediately in the pressure instruments. The Pilot will have to hold the new attitude for a few seconds before the indications on the ASI, Altimeter and VSI settle down.

When performing a particular flight manoeuvre, the Pilot must comprehend the picture indicated by the instruments and then determine what control movements he will make. With practice, the time taken to comprehend and then to act shortens. Flying on instruments then seems to happen 'naturally'.

To change from one particular flight condition to another, use the same sequence as in normal visual flight:
- select the Power and the Attitude appropriate to the desired flight performance (keep the aeroplane in balance with rudder);
- hold the new attitude, which may require checking (stopping) the control movement, and allow the aeroplane and instrument indications to stabilise (which may take some seconds);
- adjust the attitude and power until the actual performance equals the desired performance;
- trim.

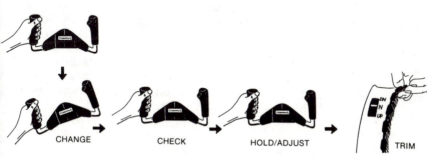

CHANGE   CHECK   HOLD/ADJUST   TRIM

Fig.19-9. Change – Check – Hold – Adjust – Trim.

NOTE: Heavy loads can be trimmed-off earlier in the sequence to assist in control (e.g. in a go-around, where a strong nose-up tendency will be experienced), leaving the fine trimming until later.

ATTITUDE AND POWER CONTROL.

For proper control of the attitude in both pitch and roll, the Pilot must:
- be able to hold a constant attitude;
- know when, and by how much, to change the attitude; and
- be able to change the attitude smoothly.

The Attitude Indicator will give you an immediate indication of both pitch and bank attitude, hence it is most useful as the primary instrument when making attitude changes.

Pitch Attitude Control. The index aeroplane with the dot in the centre of the wings allows you to make precise changes in pitch attitude relative to the artificial horizon using the control column. The attitude changes are often referred to in terms of 'bar widths' – one bar width being the thickness of the horizon bar or model aeroplane – or in terms of degrees, depending upon how the Attitude Indicator is marked. One bar width is usually about 2° in pitch. Quite large changes in pitch attitude are reflected in seemingly small movements on the Attitude Indicator.

Bank Attitude Control. The Bank Pointer at the top or bottom of the Attitude Indicator, and the angle the wings of the model aeroplane make with the artificial horizon, allow you to make accurate changes in bank angle. The bank scale is usually marked at 0°, 10°, 20°, 30°, 60° and 90°.

Balance Control. The Balance Ball allows you to keep the aeroplane in balance during all flight manoeuvres, and during power changes.

Power Control. Throttle positions to achieve certain power settings soon become familiar. Correct power can be set (at least approximately) by feel only, with a glance at the rpm indicator (tachometer) to make final adjustments. Power will remain constant with only occasional attention required from the Pilot.

Trim. Use of the correct trimming technique is essential if you are to achieve smooth and precise control when flying on instruments. Hold the desired attitude with the control column, ball centred with the rudder, and use the trimming device(s) to remove any steady control pressure. Any change of attitude, power or configuration (flaps) will probably require control pressures to maintain the desired performance. These pressures should be trimmed-off. Trim should be used only to remove control pressures, **not** to change attitude.

AIRMANSHIP

Only practise instrument flying with a Flying Instructor on board.

Exert firm, positive and smooth control over the aeroplane.

AIRWORK 19 — INSTRUMENT FLYING

The basic manoeuvres will be practised initially whilst you have visual reference to the outside world, and then when you have reference only to the cockpit instruments.

This **Introduction to Instrument Flying** may best be handled in the following four separate exercises:

(A) Straight and Level;

(B) Climb, Cruise and Descent;

(C) Turning;

(D) Recovery from Unusual Attitudes.

AIRWORK 19, (A) —

AIM: *To maintain a steady cruise straight and level with reference to the flight instruments only.*

(1) To Establish Straight and Level Flight:

- Select power for level flight;
- Set pitch attitude for level flight by positioning the index aeroplane on the artificial horizon;
- Hold the attitude and allow aeroplane to settle down to a new and steady performance;
- Monitor: AI—ALT—AI—DI—AI—ASI—AI—VSI—AI—TC—AI—ALT, etc.;
- Trim the aeroplane 'hands-off' carefully.

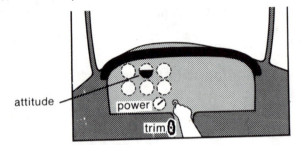

(2) Raising the Nose at Constant Power:

- Place the index aeroplane a little above the artificial horizon on the AI (say one-half or one bar width) and hold;
- The ASI will show a gradual decrease and finally settle on a lower Indicated Air Speed (IAS);
- The Altimeter, after some lag, will start showing an increase in height;
- The VSI, after some initial erratic behaviour, will settle on a steady rate of climb.

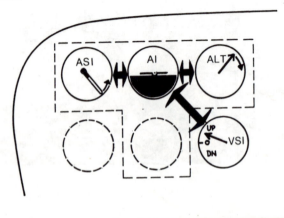

FLYING STRAIGHT AND LEVEL
ON INSTRUMENTS

(3) Lowering the Nose at Constant Power:

- Place the index aeroplane a little below the artificial horizon on the AI and hold this attitude;
- The ASI will show a gradual increase and finally settle on a higher IAS. Note the large airspeed change for what seems a small change in attitude;
- The Altimeter, after some lag, will start showing a gradual decrease in height;
- The VSI will eventually settle on a steady rate of descent.

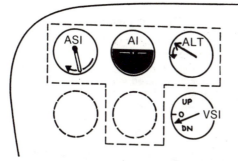

(4) Maintaining Straight and Level at Constant Power:

Adopt 'Selective Radial Scan' pattern, as shown:

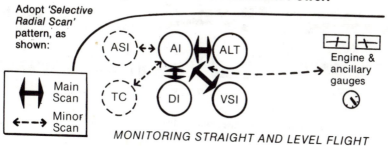

MONITORING STRAIGHT AND LEVEL FLIGHT

- Correct Variations in:

ALTITUDE —
by making very small changes in the position of the index aeroplane relative to the artificial horizon. Within ± 100 ft acceptable*.

- Keep in Trim.

DIRECTION —
by using small bank angles and checking that the aeroplane is in balance. Within ± 5° acceptable*.

AIRSPEED —
by adjustments in power, followed by, as a consequence, a small change in attitude. Within ± 5 kt acceptable*.

*A disciplined instrument pilot will aim to have airspeed, altitude and heading 'Spot-on'. If they are not, he will immediately do something about it.

(5) Changing Airspeed, Straight and Level:

(a) To Increase Airspeed at a Constant Height:

- Add power with the throttle (balance with rudder and forward pressure on the control column);
- Gradually lower the pitch attitude to avoid climbing and allow the airspeed to increase to the desired value;
- Adjust power to maintain desired airspeed and hold the pitch attitude;
- Trim.

(b) To Decrease Airspeed at a Constant Height:

- Reduce power with the throttle (balance with rudder and hold nose up with elevator back pressure);
- Gradually raise the pitch attitude to avoid descending and allow airspeed to reduce to desired value;
- As the desired airspeed is approached, adjust power to maintain it and hold the pitch attitude;
- Trim.

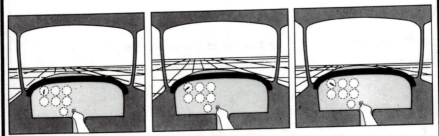

NORMAL CRUISE   FAST CRUISE   SLOW CRUISE

Different pitch attitudes for different speeds.

END OF PART (A)

AIRWORK 19, PART (B) —
CLIMBING, CRUISING & DESCENDING ON INSTRUMENTS

AIM: *To climb, cruise and descend, and to change from one to another, with reference only to the flight instruments.*

(1) Climb, Cruise and Descent at a Constant Airspeed

(Climb, cruise and descent speeds are usually different. By keeping the airspeed constant in this initial manoeuvre, we simplify the task by removing one of the variables).

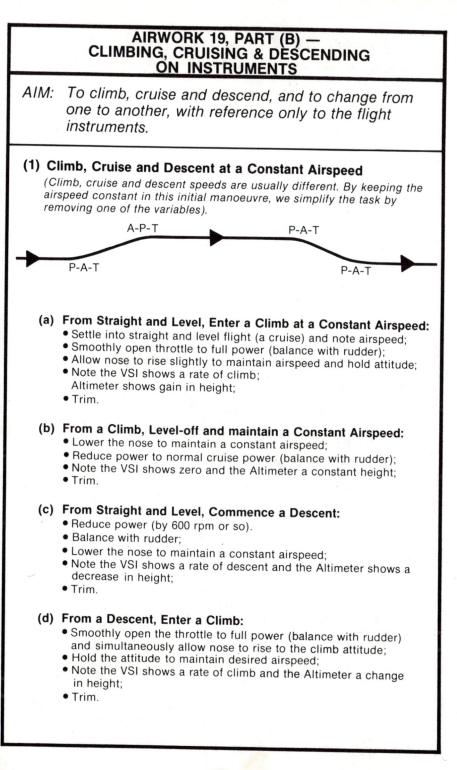

(a) From Straight and Level, Enter a Climb at a Constant Airspeed:
- Settle into straight and level flight (a cruise) and note airspeed;
- Smoothly open throttle to full power (balance with rudder);
- Allow nose to rise slightly to maintain airspeed and hold attitude;
- Note the VSI shows a rate of climb;
  Altimeter shows gain in height;
- Trim.

(b) From a Climb, Level-off and maintain a Constant Airspeed:
- Lower the nose to maintain a constant airspeed;
- Reduce power to normal cruise power (balance with rudder);
- Note the VSI shows zero and the Altimeter a constant height;
- Trim.

(c) From Straight and Level, Commence a Descent:
- Reduce power (by 600 rpm or so).
- Balance with rudder;
- Lower the nose to maintain a constant airspeed;
- Note the VSI shows a rate of descent and the Altimeter shows a decrease in height;
- Trim.

(d) From a Descent, Enter a Climb:
- Smoothly open the throttle to full power (balance with rudder) and simultaneously allow nose to rise to the climb attitude;
- Hold the attitude to maintain desired airspeed;
- Note the VSI shows a rate of climb and the Altimeter a change in height;
- Trim.

(2) Initiating a Climb at Normal Climb Speed:

Generally the normal climb speed is less than cruise speed.
As in normal visual flight, a climb is initiated in the sequence
'P-A-T': Power – Attitude – Trim.

Procedure:
- Settle in straight and level flight and note the airspeed;
- Increase power to the climb figure (balance with rudder);
- Raise the nose to the pitch attitude for climb;
- Hold the new attitude as airspeed decreases to the desired climbing speed. The VSI will show a rate of climb and the Altimeter an increase in height;
- Make minor pitch attitude adjustments to achieve and maintain the correct climb airspeed;
- Trim.

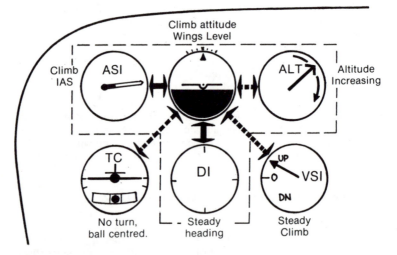

NOTE:
You can trim earlier in the sequence when holding the new attitude as airspeed decreases, if you wish. This will off-load some control column pressure, but a final trim adjustment will need to be made. Do not use trim to change the attitude; this must only be changed with elevator. The trim is used to relieve residual control pressures.

A steady climb is maintained with reference to all flight instruments, with the ASI confirming you are indeed holding the correct attitude for climbing, as shown in the AI.

CLIMBING, CRUISING & DESCENDING ON INSTRUMENTS

(3) Levelling-Off from a Climb:

As in normal visual flight, levelling off from a climb follows the sequence 'A-P-T': Attitude–Power–Trim. Since cruise speed is normally greater than climb speed, acceleration is allowed to occur before the power is reduced from climb to cruise power.

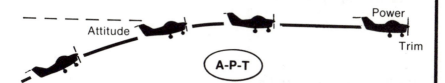

To Level-Off at the Desired Height:

- Smoothly lower the nose to the cruise position slightly before the height is reached — the amount of 'lead' being approximately 10% of the rate of climb.
  (For example, at 500 ft/min, commence lowering the nose 50 ft prior to reaching the desired altitude.);
- Allow the airspeed to increase towards the cruise figure;
- Reduce power to cruise r.p.m. as the cruise speed is reached;
- Make minor adjustments to hold height, heading and airspeed;
- Trim.

NOTE:

Steady straight and level flight is maintained by reference to all flight instruments, with the Altimeter confirming that you are holding the correct attitude for straight and level, as shown on the Attitude Indicator.

AIRWORK 19, (B) (cont'd) —

(4) Initiating a Descent on Instruments:

As in normal visual flight, a descent is initiated in the order 'P-A-T': Power-Attitude-Trim. Descent speed is usually less than cruise speed – deceleration to descent speed occurring at the cruise height before lowering the nose to descend being the generally accepted technique.

The standard rate of descent in instrument flying is 500 ft/min. This may be achieved by a reduction of 600 r.p.m. or so from the cruise power setting. This is not to say, however, that you may not remove all of the power and descend at a greater rate.

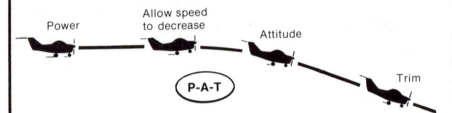

Procedure:
- Reduce power (balance with rudder and exert back pressure on the control column as necessary to maintain height);
- Allow the airspeed to decrease towards descent speed;
- At descent speed lower nose to descent speed attitude;
- Hold new attitude to maintain desired descent speed — (VSI will show rate of descent and Altimeter height decrease);
- Make minor adjustments to maintain desired descent speed and rate of descent — (control airspeed with attitude and rate of descent with power);
- Trim.

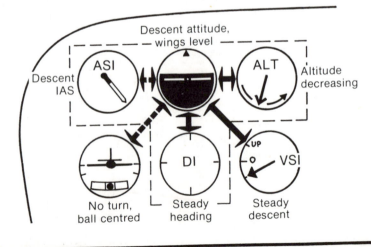

CLIMBING, CRUISING & DESCENDING ON INSTRUMENTS

NOTE:

A steady descent is maintained with reference to all flight instruments, with the ASI confirming you are holding the correct attitude for descent, as shown on the AI.

(5) Controlling the Rate of Descent at a Constant Airspeed:

To achieve any desired rate of descent whilst maintaining a constant airspeed, both the power and attitude must be adjusted.

Rate of descent is indicated to the pilot by the:
- *Vertical Speed Indicator (primarily),*
  or the
- *Altimeter and Clock.*

(a) To Increase the Rate of Descent:
- Reduce power;
- Lower the pitch attitude to maintain airspeed;
- Trim.

(b) To Decrease the Rate of Descent:
- Increase power;
- Raise the pitch attitude to maintain airspeed;
- Trim.

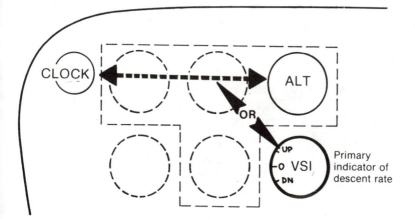

AIRWORK 19, (B) (cont'd) —

(6) Levelling-off from a Descent:

As in normal visual flight, levelling-off from a descent follows the sequence 'P-A-T': Power – Attitude – Trim.

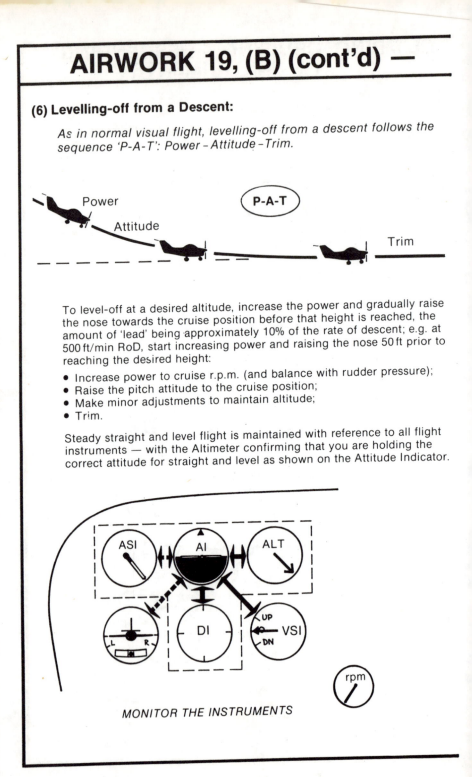

To level-off at a desired altitude, increase the power and gradually raise the nose towards the cruise position before that height is reached, the amount of 'lead' being approximately 10% of the rate of descent; e.g. at 500 ft/min RoD, start increasing power and raising the nose 50 ft prior to reaching the desired height:

- Increase power to cruise r.p.m. (and balance with rudder pressure);
- Raise the pitch attitude to the cruise position;
- Make minor adjustments to maintain altitude;
- Trim.

Steady straight and level flight is maintained with reference to all flight instruments — with the Altimeter confirming that you are holding the correct attitude for straight and level as shown on the Attitude Indicator.

MONITOR THE INSTRUMENTS

(7) Climbing Away from a Descent:

The procedure is the same as levelling off from a descent, except that climb power and climb attitude are selected.

Be prepared for a strong nose-up tendency as climb power is applied.

Even though the climb attitude is higher than the descent attitude, it may initially require forward pressure to stop the nose rising too far. Rudder will of course be required to balance the increase in slipstream effect.

Trim-off any steady pressure remaining on the control column.

Procedure:

- Apply climb **Power**, balance with rudder;
- Set the desired pitch **Attitude** for the climb;
- **Trim**.

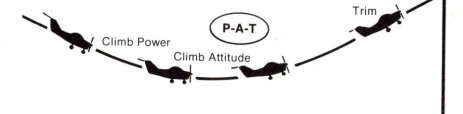

Climb Power   P-A-T   Trim

Climb Attitude

END OF PART (B)

AIRWORK 19, (C) —

AIM: *To turn the aeroplane solely using the flight instruments.*

(1) A standard Rate One Level Turn:

The required bank angle for a Rate 1 turn will equal '1/10th of the airspeed plus 7'. At 90 kt. the bank angle required will be 16°. (If your ASI is calibrated in m.p.h., use '1/10th of the airspeed plus 5'.).

- Trim for straight and level flight.

To enter and maintain the turn:
- Roll into the turn using ailerons and balance with rudder pressure;
- Hold a constant bank angle and keep the balance ball centred;
- Hold the correct pitch attitude to maintain height using elevator;
- Do **not** use trim in a turn, since turning is only a transient manoeuvre.

The rate of turn is indicated to the Pilot by:
- The Turn Co-ordinator (Rate 1 = 3°/sec or 360°/2 min);
  or:
- The Direction Indicator and the Clock.

To stop the turn on a desired heading, anticipate and commence recovery from the turn about 5° prior to reaching the desired heading;
- Roll the wings level and balance with rudder;
- Lower the pitch attitude to that required for straight and level flight;
- Trimming may not be necessary, as trim was not used during the turn.

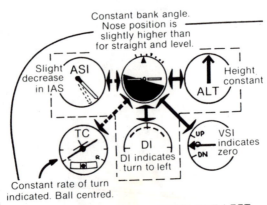

Constant bank angle. Nose position is slightly higher than for straight and level.

Slight decrease in IAS — ASI

Height constant — ALT

Constant rate of turn indicated. Ball centred. — TC

DI indicates turn to left — DI

VSI indicates zero — UP DN

A RATE 1 LEVEL TURN TO THE LEFT

TURNING USING THE FLIGHT INSTRUMENTS

A Rate 1 turn may also be achieved by using the Clock and the Direction Indicator. By holding the calculated bank angle, you should achieve a turn rate of 3°/sec, which will give a 45° heading change in 15 seconds, a 90° heading change in 30 seconds, a 180° heading change in one minute and 360° heading change in two minutes (hence the two minutes that is marked on many Turn Co-ordinators).

(2) A 30° Banked Level Turn:

At the speeds achieved by most training aircraft, a 30° banked turn is greater than Rate 1. A steeper bank angle requires a greater back pressure to maintain height, so the airspeed will decrease a little further – by about 5 or 10 kt. The pitch attitude will be slightly higher than for straight and level.

The rate of turn can be estimated from the Turn Co-ordinator or by using the Clock and the Direction Indicator (bearing in mind that the Turn Co-ordinator may be limited by stops at about Rate 2 – so that steeper bank angles will not be accompanied by an increased Rate of Turn indication).

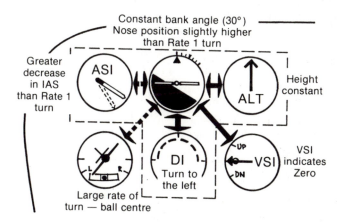

A 30° BANKED LEVEL TURN

AIRWORK 19, (C) (cont'd) —
TURNING USING THE FLIGHT INSTRUMENTS

(3) The Climbing Turn:

The climbing turn will normally be entered from a straight climb.
Do not exceed a 20° bank angle in a typical training aeroplane or climbing performance will be destroyed.

The pitch attitude will have to be lowered slightly to maintain a constant airspeed in a climbing turn. (In climbing and descending turns, speed is is maintained with the elevator whereas, in level turns, it is height).

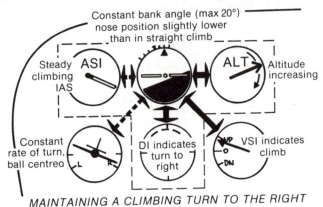

MAINTAINING A CLIMBING TURN TO THE RIGHT

(4) Descending Turns:

The descending turn will normally be entered from a straight descent.

The pitch attitude in the turn will have to be lower to maintain airspeed. The Rate of Descent will increase — it can be controlled with power, if you wish.

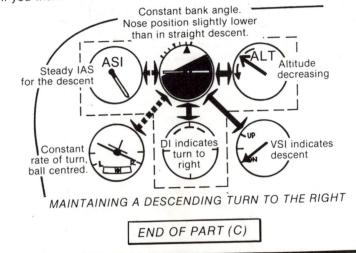

MAINTAINING A DESCENDING TURN TO THE RIGHT

END OF PART (C)

AIRWORK 19, (D) —
RECOVERY FROM UNUSUAL ATTITUDES ON INSTRUMENTS

An **'Unusual Attitude'** is considered to be an attitude where either:
- the aeroplane's nose is unusually high with the airspeed decreasing, or
- the aeroplane's nose is unusually low with the airspeed increasing.

The aeroplane may also be banked.

The easiest 'recovery' from an unusual attitude is not to get into one!

In extreme attitudes, the Attitude Indicator (a gyroscopic instrument) may topple, depriving you of your most important instrument. Most of its information can be derived, however, from other sources.

- Approximate Pitch Attitude can be determined from the Air Speed Indicator (increasing or decreasing airspeed) and the Altimeter and Vertical Speed Indicator (descent or climb). A decreasing airspeed indication and a decreasing rate of climb would indicate an unusually high nose-up attitude; conversely a rapidly increasing airspeed and rate of descent would indicate a nose-low attitude.

- Turning can be detected on the Turn Co-ordinator. The Direction Indicator (a gyroscopic instrument) may have toppled and the Magnetic Compass will probably not be giving a steady reading if there is any significant turning. The Turn Co-ordinator is gyroscopic but it will not topple.

THE AIM of this exercise is for you to recognise an unusual attitude before the Attitude Indicator topples, and to correct it.

---

(1) Nose-high and Steep Bank — Beware of Stall.

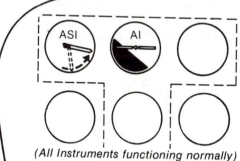

(All Instruments functioning normally)

A NOSE-HIGH UNUSUAL ATTITUDE.

Recovery Procedure —

(a) If Close to the Stall, simultaneously:
- Lower the nose to the level pitch attitude (referring to the AI);
- Apply full power (balance with rudder).

As speed increases, level the wings, (refer to the AI).

(continued)

(1) Nose-high and Steep Bank (cont'd) —

(b) If Not Close to the Stall:
- Select straight and level flight (refer to AI):
  - control column forward;
  - roll wings level with aileron, (aileron can be used as wings are not stalled);
  - balance with rudder.
- Add power as necessary.

(2) Nose-Low and High Airspeed —
Beware of an Overspeed or a Spiral Dive.

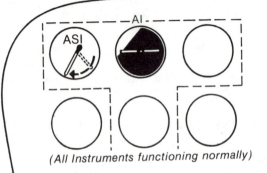

(All Instruments functioning normally)

A NOSE-LOW UNUSUAL ATTITUDE

Recovery Procedure:
- Reduce the power (throttle *CLOSED*);
- Roll the wings level with aileron and rudder;

- Ease out of the ensuing dive into S & L attitude (AI);
- Re-apply Power to regain height, if necessary.

THE END

APPENDIX
The General Flight Test (GFT)

The following is reproduced from CAP 53 (The Private Pilot's Licence and Associated Ratings). It is an outline of what you can expect to be asked to demonstrate for your PPL(A), in a Group A aeroplane.

The oral examination – Aircraft (Type) is also covered at the time you take your flight test. Details of this test are included in Vol. 4 of this series – The Aeroplane – technical.

During the course of your training, an additional flight test is also involved – the Navigation Flight Test (NFT). This is included in an Appendix to Vol. 3 of this series – Air Navigation.

This syllabus lists all the items which should be covered during training and which will be examined during the GFT. It applies to the test for aeroplanes of Groups A, B, and D and the SLMG except where otherwise specified.

The GFT will cover the following items and the candidate will be required to demonstrate satisfactory standards of knowledge and handling in each.

Preparation for Flight

Self briefing, weather suitability, aeroplane documentation, personal equipment check, weight and balance (calculate), weight and performance (calculate), fuel and oil state, aeroplane acceptability, ATC booking-out, and pre-flight inspection.

Starting, Taxying and Power Checks

Pre-start checks, post-start checks, taxying techniques, and power checks.

Take-off

Pre-take-off checks (vital actions), assessment of cross-wind component, during and post take-off checks, normal take-off, and cross-wind take-off.

Aerodrome Departure Procedures

Climbing

Straight and Level Flight

Descending with Power/Flap

Turning

Level, climbing, descending, high angles of bank.

Stalling/Incipient Spinning/Unusual Attitudes

Checks before stalling/spinning; flight at V_{s1} +5 kts and at V_{s0} +5 kts in straight and level, climbing, descending, and turning flight; recognition of incipient stall, recovery from incipient stall, recognition of incipient spin (Group A, SLMG and Group D dual only), recovery from incipient spin (Group A, SLMG and Group D dual only): straight and level, turning, climbing, descending and approach configuration flight; recovery from a developed stall from straight, turning and approach configuration flight; recovery from a spiral dive; side-slips (Group D dual only).

Forced Landings without Power (Groups A, D and SLMG only)

Checks, procedure, judgment.

Flight by Sole Reference to Instruments (Groups A and B Only)

Straight and level, climbing and climbing turns, descending and descending turns, turns onto specified headings, recovery to straight and level flight from climbing and descending turns.

Navigation/Orientation

Recognition of features, assessment of position.

Circuit joining Procedures

Circuit Procedure

Approach and Landing

Pre-landing checks (vital actions), assessment of cross-wind component, powered approach, flap-less approach, glide approach (Groups A, D and SLMG only), short field landing, bad weather circuit, cross-wind landing, missed approach procedure, checks after landing.

Simulated Emergencies

Engine fire in the air/on the ground, cabin fire in the air/on the ground, engine failure after take-off, other simulated emergencies.

Engines and Systems Handling

Airmanship/Awareness

Look-out, positioning (restricted airspace, hazards, weather), ATC liaison, aerodrome discipline.

Action after Flight

Engine shut down, parking and securing aeroplane, recording of flight details.